CALLED INTO LIGHT

CALLED INTO LIGHT

Meditations with
Bishop Richard Challoner
for the Christian Year

STAFFORD WHITEAKER

GRACEWING

First published in England in 2022
by
Gracewing
2 Southern Avenue
Leominster
Herefordshire HR6 0QF
United Kingdom
www.gracewing.co.uk

ISBN 978 085244 979 0

Typeset by Gracewing

Cover design by Bernardita Peña Hurtado

Cover image: mural *Noli Me Tangere* by Aidan Hart,
St Edward's Church, Lees, Manchester

You are God's special possession

that you may declare the praises of him

who called you out of darkness into his wonderful light.

1 Peter 2:9

CONTENTS

FEBRUARY

Contents

Contents

Contents

Contents

Contents

Contents

Contents

Contents

FOREWORD

NLESS ONE KNEW otherwise, it is possible to imagine that Bishop Richard Challoner (1691–1781) had done nothing else in his life than devote it to "the composition of the many works he has left us in defence of true faith and of sound morality".[1] It is one of those "many works" that, two hundred and sixty years later, has provided our editor with the inspiration to write this book.

Called into Light—Meditations with Challoner for the Christian Year has been inspired by Richard Challoner's *Meditations for Every Day of the Year*, published in 1753 and a beloved book in many Catholic and non-Catholic households. Unlike our own more ecumenical times, this was a period when there were anti-Catholic laws and anti-Catholic feelings ran high.

Challoner's writing was prolific in the belief that two needs could be met by the printed word for eighteenth century Catholics. The first was to instruct and strengthen them in their faith, and the second was to defend that faith against misconceptions and attack.

The middle years of the eighteenth century were more than challenging for the Church: many people had become disillusioned with the slow pace of recovery. Emancipation was slow in coming; persecution and imprisonment remained a threat, even though it was some fifty years since the last execution. Through the apostolate of his writing, Challoner sustained and encouraged the faithful flock to persevere.

Today, perseverance is called for in the flock of Jesus, as many challenges have to be faced by the Church. Beyond identifying them, today's editor sets about how they are to be addressed. It is by reading the Scriptures, by *listening to* and not just *hearing* the teachings of Jesus, by prayer, fasting,

---

[1] Bishop John Milner, *Funeral discourse for Richard Challoner*, 22 January 1781.

almsgiving, service in charity, self-sacrifice and in the sacraments and fidelity to them that we are to make a difference to our world—because Jesus has made a difference to *us*. As the editor says, if using these meditations brings you closer to God, then they have served their purpose.

Unsurprisingly, having revised the Douay Bible with notes (1750) making it even more accessible to his own generation, Richard Challoner used many scriptural quotations to illustrate or make a point in his *Meditations*. Our editor greatly multiplies the use of scripture throughout the volume, and states clearly *The Word of God is always triumphant.*

The sentiment express in the 22 January mediation here that *to listen to the Word of God and to live by it is the one necessary thing* has been the underlying theme of Pope Francis' ministry from the earliest weeks of his papacy to his Apostolic Letter *Aperuit Illis* (30 September 2019) instituting the *Sunday of the Word of God* which begins with the words from St. Luke's Gospel *He opened their minds to understand the Scriptures.* (Luke 24:25).

Also drawing on the rich treasures of Christian writing, religious and monastic, lay and secular our editor fleshes out his own thoughts and words. In the framework of meditations day by day through the year, he uses the liturgical calendar with its seasons and feasts, Mass and the Sacraments, the *Liturgy of the Hours*, sermons of Jesus, various well-known prayers, writings of the Church Fathers, and articles of faith. He is not afraid to be forthright and to ask hard questions of us in the manner of the second chapter of the First Letter of St John. He employs a variety of genres: descriptive, instructive, reflective, formative, admonishing, personal, and comforting to create an armoury for the Christian soldier or disciple (2 Timothy 2:3; Luke 14:31) to live life in to-day's challenging world.

Throughout the work and in every way our editor is inviting us to engage with God and *to listen with our heart, because it is from this kind of inner hearing that love springs.* (see Mediation below for 11 July).

Inspired by Richard Challoner's *Meditations for each day of the year* the editor's objective is to provide for us a contemporary version of those meditations in the context of the religious freedom we enjoy to let the light of Christ shine into every corner of our lives and thus refine and purify those lives that we might be what we are called to be (Ephesians:8–9) and so ourselves to become light to the world (Matthew 5:14)

I am glad of this book, and strongly recommend it, as it not only provides a wealth of catalyst for prayer and reflection but it also reminds us of the now often forgotten or ignored *Meditations* of Bishop Challoner and of the revival which they helped to bring about at another challenging time in the life of the Church. While I know that in humility our editor would not want that acclamation for himself, he would be delighted if *Called into Light* had but a fraction of the same beneficial effect.

Take a year or more to savour all it has to offer, for it is a rich feast. Following its wisdom will lead to a greater banquet yet (Revelation 19:9)

✠ Peter M. Brignall
Bishop of Wrexham

INTRODUCTION

HIS BOOK *Called into Light — Meditations with Bishop Richard Challoner for the Christian Year* is based on the 1753 book, *Meditations for Everyday of the Year,* written by the Roman Catholic bishop and scholar, Richard Challoner (1691–1781). He is also the author of the revised *Douay-Rheims Bible,* still in use up to our own day. Bishop Challoner wrote at a time when Catholicism was still officially outlawed in Britain, even though executions of the faithful had ceased. In many places today's Christians and not just those of Catholic confirmation, labour under great difficulties in practicing their faith just as they did in Bishop Challoner's day. Sadly, Christian martyrdom still happens somewhere in this world today.

First published in 1753 and frequently reprinted and often used by non-Catholics, Challoner's book of meditations remained in print for some 200 years. His meditations inspired this book, *Called into Light.* These new and revised meditations cover important aspects of the spiritual life. In general they follow the plan of Challoner's book and even some of the original phrasing of Challoner's text in more modern language, but these new meditations are an original work following the current Catholic liturgical calendar.

It is my intention and hope, as a baptized follower of the teachings of Jesus the Messiah, that these meditations will prove helpful for anyone in the practice of their Christian faith as well for all who seek God and honour him as the one God through the faiths of Abraham's children, who are the Jewish, Islamic and Christian peoples. It is hoped too that these mediations may prove of benefit to those of other faith persuasions and to those who have not yet begun their spiritual journey but are seeking meaning and peace in life.

The meditations in this book are based on my personal use of Challoner's original meditations for over thirty years. I discovered his book in the library of the Benedictine monastery to which I was attached at the time and used it in my daily contemplation. When I left this community to enter the life of a hermit, the Superior of the monastery gave me Challoner's book. It has accompanied me every day since then as a servant of God in a life of prayer.

No matter where or how God has shown me his plan for my life, Challoner's meditations have helped me renew my faith when it faded, helped me to repent when I sinned, and encouraged me to be reconciled with God and remain in his presence as best I could. The principles and values of trying to live such a holy life underpin the meditations of Challoner and those in this book, because there is a new life in God through Jesus the Messiah. In this new life with God is to be found consolation, joy, hope and the contentment of knowing we are loved.

We are clearly told what to do in making this new life with God: *You must be made new in mind and spirit, and put on the new nature of God's creating.* (Ephesians 4:23–24)

Therefore, the mediations in this book are written, like those of Challoner, around the unifying acts of repentance for lack of virtue and of renewal for a life of dignity, wisdom and virtue so that we are reconciled with God and please him. Without repentance and renewal we cannot live as God commanded: *Be holy, for I am holy.* (1 Peter 1:16)

Using these meditations

These meditations are reflections on the *Old Testament* and the good news of the *New Testament*. They are not meant to be a substitute for the instructions of God or the teachings of the Messiah, his incarnate *Word*. If these mediations lead you to prayer and to the bible, then they have served the purpose of bringing you closer to God.

Now God does not *need* our praise but as his servants we do need to glorify him for the benefit of our earthly and eternal lives. So let us pray and meditate often on his *Word* and if possible daily, because here is the strength and wisdom to live a life pleasing to God and one which leads to eternal union with him.

Meditations in this book are arranged in accord with the current *Roman Catholic General Calendar*. All feasts are kept but only a selection of memorials for saints when it was felt that these have a special relevance for the general spiritual life. The saints celebrated in this book are men and women who by the example of their lives teach us how to live by the commandments of God and to believe in his promises. They show us too that consolation and joy are to be found in a holy life with God through obedience to him with a faith that perseveres.

Biblical and other references in these meditations refer to the passage in the *Old* and *New Testaments* upon which the meditation text is based or arise from the writings of sources such as the *Second Vatican Council* or from men and women who have been deemed important in the development of Christianity in the lives of the faithful such as popes, bishops, theologians, and many anonymous disciples of Christ who have willingly submitted to the authority of God. All dates given are as *BC* (Before Christian Era) or *AD* (Christian Era after the death and resurrection of Jesus Christ).

The Word of God is triumphant

Should you pause to read a biblical reference, then go to that scriptural passage and stay with that *Word of God*. Let it open your heart to the Holy Spirit. It does not matter if you return to the meditation in this book. Stay with the *Word* for there you will find all the basic truths of living, the promises of God, and the hope and courage you need.

The mysterious purpose of the *Word* is to take you to God, to help you please him, to strengthen your faith, and to keep you near his mercy and compassion. So if you fall into holy contemplation then stay there, because you are with God. It is a wondrous moment of union.

A meditation by anyone, no matter how holy or of what high social or ecclesiastical rank, does not have any great weight when measured against the *Word of God.* If a meditation in this book takes you to the *Word* and prayer or contemplation, then it has served its purpose. The *Word of God* is always triumphant. Here is the help we all need to be God's true subjects. *Come close to God, and he will come close to you. Humble yourselves before the Lord and he will lift you up.* (James 4:8 & 10)

About repentance and renewal

Real repentance is difficult, because we must look deeply and honestly into ourselves. Having done that, we can acknowledge how we have failed to live up to the standards set by God. This *knowing yourself* is the hardest of all things for us to do, because none of us like the dark part of our heart. Yet, this examination of self is what we must do if we are to repent when we have succumbed to temptation.

While we often know when we are guilty of *sins of commission,* that is acts that displease God, we frequently do not realize those other more hidden faults like spiritual pride and the love of our power, social prestige or wealth.

We hardly ever contemplate our *sins of omission* when we did not practice what Jesus taught, such as charity to the poor or not making judgments about other people. Usually we just ask God in some formula of prayer to forgive our sins whatever they may have been. This confession is pleasing to God, but it is almost always superficial. We can do much better at our self-examination if we do not fear to enter the dark part of our soul.

Sometimes a shallow examination of our inner self may bring that regret that leads us to true repentance, but often much more is demanded before our heart cries out in sorrow at our offenses. We may fool ourselves but God knows everything about us, including when we have fallen prey to temptations either in mind or body. (1 John 3:20; Psalm 139; Matthew 5:28)

So repentance means a true self-examination and looking at how we *really* are as a human. Such a look into the darkness of your self can be very frightening. We see things in ourselves we have hidden to fool ourselves about the truth. It can be an unpleasant experience often bringing despair. But out of such despair arises hope. With hope comes regret and, finally, an acceptance of how we truly are. This knowledge of ourselves tells us of any wrongdoing. We repent. We ask for forgiveness. With such confession to God comes reconciliation for God is All Merciful and All Compassionate.

With reconciliation comes that renewal with God that returns us to love, a purity of spirit, and the joy of living.

Called into Light

Under the impulse of grace, this invitation, this *Called into the Light* by God demands a change in us, a putting to one side all temptation to sin and being holy as God himself is holy.

Now change of any kind is hard to accept and a change in the deepest part of your self is the hardest change of all. Yet, such change begins by an awareness of who and what we are. With every hidden secret of ourselves exposed and with no dark corner of ourselves left unexplored, we may find a true acceptance of who and what we are. This awareness is not something we want the world to see. Indeed, we hide it even from ourselves, but God knows us with an intimacy that is complete knowledge. We can hide nothing from God. Our good points and our sins lay before him like the open pages of a book, a book of a life he reads with understanding and love. While promising a final judgment, he meanwhile exercises mercy and compassion, giving us another chance to be his faithful servant.

By this example of love, we may be sure that we have found the encouragement for our deepest reflection about ourselves. We no longer need fear the darkness of our soul.

Here lays our reconciliation with God, because he wants us to come before him with complete honesty. Such reconciliation is always possible. It does not matter if you are rich or poor, powerful or powerless, imprisoned or free, under democracy or dictatorship, educated or illiterate, in good or poor health, doubtful or certain of holy truths, in the darkness of sin or in the dawning of God in your life, that holy light to which you have been called to that same one God.

What does God ask of you? Only this: *to fear the Lord your God, to follow his ways, to love him, to serve the Lord your God with all your heart and all your soul.* (Deuteronomy 10:12)

JANUARY

Theme: A New Year and a New Life in Jesus the Christ

You must be made new in mind and spirit. And put on the new nature of God's creating.

Ephesians 4:23–24

ACH CHRISTMAS WHEN we celebrate the birth of Jesus Christ, we have a chance to begin afresh in a Christian life. It is time for turning our eyes heavenward and away from worldly values and goals. It is a time to renew our pledge to be obedient to God's commandments A time to live according to our faith in the Messiah, who was created and sent to us from God.

It is a day for recovery not just from the pleasure of celebrations of Christmas and New Year, but for the fullest possible recovery of our relationship with God. It is a time of healing.

However, this day of joy should be also filled with a certain sense of sadness for this past year when we neglected, doubted or deserted God. We must not forget to regret those days in which we did not live our lives as God intended and allowed despair and lost hope dominate our thoughts and actions, forgetting that like every man and woman, we were born for joy. (Psalms 93:19, 47:1; Ecclesiastes 9:7; 1 Peter 1:8–9; Romans 14:17)

So, let us take as much time now as is necessary to examine how we stand in our life and with God. Let us not hurry. Let us put to one side all our worries and responsibilities for as long as it takes to replenish ourselves with God and let his mercy and his promises fill us with hope and love. Let us submit to his will in all things. (Matthew 10:37,38,39; Luke 14.26,27)

Begin this renewal of faith by thinking deeply into how you are actually living your life. Ask yourself: *If I don't have the joy that God intends for me, then why not?* It takes time to reflect on your life with real honesty and a great deal of courage, so do not hurry.

1 January — Solemnity of Mary Mother of God

 E MAY KNOW about very few of the events in Mary's life, but what we do know points the way in every case to Jesus the Christ. Each of those events is vital to our faith, because they show us the way we are to follow if we are to be faithful servants of God. Mary tells us exactly what we are to do as a follower of Jesus: *Do whatever he tells you.* (John 2:5)

By her obedience to God's will, Mary shows us the kind of loving submission to God and trust in him that we should all make. Through such obedience, she becomes not only the mother of Jesus, but also the eternal *New Eve* of all men and women. She replaces the disobedience of the first Eve and, by doing so, gives birth to our salvation.

By Mary's refusal to be intimidated by the society and its worldly values in which she lives, she shows us another dimension of our discipleship in Jesus. This is to put the values of God first and above those of any nation, society, tribe or culture in which we may live. Mary willingly did this and was not seduced by the pressures and values of the world. By agreeing to become an unmarried mother, she knows she may be shamed and condemned by the standards of her society, family, and neighbours. In her bravery Mary shows us that great courage is sometimes necessary in order to do as God wants and not what the world may think best or proper. God helped Mary to achieve his holy plan for her as he helps all who freely keep faith with him. Such is the mystery of God's mercy.

Through her holy role as bearer of the redeeming Christ, Mary shows us that we too are to personally bring Jesus into the world for others. This is a great example to set before us, since she is confirming us as ambassadors for the Messiah, his chosen messengers who are to be bearers of his light in this world. Jesus confirms this when he tells us never to hide that light but to always keep it shining. (Matthew 5:15,16; 2 Corinthians 5:20) This light is no less than the illumination of the path to peace, the way of Christ.

Thus, the proper work of our life is to be bearers of this holy illumination and there is no better place or way to start than with this day, a new year in Jesus the Christ, the beginning of your true life of love.

2 January—On beginning a new life with a new year

HAT A SAD thought it would be if during all these years you have lived, instead of storing up provisions for a happy eternity, you have been only adding to the anger God will have towards you when his judgement is made. (Romans 2:5,6)

But consider how changing ourselves often seems impossible. Old habits die hard, because we are so comfortable with what we know already even if it is displeasing to God. To change can be scary for we think we are entering an unknown, perhaps very dangerous, territory, but the way of Jesus has been make clear to us. So there is nothing to fear from changing to his path of love instead of the world's path of self-interest.

Yet, when our resolutions grow weak and we are on the verge of failing, it is just the right moment to ask ourselves just how much time we have spent in the service of God. Remember that your faith without your actions is a worthless thing because it is not alive with love. (James 2:26) Have you failed to love as you were commanded?

How then do matters stand between you and God at the beginning of this New Year? What would you think if this day you were to be judged by the present state of your life?

Think how few of us live in the manner in which we would be glad to be found when death should take us away. Yet, we know that death most often comes when least expected and that, generally speaking, as people live so they die. Your time may be much shorter than you are willing to think, so do not deceive yourself. Do not pretend that death is not your mortal fate nor believe for a second that the beauty or riches or earthly love you now have will last forever. Perhaps until now you have been like the barren fig tree in God's eyes, planted in his vineyard but bringing forth nothing but leaves. (Luke 13:6–8)

Yet, God has safely taken you to the beginning of this New Year. Do not refuse him the fruits he expects. Why not set yourself in order now and live, as you would desire to die? Resolve to take this new self into the New Year. (Psalm 126:1–2)

3 January—The rule of life that comes from Jesus

HE REASON MOST people fall into ungodliness is because it is so hard to give up worldly ambitions and pleasures. Instead of dedicating ourselves to God by giving him our whole heart, we give it instead to empty amusements and the follies of vanity. To become ungodly is a kind of idolatry, because we prefer the creature that is ourselves before the Creator, who is God. This wrong preference is the very bane of our world. Let us detest such celebration of humanity whether of ourselves or of others. Let us move away from the way we think and act that is not a sign and action of our love for each other and for God.

Evil, the opposite of love, is always at work to draw us away from God, because evil sets before us a tempting, if deceitful, feast of worldly honour, profit, and pleasure. With these temptations men and women are lured to the service of evil. These temptations are the gilded fruits, which poison your spirit. These are the treacherous but delicious baits hiding the hook of sin. A hook that everyday catches millions or men and women and pulls them into eternal darkness. (1 John 2:15–16)

It is on account of these false values, which abound in our everyday life that the world is passing away. (1 John 2:17) If we desire to be godly, we must declare a perpetual war against these worldly appetites, which corrupt nature and harden our hearts against God. Let us be strong for Christ then, remembering that God's word is founded on truth and his degrees are eternal. (Psalm 118: Aleph & 153–160)

Conclude to belong to God, seeking your happiness in other kinds of honours, riches, and pleasures such as the world cannot give and which may stay with you forever. Make your treasure in heaven. (Matthew 6:19–21) This is the rule of life you need.

4 January—On the rules of a new life in Jesus Christ

OW OFTEN WE want someone to help us with guidelines about living a life of happiness. How often we wish for the wisdom of good advice. The Apostle Paul did just that. He told us in a few words the rules we are to follow in living a Christian life. What we are to renounce. What we are to practise. What we are to look for. What are to be our values for daily living.

So listen again to what Paul tells us, because these rules are from the teachings of Jesus and, thus, they are of God:

> God's grace has been revealed to save the whole human race; it has been taught us that we should give up everything contrary to true religion and all our worldly passions; we must be self-restrained and live upright and religious lives in this present world, waiting in hope for the blessing which will come with the appearing of the glory of our great God and Saviour Christ Jesus. He offered himself for us in order to ransom us from all our faults and to purify a people to be his very own and eager to do good. (Titus 2:1–15; Letters 1 & 2 of Peter)

Since we belong to God, we cannot act or live in any way other than according to his teaching through Jesus the Word. Here are found the rules of life in all we do. So, renounce all that you know to be displeasing to God and pursue what you have been told repeatedly by the prophets and Jesus to be agreeable to God. After all, you are not your own property for you have been bought at the greatest price through that sacrifice which brought you salvation.

So in using your mind and body for the glory of God, you should take the holy will of Christ for your rule of life, since you are belong to God. (1 Corinthians 6:19–20) In consequence of Christ coming among us, we are not only to avoid all evil but are also to do good, giving up everything contrary to our religion and to live upright lives in this present world. (Titus 2:12–13)

5 January—On the life we are to lead as a Christian

 HIS RULE OF life for Christians has three branches. One relates to the regulating of self, another regards your neighbours, but the third and most important of all, relates directly to God. We comply with all these requirements when we live moderately, justly, and holy, because by living moderately we keep ourselves in balance and away from excesses, by living justly we behave to our neighbours in all things as we ought, and by living holy we dedicate our lives to God.

These three branches of a Christian's duty reach deeply into us. Just think how much this moderation, this justice, and this holiness demand of us. It means we must love without expectations. It means understanding the good and the hidden darkness in us. It means not judging others. It means seeing Christ in every man and woman you meet. In effect, it means changing everything about yourself that goes against the commandments of God. To live such a life would be impossible in its demands without the presence of God's grace.

Christian moderation is a self-restrained living that not only includes eating and drinking in moderation, but also applies to all other excesses that may carry you away. To be truly self-restrained, we must hold back our pride by humility, our anger by meekness, our lust by purity, and all our unsettling desires by a general moderation. It calls us to live a balanced life. In this way, we maintain with discipline and patience our whole person in a harmony of spirit and body. This harmony makes for good health, contentment, and gives meaning to life.

Ask yourself: Don't I want good health? Don't I desire contentment? Don't I seek the meaning of my life?

Now justice for a Christian means living an upright life. It regulates our whole conduct toward our neighbours by that golden rule of always treating others as you would like them to treat you. (Matthew 7:12) This means we shun every thought, judgment, word, or action that in any way may be to the disadvantage of someone else. Here is the practice of love.

Lastly, to live truly holy lives means we seek God in all things and above all things. As our first and most important priority, it consecrates all our talents and passions to him through our actions, recollections, meditations, repentance, praise and prayers. Above all, we keep God in the present moment of our life, never forgetting him and always begging for his mercy. The truth of the Jesus Prayer never ceases to echo in your mind. Your heart prays continually: *Lord Jesus Christ, Son of God, have mercy on me, a sinner.*[1]

In this way, those three branches of our Christian living establish the peace of Christ in us. We are at rest, then, in the embrace of holy love. So begin this New Year determined to advance daily in this happy way of a Christian's rule of living, a way which leads to the life which never ends, the way of Christ.

---

[1] The Jesus Prayer, says Metropolitan Anthony Bloom, "more than any other," helps us to be able to "stand in God's presence." This means that the Jesus Prayer helps us to focus our mind exclusively on God with "no other thought" occupying our mind but the thought of God. At this moment when our mind is totally concentrated on God, we discover a very personal and direct relationship with Him.

6 January — Solemnity of the Epiphany of the Lord

HE CHURCH KEEPS this day with great solemnity as one of the principal festivals of the year. It is called the *Epiphany*, that is to say the manifestation of our Lord, because on this day he was first made known to the wise men of the east that were Gentiles. They were guided to him by the appearance of an extraordinary star and inspired to pay him homage and worship. This day was the first call to the knowledge of Christ for the Gentiles. If this single event had not happened we might have been left to dwell in darkness like the dead, long forgotten. (Psalm 142:3)

Divine Providence prepared both the Jews and Gentiles to expect the coming of the Messiah. To the Jews by an Angel sent to the shepherds and to the Gentiles by a star that appeared to the wise men of the east. But how few, either of the one or the other, responded to this great call. Is this not the case of millions of men and women even now? People who continue to live by the values of this world and ignore that real light that gives light to everyone. (John 1.6–13) One day we may see that there was nothing wanting on the part of God's plan to bring us to himself, but that we were wanting in not responding to his call.

Can you see then, the difference between a ready and willing compliance with the inspirations of God and the neglect of such calls? This difference produces the distinction between the saint who follows God's calls and the sinner who neglects them.

Conclude then to pay attention to all those inspirations by which you are invited to follow Jesus. How many of these holy stars that have arisen in your heart have you so far neglected or darkened by the shadow of your desires for pleasure and power? Set out now by the guidance of this divine light to make your way home to God. It is never too late to be obedient to God's call.

7 January — In the beginning of your new life

OT SO VERY long ago everything on earth was bigger than you, because you did not yet exist. Think about who it was that drew you out of nothing into this being which you now enjoy. Who gave you the power of thought, a consciousness of life, a will, a memory, and the capacity to understand and love? Who gave you a body full of wondrous workings and a spirit thirsting to find holy meaning in this life? No other than God, the one who created you as he did universe upon infinite universe with all their stars, planets, light, and mysterious darkness.

How is it, then, that this immense God of all creation should think of making you? What did he see in your nothingness that could move him to bestow earthly life on you? Do not question this holy event but, rather, accept that your whole being was simply a gift of love. Should you not then raise your voice in song and your heart in praise and embrace God with your whole self? (Psalms 148/149)

As if giving you an earthly life was not enough, God made you after his own image and likeness so that he might help you to love him even more. (Genesis 1: 26–27) This image and likeness is stamped in your soul which is the centre of your spiritual being. Here are your spiritual powers, which hunger to be united with God. They will be satisfied with nothing less than this holy embrace. It is your free will that unchains your spirit and lets it take wing. By this means you are capable of soaring above all things, visible and invisible, and reaching to the contemplation of God himself. Do not let such a noble spirit, which is what you are, lie grovelling in the dirt of earth, a slave to the vanities of the flesh and the conceits of self-interest.

Never forget this wonder of your being alive. Be mindful that once you did not exist and that all you are now is the pure bounty of God. Remembering this truth will teach you to have humility about yourself.

8 January—Feast of the Baptism of the Lord[2]

ESUS' BAPTISM REPRESENTS the start of a new creation for this world. (1 Corinthians 15:45–49) He begins his public ministry by showing us through his baptism that we are lead to freedom in God by repentance and submission to God alone. We are above earthly powers for we belong to God above everything in this world. To be baptized is to be reborn.

First, Jesus by his baptism shows that he is obedient to God's plan for him, whatever that plan should be. This is a willing and free obedience. So we too must recognize our need for the mercy of God, which arises through our own obedience to his plan for our life.

Secondly, Jesus shows us by this act that he was truly immersed in our human condition but without sin. By this baptism, Jesus shows us we that we too must turn to God with an undivided heart. We must, like Jesus, trust in God.

Thirdly, by his being there by the river with sinners, Jesus showed solidarity with each of us. Did he not say: *I came not to call the righteous, but sinners to repentance.* (Luke 5:32; Matthew 9:13; Mark 2:17)

Such solidarity expresses the nearness of God. It is a manifestation of his compassion for us. It demonstrates his understanding of our human fragility and failures and our need for forgiveness and mercy. In baptism, there can be no divided heart. Our mind does not pose questions. Our body is at peace. Our own will is but vanity and we give ourselves to faith in the promises and will of God.

Let us admire the humility of Jesus who associated himself with sinners at his baptism and was willing to pass for one of them even though he himself was without sin. (John 1:

---

2   Note: Where the Solemnity of the Epiphany is transferred to Sunday, if this Sunday occurs on 7 or 8 January, the feast of the *Baptism of the Lord* is celebrated on the following Monday.

29–30) Such humility conducts us to God. But note carefully also how much is profoundly and wonderfully happening by this one act of baptism by Jesus.

The chief mysteries of our religion are displayed at this moment as the whole blessed Trinity manifests itself: the Father by his voice from heaven, the Son visible before us in his human nature, and the Holy Spirit descending as a dove. See how the mission and the whole Gospel of Jesus Christ are here solemnly authorized with a formal consecration and heavenly declaration. See how the Son of God descending into the waters sanctifies them in order for the great effects of regeneration and renovation of the soul to take place through baptism. See how God brings forth the new man, opening heaven in his favour, imparting to him his Holy Spirit and the title and dignity of Son of God.

Let us never forget the rebirth that our baptism brought us. Remember that to be baptized is to be reborn. So let us be of the new Adam, Jesus and of the new Eve, his mother Mary. Let us belong to the will of God without doubting or questioning as they did.

9 January — On the lessons Jesus Christ gives us in his early life

HEN HIS PARENTS found the child Jesus in the temple after searching everywhere for him, he was astounding the religious teachers with his knowledge of religious matters. His mother told him how worried she and Joseph had been, but Jesus simply asked her: *Did you not know that I must be in my Father's house?* Mary and Joseph did not understand then what he meant. (Luke 2:46–50)

Later in his ministry, when he returned to the temple to teach, everyone was again astonished at his wisdom. Jesus reaffirmed and made clear by echoing then what he had said to his mother all those years before as a youngster: *My teaching is not from myself, it comes from the one who sent me.* (John 4: 34) This knowledge of his purpose in living was his daily nourishment during his life on earth. *My food,* he said, *is to do the will of the one who sent me and to complete his work.* (Ibid) This then was the foundation of his private life that Jesus spent in obscurity, living and working under a carpenter's roof. (Luke 2:51–52)

> Yet, in all those years about which we know nothing, Jesus remained a devote Jew, obedient to God's glory. This is the only aspect of his growing up years that we need to know, because it teaches us this important lesson: We came into this world for nothing else but to do the will of God and all our thoughts, words, and actions must be directed to him. Our mission and purpose in life is to be holy. (Ephesians 1:4; Peter 1:16)[3]

Let us begin to be in earnest in building that divine framework for our lives so that we are holy. It is created when we are obedient to the instructions of God, no matter our

---

[3]   Pope Francis, *Gaudete et Exsultate*, Apostolic Exhortation on the call to holiness in today's world, 19 March 2018.

work, no matter what we possess, and no matter how we rank judged by worldly values. All of us need to make continual progress in this way every day, advancing from virtue to virtue until we become that person fully mature with the fullness of Jesus the Christ himself. (Ephesians 4:13) We have been told repeatedly what pleases God; so let us not wait any longer before we follow the example of the Messiah in following our call to God.

10 January—On imitation of the Holy Family

 N SPITE OF poverty and living three days travel away, which in those days was difficult and slow, the Holy Family still went every year to the temple of God in Jerusalem in order to celebrate to celebrate the Passover festival. (Luke 2: 41)

There they assisted at public worship in the Jewish customs, praising God, and offering sacrifices. This is a great example for Christians, because we learn from the Holy Family the importance of diligence in our religious practices and how we should join others in public worship of God at holy celebrations.

Learn, therefore, to put aside every trifling difficulty that might hinder your attendance in God's temple and do not neglect holy feasts and solemnities, not just because you are told it is your duty or obligation to go to them, but because you want to celebrate with your fellow Christians in such worship of God.

Strive then to imitate the Holy Family and do not think about the time or costs of your journey or find other excuses not to go to church.

11 January—On the happiness of having Jesus in your life

EMEMBER WHAT HAPPENED when the Holy Family had gone up to Jerusalem to celebrate the Passover Feast? When it came time to return home, they innocently assumed that Jesus was safely among their many relatives and friends returning with them. But when night fell, they could not find him. Just imagine their anxiety and fear over their child, made even more stressed by thoughts that it was somehow their fault. What anguish they must have felt.

Learn from this story in the life of Mary and Joseph what value you ought to set upon the happiness of having Jesus in your life and how much pain and regret you would have at the loss of him.

However, if sometimes you experience a feeling of the loss of our Lord perhaps by dryness in your devotions or through a sudden spiritual desolation, do not be discouraged nor give yourself up to excessive anguish. Jesus Christ never deserts you. He is never far away and you only imagine him to be lost. The remedy is to keep Jesus in your heart and to reach out to God with hope. Keep praying, no matter how you feel. Imitate Mary and Joseph and keep seeking Jesus.

12 January — On the Wise Men's journey to Bethlehem

HE WISE MEN believed an ancient tradition and prophecy, which said that a great star would be seen in the sky when the king who was to rule the world was born. (Numbers 24:17) Naturally, they expected to hear news of him in Jerusalem, the capital city of Judea. *Where is he, the one born king of the Jews?* they asked when they arrived in the city. *We have seen his star in the east, and have come to adore him.* (Matthew 2:1–2)

But Jesus's kingdom was not of this world and was to be established upon no foundations as in human empires. His kingdom was to be built in the immortal souls of people and upon the ruins of worldly pride and vanities. So a stable in Bethlehem and not the great city of Jerusalem was the birthplace of the Messiah. The choice of Jesus' birthplace by God is our first lesson in *humility*.

Many people then, as in our own days, were so wedded to this world and its beguilement as to be afraid of parting with them in order to find an eternal kingdom. It was easier then, as now, for most people to remain comfortable with what they knew and practiced in their various spiritual beliefs and in the ways of the world. They did not follow the great star to Bethlehem. Just as in our day, most people preferred a clouded vision of reality to faith in the prophecies and promises of God. How much more happy were those wise men, who wanted to find the new king, the promised Messiah, than these people.

Here then, our first prayer arises, because we are answering God's call. It reflects those wise men when we pray: *Lift up the light of your face on us, O Lord.* (Psalm 4:7)

That bright star is now in the sky of our hearts and held aloft there by the Holy Spirit still guiding the way to Jesus.

To seek this heavenly light means we must rejoice in the blessings we get along the way and suffer with patience the wounds we are given as well. But like the wise men, we must persist. Here is our first lesson in *holy perseverance.*

Try then to imitate the wise men in their obedience to the divine call and diligence in seeking Jesus, no matter how difficult or long your spiritual journey. This shows your holy perseverance.

Remember too that the great star still shines, waiting to light your way to Christ. In finding him you will return to God.

13 January—On the faith and offerings of the Wise Men

HE WISE MEN expected to find an infant king. A king attended with all those displays of wealth and pompous ceremonies suitable for someone born to be monarch of the universe. Instead, they found a baby in a stable cared for by a young woman and a humble tradesman with only some domestic animals as companions.

Most people would have turned away in shock with their expectations unfulfilled, but not these wise men. They did not look upon that scene with worldly eyes but with the eyes of faith. Not deceived by appearances, they threw aside all expectations and adored this infant as their King.

How happy are those whose faith, like that of the wise men, takes no shock or scandal or disappointment at either the crib of Jesus or at the cross of Christ, but rather finds in them that eternal donation of his love which unites them more closely to God.

Do we imitate these wise men by any similar humility, reverence, and adoration when we appear before the same Lord in our prayers? Do we kneel in humility?

The Wise Men made offerings of gold, frankincense, and myrrh to signify their honour of him. The gold was a tribute to him as their king. The frankincense, which was used in divine worship, was offered as to their God. The myrrh, which was used in the burial of the dead, as fitting tribute to a mortal man who came to redeem all people by his death.

We may not have gold, frankincense or myrrh to offer, but we have something even more precious to offer: *a pure heart*. Here is our first and best homage to Jesus the Messiah.

14 January—The offerings we are to make by the example of the Wise Men

HE GOLD, FRANKINCENSE, and myrrh offered to our new-born Saviour by the Wise Men are more than what they appear to be. They have mystically deep meanings and it is in these deeper meanings where we find what we can offer to Christ.

For example, let us take gold. When asked about the giving of tribute to Caesar, Jesus held up a coin, imprinted with the image of Caesar, and declared they were to render to Caesar the things that were Caesar's. (Mark 12: 17) This was to give to Caesar what was stamped as his. The same is true for our own life, which is stamped with the image of God. So we render to God the things that are God's. (Matthew 22:19–22) We can do this by offering ourselves—our mind, body and spirit—to God by acts of love. In this way, you give God your finest gold.

In scripture, frankincense is considered as an emblem of prayer and expresses worship. By sending up to Jesus the Messiah the perfume of our devotions to him, we offer incense fragrant with our love. Prayers, then, are the frankincense we should offer to him every day. We should try to have this wonderful perfume of devotion scent all our actions and not just when we are at prayer. If we do this, our life, as we go about our daily work and chores, becomes an offering to God and expresses our worship. In this way, we become living frankincense, a gift to God in the flame of our faith.

We must also offer myrrh, a tree resin whose name means *bitter*. When myrrh is harvested the trees are wounded and bleed this gum. Yet, this precious substance is also one with great powers of healing. This is perhaps the most mysterious of the gifts that the Wise Men offered, because in this gift lies the invisible prophecy of our Lord's suffering and death and the healing redemption of his willing sacrifice for our salvation. Like the tree that gives myrrh, we too are often wounded in the course of living, but unlike that tree we can offer our trials and tribulations to God. In this way, our own suffering becomes healed through God's mercy. We are like myrrh—bitter by our wounding but healed by our faith.

Such myrrh in us always includes self-denial. This makes the wounding of ourselves deep and painful, because we discard those passions and inclinations, which are usually bitter and disagreeable to our nature to give up. We replace them with the rule of virtue. (1 Corinthians 9:24–27; Luke 14:26–27)

So, do not let a day pass without frequently offering to God the gold of your charity, the frankincense of your prayer, and the myrrh of your suffering and self-denial. God will surely accept such offerings, reflecting, as they must, that you are in his service and believe in his promises. In exchange, you will feel the presence of God in your life, because whoever does the will of God remains forever with him. (1 John 2:19–22, Matthew 19:27–29, Mark 10:28–30, Luke 18:28–30, 2 Corinthians 4:16–18)

15 January—On how we belong to God

E BELONG TO God, because he created us. We have been confirmed in this when we were dedicated to him in our baptism. By such consecration, we have affirmed that we belong forever to God by our creation, through our protection in daily life, and by our redemption in the death and resurrection of Jesus the Christ.

By our *creation*, God made us for himself and gave us a spirit capable of knowing, loving, and enjoying him. This spirit is not able to find any true rest or satisfaction but in God.[4] Our body with all its powers, senses, and faculties belong to him as well.

Indeed, all that exists in us whether conscious and visible or unconscious and invisible belongs to God. Since all belongs to him, then like a fig tree in a garden, the fruit we bear is his harvest. Being entirely his possession, we are obliged to produce by our talents, thoughts, words and actions the finest and most acceptable fruit of thanksgiving and praise we can produce. If we do not try to use the gifts he has given us, which spring from our *creation*, then we have failed to consider this obligation to bear fruit.

By his *protection* of our lives, God preserves and maintains the person we are until such time as he deems it time to return to him. Since he is so ready with his grace and mercy to help us continue to live, surely we should live as perfectly as we can by being the person he first created. Surely we should find joy in our just being alive.

We belong to God by our *redemption*, which Jesus purchased for us with his own blood. This redemption brought us salvation. By virtue of this single act, God publicly claimed us as his very own. How can we dare to treat this blood of his covenant as if it were not holy? (Hebrews 10:29)

---

4   St Augustine, *Confessions*, Bk 1, Ch. 1.

As the sovereign of endless universes and the being of all beings, God does not just endow us with these profound ways of belonging to him through our *creation, protection,* and *redemption* He also challenges our love and service by allowing us *free will.* We should not waste time in worrying about why he chooses to give us this power of choice. When we face challenges of living, we can choose whether to fall into temptation or cling to virtue. We have *free will.* We *can* chose. At such a moment, it is helpful to remember that we belong to God.

By our choosing virtue over vice, we reaffirm ourselves as belonging to God by our *creation,* through his *protection* of our daily life, and by our *redemption* in the death and resurrection of Christ. Thus, we are continually healed into joy. We give to God the good harvest of ourselves.

16 January — On the sacred name of Jesus

 EGIN BY MEDITATING on these words about Jesus spoken by the Apostle Paul: *God gave him the name which is above all other names; so that all beings in the heavens, on earth, and in the underworld, should bend the knee at the name of Jesus and that every tongue should acknowledge Jesus Christ as Lord to the glory of God the Father.* (Philippians 2: 7–11)

So the name *Jesus Christ* signifies not just *a Saviour*, but also a Saviour that would deliver men and women from their sins. He would reconcile each lost soul to God and purchase salvation for each person. He would make each an heir of heaven. By all these ways he would give each man and woman a share in his own divinity. None but Jesus the Christ, the *Emmanuel* that is *God with us*, could do this and be to us such a never-failing source of all true good. Christ is the Saviour of the world, the king of kings, the one who was sent to save us, the one sitting at the right-hand side of God. (1 Timothy 6.15; Revelations 17:14, & 19:11–16; 1 John 3:17, & 4:9; Luke 22–69)

Jesus Christ is a name of profound virtue and great power in this world. In this name, the churches of God were planted throughout the earth. In this name, the Apostles wrought all kinds of miracles and even raised the dead to life. By this name, millions of martyrs have overcome death in all its forms. In this name, whole nations have risen up and formed themselves into new and better societies. The cry for *liberty*, *fraternity* and *equality* finds itself in the very meaning of his life and the lessons he taught. This name has peopled the deserts with holy solitaries and every nation of the world in every age with innumerable saints, men and women who kept their hearts fixed on Jesus Christ in the hope of bringing their faith to perfection (Hebrews 12:2) To this sacred name many kings have yielded themselves captives, submitting both themselves and their kingdoms to God. Millions upon millions of men and women have in his name overcome the world, the flesh, and the devil and now stand victorious. (Revelation 3:12 & 21)

Yet, even as the name of *Jesus Christ* carries with it the grandest majesty and power, it remains tempered by humility and love, because this is the character of the divine person who became incarnate to save us. (Colossians 1:15–20) God said, *Be!* And salvation was given to us through the Messiah's life, death, and resurrection. This salvation in Christ promises forgiveness and reconciliation. It preaches to all people the deliverance from their bonds and the healing of all their maladies, visible and invisible. It opens a refuge in all dangers, a place that no one may enter except for the sake of faith and love. This holiest of names encourages us to pray. It draws us to a desire for union with God. In splendour and with all purity, it conquers the world and the flesh. The spirit of Jesus the Christ is resurrected by our faith, attended by our joy, and always present by our side. You have never to doubt, never to have a divided heart, and always to believe.

Here then are a multitude of reasons to always venerate the divine name of *Jesus Christ*, never allowing it to fall from your thoughts, keeping it safely in awareness as the principal object of your Christian faith and the strongest inspiration of your hope. As often as you hear the name *Jesus Christ*, whether in the external world or in your soul, you will be reminded to exercise the three virtues of faith, hope and love.

17 January—Memorial of Saint Anthony of Egypt

 AINT ANTHONY IS considered the father of organized Christian monastic life. His monastery near the Red Sea, *Dayr Mārī Antonios Hermitage,* is still a community of monks.[5] But what can we learn from Saint Anthony's long life of over 100 years that helps us in today's busy world, a world far from the quiet of a monastery in the desert like Saint Anthony created?

In answering this question, we must not forget that such a withdrawal does not mean that such a person, even a religious hermit, leaves this world because he or she hates it.[6] Just the opposite is true as Saint Anthony and many hermits have shown us, because a person enters such solitude in order to face the inner reality of self and to seek God. Thus, withdrawal from the world does not mean to deny or love other people less. On the contrary it leads to more love for others, more prayers for their needs, more awareness of their sorrow and their joy, and more humility as a servant of God.

All solitaries, once they withdraw to such stillness and introspection, must deal with the darkness within themselves—all those vanities, unworthy desires, guilt, denials, lack of love, and other parts of the self until now so carefully hidden away. All these must be brought into the healing light of God, since God knows everything about us anyway. Nothing is hidden from him. None have secrets from him. So the solitary must face squarely up to the laws of God and live the way of life that God showed the world through his Messiah, his prophets and his messengers. This is the only way forward for anyone who withdraws from the world to

---

5   St Athanasius, *Vita St.Antoni,* Vol 4. (written between 356 and 362 AD)
6   *CIC* 603.

seek God. Nothing less will do than total faith in God and love for all men and women.

Now, such a withdrawal to a place of solitude does not have to be to some physical place. For example, a desert as Saint Anthony did or a cabin in the far mountains or other isolated place. Places remote from a busy world may help the solitary, but they are *not* necessary. What *is* necessary is for the solitary is to withdraw into his or her inner world of stillness, an inner world that abides in all of us. It is an interior place Saint Teresa called *the divine dwelling place of God.*[7]

This inner divine place is a place of deepest self, a place where only God and you may enter. It is a place of peace away from the worries and stress of this world, a place of true solitude. You can go to this inner space, this spiritual palace of God's indwelling, no matter who you are. Rich or poor. Home-based or homeless. Emotionally stable or trying to over-come addiction to substances or bad relationships. In prison or in society. Nothing stands in your way of going to this inner space. You can go there no matter where you are in life at this time. You need not be a saint or even greatly holy. After all, Jesus the Messiah was sent for sinners, not the righteous—and we are all sinners one way or another. (Mark 2:17; Luke 5:32)

However, you must not have a divided heart. Your faith must be strong, because as Saint Anthony and many others have found out this interior pilgrimage of the person seeking God is long, difficult, full of hidden temptations, and both good and bad surprises. To seek God takes great courage and great humility.

We arrive in this inner desert of ourselves by the way of stillness, reflection about the realties of our life and, most of all, and a fervent desire to be with God. In this desert or solitude, we want to be embraced by God's mercy, to be cradled in his love, and to be at peace with ourselves and the

---

[7]   *Selected Writings of Teresa of Avila*, Ch. 4.

world with that peace promised by Jesus. (John 14:27) What this means is that we want God above all things on earth and in heaven.

We do not have to be solitary or a hermit unless we feel God has called us to that form of life in his service. Nevertheless, we all need as often as possible to go into such solitude, such stepping out of our daily routines and responsibilities, such aloneness with God. Otherwise we remain too busy, too preoccupied with this world, too concerned with everyday duties and worries.

So imitate Saint Anthony by discarding your self-concerns and vanities to discover that inner solitude, this desert within, that divine dwelling place of God where rewards of heavenly grace await you. Here you will find the true identity of who and what you are and the presence of God.

18 January — On the necessity of consideration

ONSIDERATION MEANS WE look carefully at something—a situation, an idea, or what someone said to us. To consider something means we think about what may be the consequences of it and what may happen by any action or inaction we take over it. For the Christian this means considering every act or any temptation in the light of faith and the teachings of Jesus.

How is it possible then that so many Christians should live as they do, taking those actions or putting themselves in situations that lead them to break God's instructions for how we are to lead our lives?

We could claim that such people just do not *think* before acting. This *not thinking* has nothing to do with a lack of intelligence, education, social standing or a misunderstanding of the Word of God. It is simply that such people lack *consideration*. They do not think about what they claim to believe. They act *before* they think. They do not contemplate the consequences of their choices and actions. In short, it is because as Christians they don't consider the result of an action or situation *before* it happens. They forget the teaching of Jesus and the values of God. It is just as Jesus told us: *the spirit is willing enough, but human nature is weak.* (Matthew 26:40)

So the good Christian thinks about the truths of what he or she believes. Such a person considers these heavenly truths of living. In doing so, faith is refreshed and the light of God shows what needs to be done. In this way, *consideration* brings forth the fruits of virtue.

On the other hand, the bad Christian seems unaffected with the truths of the gospel. The Word of God makes little or no impression on him or her, because their faith has fallen asleep, worn out from lack of that awakening which *consideration* of the consequences of temptation brings. Just imagine what a transformation of the world we would see if only men and women were simply to think of these truths of God and obey his command to love: No wars. No cruelty. No want of food, shelter and clean water. Peace between tribes and nations. Peace between neighbours. Peace between men and women. An amnesty made of everlasting love. A peace for which the world yearns.

To make *consideration* a part of the way you live, allow yourself time to meditate everyday on one or another of the great truths that relate to God and to eternity. You hear them when you read and reflect on the gospel. You hear them whenever you go to church. You hear them from priests, ministers, pastors, and fellow Christians. Are you listening?

Refresh yourself with the teachings of Jesus Christ. Give yourself hope by your faith in the promises of God. Give love to everyone you meet, because in each person Christ is resurrected and lives. These are the best means to secure the safety of your soul and the peace of your mind. This is to consider what God would want *before* you act, *before* you succumb to temptations, and *before* you forget you are a servant of God.

19 January — On the holy consideration of God

 E HAVE BEEN warned to never forget the many evils that may come pouring upon us when the knowledge of God is wanting. (Hosea 4:1–2) But how are we to gain and then sustain such knowledge of God? What we need is the help of *holy consideration* — that is we must think, reflect, regard, weigh, and contemplate that which is *of* God. If in doubt we have all the prophets in the Books of God to help us. In this way of *holy consideration*, we discover God and what he wants for us. With this kind of thinking comes the motives we have for obeying him.

Without this kind of *holy consideration*, we remain in a spiritual paradox that is we know these things about God yet somehow we do not know them. It is as if we were wise, yet ignorant at the same time. The trouble is that we are spiritually blind. When the light of the knowledge of God begins to dispel our darkness, we awake to a greater vision, a vision that lifts us beyond our insignificant worldly concerns, vanities, and distractions. This greater vision, shaped by all that is holy, brings us to those things, which are of God: infinite beauty and perfection, the mercy of unconditional love, and the redeeming gift of salvation given through Jesus the Messiah.

Being eternal, God has no beginning or end. He is constantly changing in his creation and, yet, he does not change. Independent of all things in all universes, he alone may say, *I am he who is.* (Exodus 3:13–15) All other things, whether living or inanimate are nothing in themselves except as his possession. They have no being but in him for he is the *being* of everything from humans to the stones of the moon and the light of the stars.[8] God is the immense, the incomprehensible, the infinite, filling all universes, maker of all that is seen and unseen from the stars above to the dust at our feet, always in

---

[8] St Thomas Aquinas, *Summa Theologiae, Treatise on the one God.*

a state of creating, preserving, moving, ruling, and supporting all things. Infinitely wise, powerful, good, just, and merciful, he is beauty and truth itself. Do you see now what an immense field of choice we have here for our *holy consideration*? Here is more than enough to employ us forever in our seeking to be always with God. Just one aspect of God is enough to meditate on for a lifetime and many saints have done just that.

In spite of all these wondrous attributes, God belongs to each of us and we to him. It is this intimacy that is the ultimate *holy consideration* of God, which brings our love of him and our willing obedience. As our Creator and eternal possession, he alone can satisfy our yearning for the meaning of our lives and the deepest desire we have for an everlasting life. We are told again and again that God wants to give us knowledge, wisdom, and faith. Did he not create Jesus the Messiah to be our very own, to walk among us, to perform miracles through him, to teach us right from wrong and, finally, to show us what love really means? How is it possible, then, for anyone to turn away from God?

Pleasing God brings meaning to every life and forgiveness and love brings happiness and contentment. Here are the very foundation stones of our *holy consideration* of God. (1 John 4:8)

20 January — On consideration of the law of God

E MUST UNDERSTAND the holy instructions and sayings of the gospel of Jesus the Christ. Moreover, we must know them in such a manner as to be convinced of their truth. Only in this way may we keep them with a full heart, knowing that any rights we think we possess as individuals are not infringed by the books of God, but enhanced by their truths.

Now such conviction infers the necessity of frequent meditation on God's Word, because without this serious attention we may easily forget the duties and obligations of our life in God. Happy indeed is the person who ponders his law day and night. Such a person will be like a tree planted beside waters and which always bears fruit. *Prosperity* is the name of this blessed fruit and it is the gift of God when you meditate on his divine rulings for your life. (Psalm 1:1–3)

God command us long ago to keep his words in our heart, to tell them to our children, and to think about them whatever we are doing, whether working or walking or sitting. His words were to be, as it were, written on our foreheads and physically on the walls, doors and gates of our house. Everywhere we were to be reminded of his commandments. (Deuteronomy 6: 4–9)

Now, if under the ancient books of God, he was pleased to require this close and frequent attention to meditating on his divine precepts, how much more does he expect it from us under the new covenant of love that is Jesus the Messiah? Here, God delivers commandments not just engraved on stone as he did for Moses but on our hearts, our souls, and our minds. (Exodus 25:21 & 31:18, Deuteronomy 10:2 &5)

Psalm 118 makes it absolutely clear that we must meditate on God's commandments. There is scarcely one verse in which the beauty and excellence of the divine law, the love and observance of it, the great happiness of keeping it, and the many advantages of meditating upon it, are not strongly urged on us. At the beginning of each day's prayers we are reminded once again *to listen to his voice*. (Psalms 118 & 94)

This kind of listening activates your spirit. It will turn your thoughts away from vain and curious searches into things of little or no real importance. It will turn you to what God requires of you by his holy law and what his will is regarding your life. Such discernment is the very business with which we need to be concerned. How little science and all our other curiosity about things matter if this first and most important instruction to listen to God is neglected.

You must cease, therefore, from the desire of trying to know everything. This unabated curiosity of *needing to know* is a curse of humanity, because in that quest there is too much distraction and deceit.

Curiosity is also often the beginning of gossip and gossip always leads to judgments about other people and we know this is forbidden because judgment belongs only to God and Jesus Christ.

In any case, information, data, discoveries of science, and other "facts" declared true today are often changed or gone tomorrow. We know our world is filled with false information and that social and political truths are frequently so hidden from us that we never discover them. Nothing is certain that comes out of this world.

Instead make God's commandments the focus of your life. These truths are holy and eternal. They do not change with time and the fashions of your society or the claims of politics, cultures, and sciences. God's commandments hold no distraction or deceit. They do not ask you to be curious but obedient.

21 January — On consideration of ourselves

ESIDES THE OBLIGATION to know God and our duty to him, there is another part of understanding that calls for your serious consideration. This is the knowledge of your self.

Know thyself is a demanding consideration that takes great courage but it is necessary. Without this, we fail God and ourselves. Lack of it makes for weak faith and disobedience to God. Lack of it leads finally to a careless attitude to others. This lack of consideration of ourselves is the very beginning of pride, envy, and self-love.

The monk Thomas à Kempis tells us that if we would truly be enlightened and delivered from all blindness of heart then this knowing ourselves is the most profitable lesson we can learn, because in knowing ourselves we are better able to correct our faults and so better imitate the life of the sinless man, Jesus. But Thomas added that *he who knows himself well is mean and abject in his own sight, and takes no delight in the vain praise of men.*[9]

In knowing ourselves, we discover our faults and this makes for a humble knowledge, rather than any pride. This kind of knowing certainly informs us, but it does nothing to boast our ego. In fact, such knowing results in humility. Hence, this learning about your self the way to humility — a humility which is essential if we are to live like Jesus, powerful through God but a servant to all men and women. (Isaiah 42:1–4; Mark 10:45; Luke 22:27) Saint Bernard of Clairvaux insisted that such humility is the mother of salvation and Saint Augustine assured us, if we are to rise to heaven, we must first descend and lay the foundation of humility. What is Christian perfection then, but the depth of humility about your self?[10] Such humility teaches us to take

---

9   Thomas à Kempis, *The Imitation of Christ*, Book 1:2.
10   Saint Isaac, *The Desert Fathers.*

no pride in ourselves, neither in our material possessions nor social status nor in our power. We discover that we are simply not better than any other person. (Galatians 3:28–29, Proverbs 22:2; Colossians 3:11) This is a hard truth to bear and many people, including Christians, simply cannot accept it. They secretly or openly believe that they are better than some people, because of their money or power and social position or talents. Aspects of ourselves that make us feel different from others often make us act superior to others, but such feelings of being different are superficial. They are without merit, because we are all equal in God. Unless we become humble about ourselves how are we to be obedient to the commandment to love?

In learning this hard truth about ourselves, we have ventured into our inner darkness and found there the spoiled remains of worldly desires and vanities. Most of all, we discover how unimportant we are in the greater scheme of life and how very little control we have over anything that happens to us or others, even the children we raise. We discover that this old saying rings true: *the local cemetery is full of people who thought the world could not do without them.* The humility brought by knowing yourself is the foundation of all other virtues and they cannot exist without it.

Now this knowledge of ourselves is not acquired without serious consideration about what we have been in the past, what we are at present, and what we shall be in the future. It is an examination of ourselves like no other. Such considerations as these take very great courage, because we must see ourselves as we really are and, finding no reason to be proud and every reason to be thoroughly humble, we are shaken to our very core. This shaking-up of our mind, body, and spirit is the beginning of humility. *Awake! Awake!* is the message we must hear. (Ephesians 5:14)

Think how very difficult it is in ordinary daily living to discern true good from that which is only appears so and how strong are our passions and self-love. Consider then how much more difficult it is to cast aside such passions and self-love and return to God. We so frequently forget that no sooner were we born than we started at once to live by the principles of this world and were in rebellion against the word of God. (Ephesians 2:1–6) Is this still the way you are today? Is true humility still lacking in you? Have you secrets and hidden vices that you have not yet claimed in repentance before God?

If so, then face up now to how soon death will be with you and return you to dust. See if this does not humble you so much that you finally place all your trust in the guidance of God. Pray daily for such self-knowledge as did St. Augustine so you may be free from sin, truly humble, and return to God: *Lord let me know myself in order that I may know you.*[11]

---

[11] St Augustine of Hippo *Confessions*; also prayed by St Therese of Jesus.

22 January — On the purpose of your life

URELY YOU HAVE often thought about the purpose of your life, especially when you are bored, stressed, having relationship problems, or depressed. Did you ask yourself then: Is this all there is? Did you wonder about the purpose of your life? Did you ask yourself: What does it all mean?

The answers lie not in the pursuits, successes, and purposes of this passing world. The answers are found in holy matters. These are much more important if for no other reason that they are eternal. They do not change with society or culture or the fashions of the day. They last. This is what you want and what you need — answers you can cling to, answers that make sense of your life, and answers that do not change.

This is where God and what he has said comes into force. It relieves your boredom. It distresses you. It puts understanding and love back into wherever relationship problems you are having at the moment. If you are depressed, it brings you out of darkness into the light and gives you hope in your life. It answers your questions about the meaning of your life.

So in these eternal values, you will find the reasons for your being and the end purpose of your earthly life.

Now, of course, you can go on pleading ignorance about these things and go on suffering. But you ought to be ashamed to pretend not to understand, because God has taught you about them. After all, were you not baptized? Have you not dedicated yourself to God through believing in him? Are you not blessed in knowing, no matter who you are, no matter whether poor or rich, no matter free or confined by law or injustice, that your life has the highest purpose, because you belong to God and not to yourself? Have you forgotten that you were born a part of the divine, a possession of God and that you made in his image? Have you forgotten that you born into this life to have joy? Have you ceased to listen with your heart to the Word and to the prophets of God?

How noble then is your being, your very life. Are you not a precious possession of God? How glorious then is your life, a life designed and destined for nothing less than heaven itself. How can you forget to what end you were made? How can any of us forget in our self-concern that we are unique and a divine creation? How can God believe in us and yet we not believe in ourselves? In remembering God, you will find the meaning of your life on earth.

The path of life you are to follow is clearly shown you in the Gospel. If you do not follow the way shown by God, then perhaps the reason is because you try to fulfil the expectations of those you love, your family and friends, or the society you live in or the political system to which you claim to belong? All these efforts are trying to please the world, when you need first and foremost to fulfil the expectations of God — expectations that he has clearly explained to you through his prophets and his Messiah.

These expectations of God is what the Apostle Luke speaks of when he tells us about Jesus admonishing Martha, when she was concerned with worldly things and forgot to put heavenly considerations first. Jesus told her and through this lesson he also told us: *Martha, Martha, you worry and fret about so many things and yet few are needed, indeed only one.* (Luke 10:38–42)

What is this *one necessary thing* that Martha and we need? Jesus is telling us that we need to rise above the material labours and things of this world and listen to the Word of God and live by it — this is *the one necessary thing*.

If you apply yourself seriously to this instruction of what is vitally important in living, all will be well with your life, because the foundation and focus of everything you do will be based on the knowledge and love of God. Neglect this *one necessary thing* and all is truly lost, however great the success you may have in the eyes of the world or how neglected and unimportant you may feel.

What, then, would anyone gain by winning the whole world only in the end to forfeit eternal life? (Matthew 16:26; Mark 8:36) Do not fool yourself and try to serve both the world and God by having a divided heart. (Ecclesiastics 1:28; John 12:25–26)

Remember that people who live too much in the world and are forgetful of God become like children exhausted by too much play. They wear themselves out with fleeting vanities, catching at bubbles and empty shadows, vain honours, false riches, and deceitful pleasures that last but a moment. It is not surprising then how many people feel bewildered, complain about a lack of happiness, and suffer unexplained depression in spite of all they possess, and are constantly searching for anything, which will give meaning to their life? Such want of God eventually empties the heart and starves the spirit. Has this been so for you? Are you confounded by a strange restlessness and a sense of dissatisfaction in the face of plenty? Do you seek answers in this world when answers lay in the Word? If true, then turn to God where you will find comfort and the fullest meaning of your earthly life. Since you were created for a life of joy, do not let such a great gift and such a wonderful grace escape you.

23 January — On Jesus changing water into wine

EDDINGS ARE USUALLY joyous occasions but imagined how especially blessed was one marriage in Cana in Galilee attended by Mary and Jesus. (John 2:1–11)

As if Jesus being there was not enough, he performs a miracle. But in this miracle, Jesus showed more than just his power from God. By his presence at this celebration, he also shows his endorsement of marriage, the virtue of being happy for others, and the pleasure to be found in being with family and friends and in sharing faith together for a marriage is a solemn exchange of vows. In summary, Jesus shows us that joy is a virtue and a thanksgiving to God for his many blessings. The wedding couple and their guests do not forget, like so many people, God's grace and protection. (Tobit 6:6 *The Fish* 17–18 to the end)

Just as Jesus through God changed the water into wine at Cana, God himself often changes events in our favour when the waters of the sea of our life are turbulent. He does this by the consolation he gives us in our worries and afflictions through the grace of his spiritual presence and that of our constant friend and mentor, Jesus the Messiah. God reminds us that we are to quench our thirst at the joyous water of life, finding in it the refreshment and fresh strength of humility as Jesus did so that we continue with our head held high as a sign of the victory of God. This leaves behind us the bitter wine of discontentment, pride, and remorse. All our foes are put behind us. (Psalm 109)[12]

Indeed, the miracle of the wine takes place every day in our lives when we celebrate Christ at the altar. It is in such a miracle, like the wedding in Cana, that God sees fit to change our situation into one of joy. We are filled with the good wine of love.

---

[12] St. Augustine, *The Confessions*.

24 January—Memorial of Saint Francis de Sales

O WE FORGET humility when anger, resentment or pride overcomes us? Is our meekness put to one side when we feel challenged by others? Does our self-assertion conquer all? Has pride too often triumphed over our resolve to imitate Jesus through humility? Even worse perhaps, is when we are guilty of *false pride*. This happens when we feel proud about how spiritual we are with our devotions, our prayers and our regular attendance at church. *False pride* is often hidden even from the person who suffers from it, because someone who seems very pious may not be humble of heart. Humility never keeps company with such pride for vice and virtue cannot exist equally in the same person. Either we are humble or we are not.

So real humility is difficult to possess, because we too often belong to the values of this world unlike Saint Francis who had a special calling to this virtue. One thing that can help us here is to turn for inspiration and guidance to that great Christian masterpiece, Saint Francis's *Introduction to the Devout Life*. This little book first published in 1609 and translated into all major languages, is still widely popular with both Protestants and Catholics.

For an example, consider *friendship*. How often do we become involved in some affair of friendship that has proven to be contrary to our faith? Saint Francis comes right to the point. He tells anyone, who becomes entangled in such an affair, not to waste time in trying to unravel the ties that bind you to the other person but simply to sever them. He declares such bonds valueless. Never hesitate, he advises, to break away with no consideration at all for a love that conflicts with the love of God.[13] If you think this to hard to do, then

---

[13] St. Francis de Sales, *Introduction to the Devout Life*, Part 3, Chapter 21. 1 & 2.

remember that the Lord will help break the chains that bind you. (Psalm 123:7)

In the breaking of such chains, Saint Francis tells us, do not think you have not been loving, because in freeing yourself you also free the other person, because that relationship which has not been good for you has also not been good for the other person.[14] In this way, your action has been done out of love for the other person and for God.

Conclude then to practice virtue in all friendships by the discernment that comes from loving your friends in spite of their imperfections but never loving such faults, especially any which conflict with your love of God. Saint Francis reminds us that friendship, indeed all relationships of any kind requires that we share the good of it but not the evil. So look again at your friendships and those whom you allow into your life. It is up to you to separate worth from dross. (Jeremiah 15:19)

---

[14] See *Introduction to the Devout Life: The Practice of Virtue,* Chap 21.9.

25 January—Feast of the Conversion of Saint Paul

 UST THINK OF the amazing grace of God in the conversion of Paul. In an instant, he was changed from a bloody persecutor of Christians to a believer in the risen Christ. Moreover, he became a disciple of Christ, zealously preaching the gospel to carry the teachings of Jesus to nations, kings and the gentiles.

The conversion of Paul is set before you as a model of a perfect conversion, because no sooner was Paul called by Christ than he immediately obeyed and gave himself up to be Christ's disciple forever. (Acts 9:3–9)

Are you ready to obey Our Lord as quickly as Paul? Are you at all times prepared to hear his call? (Psalm 94:8) Is your heart always ready to serve Our Lord or is it still divided between the demands of this world and the laws of God? (Psalm 56:8) Do you desire like Moses to be obedient and accepting of God's will for whatever happens in your life, regardless of your own individual desires? (Deuteronomy 10, especially verses 12–13)

These are questions we must frequently ask ourselves so that we remain in a state of listening to God with the ear of our heart.[15] Paul's history tell us that the conversion of anyone is possible, no matter how remote he or she may seem from faith in God or a belief in the divine creation of Jesus. Be assured that the power, mercy, and goodness of God is as great right now as it was in the time of Paul.

Therefore, never forget you have been promised that if you remain in God and his Word remains in you, you may ask for whatever you please and you will get it. (John 15:7) So never cease to pray to God for the conversion of all those who do not yet profess to belong to God and to believe that Jesus was the Messiah.

---

[15] See *Rule of St. Benedict*, Prologue, 1.

26 January — On the evil of sin

 ust as God's own goodness is infinite love, so evil is a bottomless pit. There is no end to unhealthy desires and the baggage of bad memories whether true or imagined, because these are as much evil as anything else for they lack all happiness, peace of mind and true contentment in life. After all, God did not create you to be miserable.

Do you carry such odious burdens in your life? Is the baggage of yesterday weighing you down and preventing you from looking forward with pleasure to tomorrow? Are you so emotionally unstable that you are making someone else's life a misery? Can the beauty of your body or the gracefulness of your youth or your worldly wealth or the seeming wisdom of your learning be hiding within such a monster? (Ezekiel 28:1–10, 28: 17) Has arrogance and sophistication in this world blinded you to what could be your terrible fate in the life to come as it was for the Devil himself? (Revelation 20:10)

There is nowhere a greater temptation than to sin, because it was by such sinful behaviour that the chosen angel, called *the Devil*, was transformed from a being of perfect beauty beloved by God into an object of terror. (Ezekiel 28:13–19) Sin is the death that separates us from God. (Isaiah 59:2; Romans 6:23) It is a rebellion against God inasmuch as such people turn away from God, affecting an independence from him, preferring their own will, and the gratifying of their own inclinations and passions instead of God's holy will and his divine laws. They renounce their allegiance to God and disclaim his authority and sovereignty over them. This is a refusal to be subject to his Word, to condemn his wisdom, to slight his justice, and to refuse his mercy and goodness. The sinner forgets how to love others. His or her misery is self-made.

In fact, such men and women have set up the idol of self in place of God. To this idol of their own self-love, they sacrifice everything. Can there be any other evil comparable to this?

As to all past guilt about your sin, regret it with all your heart and do penance for it and thank God for his mercy. *Repent! Repent!* is the cry of all those who would please God. (Luke 13:3)

27 January—On the many terrible things found in mortal sin

 HE APOSTLE JAMES warns us that anyone who keeps the whole of the law but trips up on a single point is still guilty of breaking it all. (James 2:10) So there is not just the breaking of one commandment in every mortal sin but also the guilt of breaking all the *Ten Commandments*.

You may consider that this cannot be so, thinking that to break one rule is not to be guilty of all the others as in worldly law. However, this kind of thinking does not work in the case of God's law, because who ever wilfully breaks any part of the divine law by mortal sin violates the first commandment by turning away from the one God.

In this primary disobedience, a man or woman has refused the worship due to God and are guilty of idolatry by worshipping the creature instead of the Creator. Most often that creature is he or herself and includes the thinking that other people do not matter. (Romans 1:25)

Never believe that you are above mortal sin. Pray everyday that you will never fall prey to this most terrible of evils.

28 January — Memorial of Saint Thomas Aquinas

 HOMAS AQUINAS EXERTED profound influence on Christian theology and Western philosophy. In spite of the considerable complexity of his ideas, his spiritual writing concerns issues that every Christian faces in their pilgrimage with Jesus. His works have been for centuries the most widely read books after the Bible itself. If you are not yet acquainted with this spiritual guide, then begin when he says: *No man truly has joy unless he lives in love.*[16]

So ask yourself "What do I *really* love?" Hardly anyone can list such things on the spur of the moment. The best thing is to make an honest list. You will be surprised at what you write down and probably unpleasantly so. But you will better understand what you are now and how much you must change in order to imitate Jesus and submit willingly to God's laws. If you desire a new life in Christ then ask God to teach you his path so that you may always walk in his truth. (Psalm 24:4–5)

---

[16] St Thomas Aquinas, *Opusc. XXXV, De Duobus Praeceptis.*

29 January — Taking time with God

 VERY SAINT IS important, because each has lived a life from which we may draw lessons that help us to become closer to God.

Many saints lived in the world, yet they were apart from it. For example, Saint Teresa of Avila lead an astoundingly busy life in the world, fulfilling her vision of the religious life and, yet, still being obedient to the requirements of her vows as a nun. Many other saints withdrew from the world by going to the desert and finding there in silence, simplicity of living, and in solitude the companionship of God. Such men and women living for God in a more complete withdrawal from human society as hermits still exist in many lands today, echoing the forty days that Jesus spent in the wilderness. (Matthew 4:1–11; Mark 1:12–13; Luke 4:1–13)

Some saints were single, some married, some had children, while others guarded their chastity all their lives. Many lived in the world but none lived by worldly values and fashions. Many died, martyrs for their faithfulness to God and Christ.

Every Christian, just like the saints and vowed solitaries, need time and space alone with God. All need time to pray. A time to assess their lives. A time to heal and renew their faith. A time to repent and reconcile themselves with God. A time to give God praise and honour. All the saints and hermits for God teach us the importance of these habits of taking time and space for God in one way or another. Imitate these examples and profit by them and they will bring you closer to God.

30 January—On the havoc sin has created in the world

 F ANGELS CAN be thrown out of heaven, just think what a mere human may suffer. (Revelation 12:7–8) Do not think for a moment that such spiritual warfare is not going on at this very moment. It is all around you. Many have grown complacent and believe that nothing prompts men and women to displease God except their own evil and that there is no spiritual force behind such holy treason. Such people have forgotten Adam and Eve in the Garden and that serpent of temptation who brought them the first lesson in what happens when you wilfully disobey God. A lesson we so often forget.

There was then, and there is now a force at work and we call this personal force *Satan, Lucifer,* or the *devil,* the fallen angel who was once the closest to God. This malignant and angry angel never rests in his work of tempting men and women to disobey God. All human–made advances and knowledge are as nothing in such a spiritual war. Only the grace of God protects you.

Look what happened when the innocence, justice, and sanctity of the first Adam and Eve were stripped away. The consequences of their disobedience inflicted upon all humans to come an inexpressible weakness with regard to the doing of good and an inclination to evil. This has filled the world with innumerable horrors in a forgetfulness of love, all caused by wilful sin both by individuals and the collective cruelty of whole nations.

If you should have any doubt of this, then look at the state of so many people around you and the terrors and fears in this world. See the shocking television or digital news. Listen to the complaining lyrics of today's popular songs. Hear the roars of protestors trying to find justice. Wonder at the many wars.

Count the refuge camps. All these events and more show you how hard it is for love to survive. How easy it is for evil to reign. How often men and women chose that which leads to evil. Indeed, such wilful sin always creates havoc, devastating the whole of creation and subjecting you along with billions of others to a slavery of corruption. (Romans 8:20–21)

Remember also that scoffers whose lives are ruled by passions and vanities will claim that the promises of God will not be fulfilled. They say that prophets and messengers always broadcast dire warnings of doom about final days. Such doubting people as these scoffers are serpents in the gardens of our soul. They make us forget that the *Day of Judgment* will happen in God's own time and not time as measured by the world. It could be in the next five minutes or in a thousand years from now. God is not slow in carrying out his promises, but he is patient for he wants nobody to be lost and everyone to be brought to repentance. (2 Peter 3:1–10)

31 January—On what sin does to a Christian

AVE YOU EVER noticed how strangely men and women are changed when they fall into the ways of sin? How love and kindness seem no longer part of their motives? This change or metamorphosis is not unlike that of the best angel changing into the worse demon. It is a butterfly in reverse. First it is a delightful beauty, and then turns into an ugly caterpillar. But a person choosing to remain in grace is a favoured child of God, a brother or sister of Jesus, and a temple of the Holy Spirit.

When a man or woman consents to a mortal sin, all honour and dignity leaves them. They are filled with unclean spirits, losing all virtue and merit. Their good values are gone. They turn into self-serving people, motivated by only that which serves their desires. From then on, nothing but unhappiness and discontent in one form or the other is the state of that person. If they have power or riches, they fear losing them. If they enjoy a great but illicit passion, it grows cold. While they can buy the world, ill health and depression still strikes them. The list is endless. Just when it seems nothing can get worse, death comes. The soul is trapped. The Holy Spirit has fled. Their disobedient hearts are empty of love. They are quickly forgotten. They remain dust forever.

Are you enduring such wretched conditions right now? Is your life so dark that your life seems meaningless? If so, then open your eyes now to your deplorable state. Recognize that this burden is your own fault. No one else is to blame, no matter what scapegoat you want to pick. It is caused by your refusal to be obedient to God's commands and the teachings of his Messiah.

The solution is singular. You need to return to God as soon as possible. You need to find the repentance that alone can release you from this burden you carry and which will raise you from something dead to the joy of living. (Tobit 13: 10; Psalm 12:6)

It is the spirit of a person that gives them vitality, courage and creativity and all those other attributes, which we so rightly admire. This spirit, which is the true nature of the soul, exists by the grace of God. This is its source of life, the *being* of its existence.

FEBRUARY

Themes: *Pleasing God and what God offers in return. Preparing for Lent.*

 SALM 56 LINE 8 declares, My heart is ready, O God, My heart is ready. I will sing, I will sing your praise. But is your heart really ready for God? Think about what Saint Thomas Aquinas said: The things that we love tell us what we are. Try going back to that list of what you love that you made on the feast day of Saint Thomas.

Well then, what do you love?

1 February — On little offenses to God

E FREQUENTLY FORGET the little offenses to God that we do everyday. We excuse ourselves, thinking such offenses do not matter for they seem so small and unimportant in the greater scheme of things. It was if it was only deeds like murder, torture, or theft really counted. How wrong we are to think this way.

These *little offenses* do not break our friendship with God, but they injure it through disobedience to his teachings. Even though we know right from wrong, we often do the wrong thing by God because it is considered the right thing by the world. For example, do you think this way when you fear incurring the displeasure of a friend and take refuge in a phoney apology, believing this insincerity of regret, which is a lie and the wrong choice by God's standards, will heal your friendship? Do you indulge yourself in vanity, curiosity, sensuality, anger, impatience, and other bad habits, because you think these are just *little offenses*, and, therefore, need not be regarded seriously? Is your repentance just a phoney apology without depth of feeling or true regret? If the truth were known, are you sometimes even guilty of making a half-hearted confession at church? Do you tell *little lies* to just get by?

God knows you better than anyone else, because he reads your heart and knows the truth of you. Unlike a social friend, he is never fooled. *Little offenses,* then, are important.

When you continue to make light of any displeasing of God you are in a dangerous situation, because if you disregard the importance of smaller actions in your life, you sink slowly but surely into worse evils. (Ecclesiastics 19:1) Such behaviour eventually makes for bad habits. Such bad habits become harder and harder to shake off. They weaken and cool your desire for God's mercy and love. They lessen your time at prayer and contemplation.

In this way, bad habits may start as *little offenses* but they result in hindering the full work of the Holy Spirit within you. They set up, as it were, roadblocks on your pilgrimage to God. You begin to stumble. Slowly, your life becomes one of good intentions but no resulting good actions. You sink to your knees in self-love and frustration with your life. You find excuses not to go to church. Prayer time slips away. Thinking of holy matters is forgotten. You are overcome with worries and anxieties. In short, you stop your holy pilgrimage with Jesus.

Such is often the result of not paying attention to *little offenses*. This leaves your soul languishing and half-asleep so when a greater temptation arrives you easily yield to it.

It is hard to reconcile the indulging of what may seem harmless habits with the commandment to love. But we cannot expect the divine love of God to dwell in our hearts if we continually slight him by forgetting that love is given in small ways as well as grand ones. If you cannot love in the many small ways of daily living, how do you think you are going to act when the challenge to love is a difficult one? Indeed, how will you ever be able to love your enemy? (Matthew 5:44)

The world in its quickly changing ideas of what is right and what is wrong may continue to mock those who strive for purity and innocence, but such hopeful goodness pleases God. So make a sincere resolution to ignore the cynicism of this world, not to let wicked ways ensnare you, and to stop consenting to sin no matter how slight it may seem to be at the time. (Psalm 118: Aleph) There are no places for *little offenses* in your life where love is concerned and love is what our religion is about.

2 February—Feast of The Presentation of The Lord

E CELEBRATE THIS day as special for it holds much that pleases God and keeps us faithful. On such a day, Mary, according to the rites prescribed by the ancient law of the Jews, came to the temple of God to be purified after her child-bearing and to make an offering of thanksgiving according to what her poverty allowed. In her case, she brought a pair of pigeons, one for an offering and one as a sacrifice for sin. (Leviticus 12: 1–8) Notice here that Mary did not consider herself, a woman singularly favoured by God, as exempt from the requirements of her religion. She was willing to be considered like all other Jewish women who had recently given birth. What humility!

This meant she joined other such women as physically and spiritually *unclean,* when in fact she was as pure as the angels, but such was the thinking of her religion about women who had just given birth. For such women, it meant exclusion for forty days from touching anything that was holy or coming near the house of God. Yet, all this time Mary was nursing the beloved Messiah sent by God.

What we should admire here and to take as an example for our own lives, is Mary's desire not to disobey God in *any* matter. It is this obedience to God in *all* things, which truly purifies. In just this one lesson of Mary's faithfulness to God through her practice of the requirements of her religion, we find those great virtues of obedience, humility, and love of purity. Here is the meaning of this feast day for us: *Obedience, humility, and love of purity.*

3 February—In the vineyard of the Lord

 E BEGIN TODAY a time of devotion in preparation for Lent. It helps to remember that in the vineyard of Our Lord we have but one concern in this world and that is to persevere in our labour to secure that harvest which is eternal life. (Matthew 10: 9). This is the thought to keep in mind as we race toward that glorious prize offered by God. *Perseverance* is what we must possess to win that prize. (1 Corinthians: 7)

4 February — On the arrogance of reason

 E HAVE PRIZED reason for many centuries as high wisdom. Reason makes us question everything. Yet, such constant questioning rarely leads to satisfaction. Once we apply reason to everything, including the mysteries of God, our minds produce endless questioning of that which we once accepted as pure and not in need of explaining or understanding by human standards. For example, we accept the purity of spiritual mystery and that faith is a gift of God. This is not the outcome of reason and rational thinking, but faith for belief in what we cannot see or explain. (John 20: 29) While reason may have its rightful place in our life, innocence is often needed. This is why faith is a heavenly grace not arrived at by reason.

For many people, reason is none other than endless curiosity to explain everything. But such curiosity brings no lasting result except a divided heart and the wilderness of unsure faith and a doubt about what is truth. Then, confusion reigns and we find we are not one thing or the other. Indeed, we are lost. None of this curiosity ultimately satisfies our burning desire to know and explain the world around us. Even less, it hardly gives any meaning to our lives.

In the end, there is always still something that needs explaining. But the human spirit gives us plenty of examples of how much about our lives cannot be explained. For example, how does one explain *courage*? How does one define *falling in love*? How would you describe *happiness*? Things, events, and feelings we hold most dear are often those we cannot fully explain. Acceptance of the mystery is the only solution. Ultimately, reason can lead to spiritual confusion, so that often innocence like a child possesses, is better. (Matthew 18:3)

5 February — On the goodness of God in waiting for sinners to repent

 HINK HOW WONDERFUL God's goodness is in his dealing with sinners. What patience he bears with them in spite of their repeated provocations. (1 Timothy 1:16; Psalm 103; Romans 15:5)

Ask yourself how long has God been patient with you? Have you been playing at the edge of his despair? Have you been within a hair's breadth of a miserable eternity? Have you tempted fate? Millions before you have fallen into that after-life of endless fire. Yet for the moment God has spared you. There is still a chance to make amends. Still time to recover your purity and virtue. Still time to turn away from all temptations and values that you know are displeasing to God.

Your life was meant to be a life of joy. Is it? (Proverbs 10:28)

6 February — On turning from sin to God

 CCORDING TO THE Prophet Jeremiah, the Lord said that every wilful sinner is guilty of two enormous evils.

The first is a sinner has forsaken God, who is the eternal spring of life itself. Secondly, they have made themselves like broken jars that can hold no water—that is they are unable to hold the everlasting water of life, which is God. (Jeremiah 2:13) In any case, what refreshment any of us may get from this world is fleeting and ultimately unsatisfying. It runs out of us as if we were broken jars, leaking and no longer fit for purpose. Like the Samaritan woman we keep coming to the well, but unlike her we do not hear what Jesus says to us and we do not turn from vice to a life of virtue. (John 4:1–42)

Yet, in spite of this we always seem to fill up again and again this jar of ourselves with more of the same self-inflicted folly. We never seem to learn that what we drink from it will not quench our thirst for peace in our lives. We read about the Samaritan woman at the well with Jesus and sometimes discuss what it means, but this does not stop us from our worldly way of life. We do not imitate the Samaritan woman and drink of the living waters that come from God. We do not heed the words of Jesus.

If we are to belong to God, then we need to discard the broken jar we have made of ourselves and to drink again at that eternal fountain of everlasting refreshment. So read again the story of Jesus meeting the Samaritan women, only this time listen with your heart to what Jesus says to her: *Go and sin no more.* (John 8: 10–11)

7 February — On the feelings of a repentant sinner

IFFERENT FEELINGS GRADUALLY take possession of someone who has turned from sin to the embrace of God's mercy. First faith, which was asleep before, is awakened by serious reflection or by hearing the Word of God or by reading the writings of holy men and women. Such persons become aware of how empty a life they were leading, how little real love they showed to others, and how far from the teachings of Christ they had strayed. This produces in such a person a fear of the justice of God. The thought of the final judgment makes them tremble. Now this fear is usually the beginning of the greatest conversions, because it is the beginning of wisdom. (Psalms 111:1 & 9–10)

Although God never abandons anyone who comes to him, such a sinner trying to follow Jesus, seeks ways to escape the temptations that continually threaten from every side in this world. (Psalm 9:10–11) Now the true source of all these temptations comes from within us. If we succumb to them, then, we ourselves make sin by our own freewill. (Mark 7:20–23)

The choice to indulge in our temptations is up to each of us. No one else is responsible. This is what *freedom of will* means. Since we know God, the all merciful, is waiting for us in our repentance, we must feel encouraged to continue on the path of Jesus the Messiah. (John 14:6–7) Only in this manner may we avoid vices arising within us. The path of happiness is before us and keeping to this way quiets the fearful heart. (Psalm 15:11)

A heart at peace is a contrite and humble heart. It is composed of three great virtues: *penance, humility,* and *divine love. Penance* fills the heart with a deep sense of sorrow for those sins committed together with an ardent desire to abolish them. *Humility* obliges a person to self-condemnation, because that person has acknowledged wrongdoing. *Divine love* teaches us to detest our sins, not just because they bring evil upon us, but for the opposition they make against God who is the perfect good of the universe.

When all these feelings are in a person, the true penitent asks for God's forgiveness. Here is that contrite and humble heart which God never despises. (Psalm 1)

8 February — On why we should do penance

 UR LORD TOLD us that unless we do penance, we would perish. (Luke 13:5) In this declaration, we learn that the virtue of penance is absolutely necessary for every man and woman who has fallen from God through wilful sin.

Such penitence is a spiritual discipline involving self-denial. It is designed to tame the body and mind so that we can concentrate on God. It frees the spirit within us. When we do penance it must include prayer, repentance, and almsgiving, because we are seeking mercy and trying to live a life of love. Almsgiving is an act of charity and, therefore, must be given for others to show our love of our neighbour.

From the beginning of Christianity, penance was the great subject of the prophets, the Apostles and all apostolic preachers in the Church. It was by such preaching of the necessity of bringing forth the fruits of penance that John the Baptist prepared the people for the coming of the Messiah. When John declared *Prepare the way for the Lord, make his paths straight paths,* what else was he saying to people except to repent and return to God so that the path of Jesus would be paved with virtue. (John 1:23; Isaiah 40:3; Matthew 3:3; Luke 3:4)

Jesus himself opened his mission to us with the same theme of penance. (Matthew 4:4). Indeed, Jesus admonishes those that had not done penance in the various places where he did most of his miracles. (Matthew 11:20) This is a powerful encouragement to get on with the necessity of penance.

However, as time has passed more and more Christians disliked the idea of doing penance through actual physical acts, because it meant giving up something that they liked, something that was innocent but brought pleasure. Even the modest penances of abstaining from meat or alcohol have found decreasing favour by the faithful. Most fasting is done today in the cause of fashion and personal-image and not for the sake of a holier life with God.

In large part the reason this has developed, especially in the Western world, is because comfort and personal expression are increasingly the goals of earthly life and believed to be the *rights* of the individual. Depriving ourselves of something we know we enjoy also can seem a senseless practice, especially when it is considered foolish by so many people in the world at large. Somehow doing penance or self-denial for God seems old-fashioned and out of step with contemporary thinking.

In short, penance of self-denial for holy reasons is thought by most as a useless deprivation that does not matter even to God. Even worse as far as many are concerned is to be *told* to do penance, which seems to them an infringement of their unassailable rights. Hence, the sacrament we commonly call *Confession* or *Reconciliation* is much less frequently undertaken and, if done, the penance it attracts is usually easy.

Yet, we have before us in saints and holy heroes many examples of the spiritual benefits that penance can bring. In order to accept this idea of penance involving self-denial, we need to grasp that our displeasing God arises from an overwhelming love of ourselves. In short, we have put ourselves *before* God.

This self-love fosters in us the wrong inclinations and passions. Pride arises and blocks the way in our walking the narrow path of Jesus. What pleases us seems irresistible. We cannot resist those temptations that bring us pleasure or power or more wealth. The trouble is that once we satisfy our little temptations we are open to greater ones. Our resistance grows weak and our sins greater. Self-love dominates our decisions. The outstanding feature of most of such inclinations and passions is that it involves the whole person, finding its expression in mind and body and, eventually, negatively affecting the state of our spirit.

It is true that we like our creature comforts and, especially, our freedom to choose that which pleases us. We seek endorsements from others that support our vanities about ourselves. We try to make expressions of our self-love acceptable to others. We want the approval of others. We become very needy and discontent. Self-love becomes the guiding force of our lives. In short, we live by worldly values and not by those of God.

So true penitence must take some form of depriving ourselves of what we like, something we really treasure, something, which we are reluctant to give up even for a short time. Nothing less will do than this chastising of the flesh. To do such a penance takes both physical and mental effort. Such penance does not divide the body from the mind as if these were two separate things, which they are not. Therefore, the whole of yourself is involved in any physically manifested penance you undertake. We no longer do penance in dust and ashes, but depriving our flesh of certain foods, activities or pleasures is a discipline that affects the mind. Thus, our spirit is also affected the whole of ourselves, because the body, the mind, and the spirit cannot be separated.

Since Jesus is resurrected and with us, we cannot lack courage in fulfilling the requirements we set out for our penance. Therefore, do not be afraid of hurting your normal self-concern by disciplining your body and mind. Your spirit will gladly join in and benefit from such acts. Do not shy away from practicing austerities that bring humility.

Let us, then, imitate as best we can that glorious penitent, King David, by doing what is most suitable for our situation and for the gravity of our sins. (2 Samuel 12:13; the penitential Psalms 6, 32, 38, 51, 102, 130, 143.)

9 February—On the manner of doing penance

HERE ARE THREE particular practices of penance. The first is that you should go in spirit to God and beg forgiveness. This is the correct beginning of your penance.

The second, which naturally arises from the first, is to offer up to God voluntary self-imposed hardships of your own free will. Such hardships have long been called *mortifications.* Few have the strength or courage to make these mortifications extreme like many of the saints in former times. Indeed, there is no reason to believe extreme penances are more affective than lesser ones, which are within everyone's ability to do. In any case, the Church today actively discourages any extreme penances. It is not the severity of our penance that matters to God but how sincere our regret. For example, rising early in the morning to contemplate the Word of God or eating, drinking or sleeping less or replacing entertainments like television, distractions, and a busy social life with more prayer, stillness, and contemplation. These all serve as penances.

The third penance is to offer up all our labours and suffering to be sanctified by a remembrance of the suffering of Jesus. This should help put an end to our complaining about our life.

Although your circumstances of life, such as strength, age or health may vary, these three forms of penance are possible in greater or lesser form to everyone. Conclude then to do penance for displeasing God in the best manner you are able to do. Start now to prepare yourself in body, mind, and spirit for the requirements of Lent. It is never too soon to begin your reconciliation with God.

10 February—On the parable of the sower

SK YOURSELF IN what manner you received the holy seed of God's Word. What is the nature of your spiritual soil, that is to say what sort of person are you? Perhaps you have a garden of the soul in which this seed of God will flourish and bear those fruits that lead to eternal life. But are you like a hard and rocky path or a place over-run with thorns and briars where such a seed cannot grow? (Matthew 13:1–32)

Being a hard and rocky path means you live in forgetfulness of God in a continual flow of thoughts. First one thought, then another, then another. So your mind is never calm. You have what is often called *a monkey mind*. You are here, there, everywhere. Always on the move. Jumping from one thing to another. Easily distracted. Never at peace for very long. Your holy garden has become a thoroughfare for everyone and everything passing through your life. Every idle amusement and current fashion, idea or event bemuses you. You have hardened your heart without probably ever realizing it. The end result is that you have no sense at all of the fear of God. (Psalm 95:8; Exodus 17:1–7) In this way, the holy seed is lost when it falls onto the poor soil of your soul.

Is the garden of your soul so over-grown with the brambles, thorns and the wild shrubbery of self-love and self-concern that there is no space and light in which such seed may spread out its holy roots? Have the hungry birds of passion, comfort, and riches arrived to pick over your spirit? In this way, the holy seed of God is lost when it falls onto the poor soil of your soul.

The remedy for unfertile soil of the soul is to plough it up by prayer and meditating on the Word of God. Weed this garden of yourself by acts of charity and by increasing your humility. By focusing on eternal truths, you can change from a person who is barren in spirit to one who is beautiful and loving. If you find yourself trampled under foot by everyone and everything, do not worry, because the least of us shall be the first in God's kingdom. (Matthew 20–16)

In letting God rule your life, your heart will soon be so harrowed and so fertile that it will enfold this holy seed offered by God. You will no longer be prey to those evil birds of your worldly appetites.

Let this seed, which is the Word of God, sink deep into the garden of your soul. Let it grow strong and beautiful, bringing forth the glorious flowers and fruits of a life rich in eternal truths and values. Let he, who is the Light of the World, shine in your life. (1 John 5) Then, how much happier and contented you will be.

11 February—Optional Memorial of Our Lady of Lourdes

 OURDES IN FRANCE is one of the three greatest places of religious pilgrimage in the world. The history of this great Christian shrine is a simple one: A fourteen-year-old poor peasant girl, Marie-Bernarde Soubirous (1844–79), known today as Saint Bernadette, received eighteen apparitions of the Blessed Virgin Mary at the Massabielle Rock by a river in Lourdes. During this time, a spring appeared in the grotto of the rock, the waters of which are miraculous for those God favours. Almost from the beginning people visited the grotto to seek cures for their illnesses and fulfilment of their prayers. For those sick and incurable, hope arises in the heart and hope is what everyone needs. It is the best of medicines.

But you do not have to go to Lourdes to pray. You can do that right now. You do not have to seek hope, because hope is already with you in the promises of God. The more you follow him through faith, the more hope you possess. This is the miracle already with you.

12 February — Against any delay of repentance

 HERE IS NO delusion more common or more dangerous than that which persuades men and woman to put off their repentance with God until there is no more time left for them. They have gone on postponing reconciliation with God until cut off by death when it was least expected. Suddenly, they have no more time left in which to make holy amends.

Such men and women, and there are millions of them, pay lip-service to their religious obligations They imagine that an occasional Sunday attendance at church or at christenings, and feast days like Easter and Christmas or going to funerals are enough. Somehow their lives are so busy with living in this world that God is forgotten or put to one side. They are busy with family and friends and keeping their home and garden in good shape. They hardly ever listen to the Word of God in private. They do not have time or inclination to go to bible study groups or regularly to church. They pray when in need, but much less often in thanksgiving and hardly ever for other people unless someone close to them is ill. Most such neglectful people die as they have lived: bewildered or fearful and not reconciled to God. Yet, such men and women call themselves *Christians.*

How can such people, falling prey to such delusion, treat God with this kind of contempt? Are they so arrogant or so ignorant or so conceited that they believe they are immortal and will never die and face a final judgment? Such half-hearted believers, who think they have endless time on their side, run the risk of God turning away from them. (Hosea 5:6; 2 Timothy 2:12; Matthew 7:21–23) This could be their earthly punishment for such obstinacy and ingratitude.

> Let them give ear, then, to God's warnings of this possibility: Since I have called, and you have refused

me, since I have beckoned and no one has taken notice, since you have ignored all my advice and rejected all my warnings, I, for my part, shall laugh at your distress, I shall jeer when terror befalls you, when terror befalls you, like storm, when your distress arrives, like a whirlwind, when ordeal and anguish bear down on you. Then they will call me, but I shall not answer, they will look eagerly for me and will not find me. (Proverbs 1: 24–28)

Accordingly, do not delay or defer or dither in being fully reconciled to God. (Ecclesiastics 5: 8–11) Keep yourself close to God through diligence in worship, prayer and study of Holy Scripture. Be like Mary and observe all the obligations of your religion.

13 February — On the folly of postponing our conversion to God

 T IS TRUE that many are called but few are chosen. (Matthew 22:14) All men and women are called to the light of Jesus the Messiah for his act of salvation was for the whole world. This call from God, formed into Jesus who took human flesh and yet was divine, is always an invitation to follow the light of the Christ sent by God. It is a call to all men and women to become fully alive in that holy light.

Perhaps it is this invitation and how you answer this call that God turns into a choosing of you as one of the few. While all may be called, no one knows in advance if they have been chosen until it happens. Today you may feel one of the many called into holy light and not one of few chosen into further service to God. But tomorrow an angel with a heavenly message may knock on your door or appear beside your bed as you awake in the night.

How is it, then, that so many refuse such mercy and honour from God as is in his invitation? Why do they refuse the table of the Lord so laden with blessings and comforts? They know full well to be *chosen* you have to have already answered his call. You are already in his holy light.

Their refusal of his invitation is not just because they may be blinded by the temptations of this world. The problem is often that they postpone a return to God and put reconciliation aside, promising that tomorrow they will repent. Sadly, tomorrow may be too late.

What an illusion this postponement is, since both reason and daily experience must make it evident that the longer this holy work is deferred, the harder it is to bring it about. How could it be otherwise, since by such delays our sinful habits grow stronger and, consequently, they are more difficult to root out. Hardness of heart sets in, which of all evils is one of the most difficult to change.

So it is a great folly to put off our conversion to God by answering his call, because in this way our bad habits grow, our heart becomes hardened, and our guilty conscience is a gnawing awareness like an open wound that never heals. We never give it the healing power of faith, which our repentance would provide. We continue to expose ourselves to the danger of judgment and being denied eternal life.

Surely, everyone would believe a person as insane, who had a mortal illness and with a remedy readily available, did not take it at once? What is this remedy in spiritual terms but to repent and to confess? In this way you make amends to your Lord, gaining not just atonement but the virtue of humility through your act of confession. Why continue to refuse the blessed remedy on offer through your priest? Why postpone your confession? Why refuse to heal your soul?

14 February — On deathbed performances

 OW OFTEN MEN and women in great fear of God's judgment on them, call in a priest to hear their last minute confession. *Saved in the nick of time* is what relatives and Christian friends usually think but do not say aloud.

But do these last-minute Christians really believe that God does not know their guilt in believing they can live disobeying God's commandments, as you might be doing right now, but then make peace with him at the very end of their lives? How arrogant to believe this. Such people will find to their loss that God is not to be mocked (Galatians 6:7)

As a general rule, what a person sows so they shall reap. This includes death and subsequent judgment, because as we have lived so shall we die. In Scripture, we have but one instance of a happy death after a wicked life, which is that of the good thief, the one who hung on a cross next to Jesus. (Matthew 27:38; Luke 23:39–43; Mark 15:27)

This example of the good thief is so singular in all its circumstances as to give little if any encouragement to such sinners as try to give the slip to God's justice by a last-minute or deathbed conversion.

These are some the ways of thinking by which men and women fool themselves: Postponement. Making many excuses for delay of the holy. Waiting to be reconciled with God until the last minutes of life. Believing somehow everything will be all right at the end. Thinking there is nothing to fear in being busy with worldly things now while letting holy issues with God wait until sometime in the future. Incredible as it may seem, millions of Christians think just this way. Are you one of them?

What is most common in forgetting God during their lifetime is that such people forget as well that they do not know when death will come. So, generally speaking, deathbed performances are often illusions of true repentance, born out of fear about final judgment and not produced by true regret.

As we start the season of Lent, let our meditations be on the wisdom of pleasing God, our prayers on forgiveness, and our hearts warm with love of God and our neighbour. But keeping the fear of God and the obligations of your faith always in mind, use this season to confess how you have disobeyed or displeased him. Do not wait or postpone this reconciliation with God. The best moment for this action is always *immediately*. Do not waste another minute before being reconciled to your Maker.

15 February — On the opposition between the world and the Gospel

HE WORLD PERPETUALLY recommends what the Gospel condemns and condemns what the Gospel recommends. For example, the world inspires a covetous spirit, the love of money and a fondness for worldly distractions, while the Gospel teaches the necessity of putting aside things if they distract you from following Jesus and God.

Everyone knows the world has always been a slave to sensual pleasures, placing its happiness in indulging the pleasures of the flesh and the rewards of self-love. The world imagines a man or woman very blessed who abounds with the most honours, the most wealth and the best social or political powers. If sex or scandal is mentioned, everyone pays attention at once for gossip is the method employed by those who would judge others. The imagined or real desires of the flesh are held most dear. Individual rights are put above the collective good. There is little forgiveness. These are the ways of the world and they always seem relentlessly present.

The Gospel on the other hand, says the blessed are the poor in this world, all those who suffer unjust injuries and affronts, who weep and mourn, and who are reviled and persecuted by men. (Matthew 5:5; Luke 6:20–21)

In short, the life of those who would follow the world is in constant contradiction of the teachings of Jesus Christ and rules of God.

The Church sets aside this time for devotion and penance as a suitable preparation for the solemn *Season of Lent*. Now is the time for all Christians to be of penitential disposition, to renounce evil ways, and to confess their sins. It signifies a turning to God with a humble heart so that Lent readies us for the great celebration of Easter. While there are many joyous events surrounding Easter such as coloured eggs, children seeking little hidden amusements, images of happy bunnies and families sitting down to feasts, be aware that this fun does not take your attention away from the true reason for Lent and of Easter celebrations. This true reason is the life, death and resurrection of Jesus Christ.

Listen closely to our divine oracles: *Love not the world or what is in the world. If anyone does love the world, the love of the Father finds no place in him.* (1 John 2:15) *Do you not realize that love for the world is hatred for God?* (James 4:4)

16 February—On the state in which we are to enter the service of God

 F WE WISH to enter the service of God, we should first pay close attention to these words: *When you come to the service of God, stand in justice and in fear and prepare your soul for temptation.* (Ecclesiasticus 2:1–5 & 14)

This tells us right away that we will need in such holy service to have much courage and persistence so as not to be discouraged by the opposition and temptations that we will meet from the world, the flesh, and the devil. Like a valiant soldier we must be determined to stand our ground in this spiritual warfare by putting on the armour of Christian justice and of the fear of God. In this way, wearing the helmet of salvation and with a humble heart full of confidence in God, we will deflect all the arrows of temptation that come our way. (Ephesians 6:13)

Now, the spiritual benefits of a humble heart are many. It allows us to endure with patience as we wait on God's grace and mercy. Such endurance and patience helps us when we are tried in the fire of a world that mocks us. From this furnace of such humiliation, we emerge more acceptable to God, because we have been schooled in the lessons of purity and obedience. We have endured with tranquillity and confidence the crosses, sufferings, and insults which are the portion of the servants of God, just as Jesus suffered them. We have tried to mirror the example of Jesus in living a life based on love.

One of the best means to continue in the happy service of God is to nourish in ourselves an earnest desire for being good, a thirst for justice, and an awareness that Christ lives in each man and woman we meet. This may be unknown to them as yet, but he is there.

So we must have an ardent love for true wisdom, which is the knowledge, love, and service of God.

> I prayed and understanding was given me, said the wise man, and I entreated, and the spirit of wisdom came to me. I esteemed her more than sceptres and thrones; compared with her, I held riches as nothing... I loved her above health or beauty, preferred her to the light, since radiance never sleeps ... all good things came to me, and at her hands incalculable wealth... For she is to human beings an inexhaustible treasure and those who acquire this win God's friendship. (Wisdom 7:7–14)

This wisdom can be your own. You need only desire it, seek it, and love it with all your heart and it will be your possession, your treasure. Why not start now to observe all these lessons that will bring you in service to God? By accepting us as his good servants, God will bless our lives and make heavenly wisdom our reward.

17 February — What is true devotion to God?

HERE ARE THOSE whose devotion consists of certain external exercises, such as going to church every Sunday or diligently observing feast days. While fully in accord with the Church and certainly commendable in themselves, these actions and others like them may still be empty of that interior spirit that is the wellspring of all true devotion.

In offering long prayers of many words, frequent self-denial, giving alms to many charities, receiving the sacraments often, or in following other religious practices many Christian may be still full of self-love, vanities, feelings of spiritual superiority, false pride, and otherwise devoid of all true charity to either God or their neighbours. So their religious practices fall into nothingness before God, because all these external actions are done without humility. We may be forbidden to judge others for only God knows what is in our heart, but we can examine our own interior spirit and make judgments about it.

To be truly devout is to give your self *fully* to God. He wants nothing less than the complete commitment of your heart to love and through this love to serve him in all you do. No matter how small or grand your actions, no matter how frequent your religious practices, and no matter how frequent your prayers, what really matters is that your devotions are true with real love for God. Since God *is* love, it is to him that we must belong. This is a total giving of your self to love in every way, because whoever does not love does not know God. (1 John 4:16–21)

While we must persist in our religious practices, since they help the pilgrimage of our spiritual life and fulfil our religious obligations. But we must examine the source of our devotion from time to time. If we judge our devotions to be merely the fulfilment of religious obligations, — good and necessary as they may be — then we must act to return to the love of God as the true motivation for all we do in church and in our lives.

18 February—On fighting under the flag of Jesus Christ

 N EARTH THERE has always been two opposing king-doms, two opposing interests, two opposing sym-bols, and two opposing cities. These opposing forces are Jerusalem and Babylon. The first stands for the city of God. The second is a city in opposition to God. Here are the two conflicting standards, that of the good and that of evil.

The Devil set up his own empire of temptations, since he first was the angel who fell from God's grace. He is a ruler of Babylon. He has endeavoured by all kinds of tricks and lies to maintain its power ever since. We know how he allures deluded men and women with glittering shows of worldly pomp, riches, and pleasures into becoming his slaves and to fight under his flag for the triumph of his empire, Babylon. He has recruited millions to his cause. Multitudes of sinners everywhere join him. Babylon never sleeps in its spread over all the earth.

The children of Babylon are unhappy, miserable, and never content, because they are slaves to passions that can never be satisfied, to negative feelings that continually drag them down and to a world of self-love that can never be contented. They are enslaved to empty vanities, childish amusements, and many follies of distraction and substitution. They labour under a variety of fears, cares, sorrows, and anxieties. Innumerable thoughts depress them. No sooner do they relax then they must be busy again. Anxiety is their unhappy lot. If they are not constantly distracted, they slump into wondering about the meaning of their lives and find only emptiness and no answers. Discontentment is always near at hand for them. Not surprisingly, they don't enjoy what little real happiness that might come their way. It is so momentary that it leaves them once again in despair without any lasting satisfaction with their lives.

On the other hand, how happy are the children of Jerusalem! Rich or poor, master or servant, successful or not by the world's standards, suffering or not, they follow Jesus the Christ, contented to be God's dear possession in this life, and looking forward to the joys of the next.

What do you chose in this life? Are you a child of Babylon or are you a child of Jerusalem? Are you under the leadership of the Christ, striving for the good that God represents or do you live in Babylon under the vanity of this world? You cannot do both so what is your choice?

19 February—On the rules prescribed by Jesus to his followers

 ESUS TELLS EVERYONE, who wishes to follow him that they must renounce themselves, bear their cross, and walk in his footsteps. (Matthew 16:24)

To follow these instructions calls for a military-like discipline, because we always have within us the potential corruption of our good intentions by our yielding to temptation. In addition, we carry interior wounds on our heart, because we have in the past turned away from God in one way or another. So like good soldiers we must maintain discipline all the time.

Such discipline is hard work, because the plain fact is that we do not have a more dangerous enemy than ourselves. We like to put the blame for our failings on others, but even the devil cannot hurt us half so much as we hurt ourselves. This is especially true when we follow our passions and freely indulge the inclinations of our self-love. So the way of life shown by Jesus is difficult to follow. Indeed, narrow the way that leads to life. (Matthew 7:13–14)

If we are to have such discipline and stay on that narrow road, then the first step is to refuse self-love of which there are three principal parts. These are *lust of the flesh, lust of the eyes*, and *pride of life*. Renounce these and you are ready to walk in the footsteps of Jesus.

Conclude to embrace such discipline, to maintain it with perseverance, and, thus, to be a good soldier in the army of Jesus. It is a heavenly discipline since he came from heaven to teach it. By its observance we return to God and his heavenly promises for us. We willingly carry whatever is our cross with holy pride.

20 February — On the remaining part of the parable of the sower

 N THE PARABLE of the sower there remains a third kind of soil, which is thorny ground. Such soil brings no holy fruit to maturity. It receives the seed of the divine word, but chokes it up with the thorns of carnal affections and lusts. Jesus tells us this kind of thorny ground yields no fruit, concerned as it is with the cares, wealth, and pleasures of this life. (Luke 8:11–15)

People suffering this way may hear the Word of God or may even be favoured with visits of graces and spiritual calls from God, but they are so overwhelmed by the thorns of bad habits that all these heavenly messages are choked out. They truly believe that they can stay in control of their lives, fearing they will lose their power and prestige if they submit to God's virtues and truths. They wonder if such submission means they will have fewer comforts, needless suffering, and fall from the social circles whose membership they prize so highly.

Such people live in constant fear. The trouble this causes is not just to them, because in their need to control their life they almost always seek to control the lives of others. This is the thorny ground of human behaviour where no divine seed may bear fruit.

Conclude to rid your soul of all the thorns that may hinder it from bringing forth the flowering and fruit of God. Here is the blessed harvest for this life and the next.

21 February—On feelings of guilt as a Christian

EELING *GUILTY* IF you do not behave socially in the way expected by others can actually serve a spiritual purpose. But it only does so if it strengthens our sense of ethics and morals.

These feelings of guilt are a by-product of our living in accord with what the Gospel teaches in spite of what others may think. It can be as simple as offering hospitality to a homeless person.

You may not have done such actions of charity up until now, because you did not want to be bothered or thought yourself too busy or were worried about what your family, friends or neighbours might say. If so, you have forgotten that Christ may live in every man and woman. You have forgotten his words: *In truth I tell you, in so far as you neglected to do this to one of the least of these, you neglected to do it to me.* (Matthew 25:40–45) In the *Rule of Saint Benedict* followed by many monasteries, it is written: *Let all guests that come be received like Christ, for he will say: I was a stranger and you took me in … let Christ be worshipped in them, for indeed he is received in their person.*[1]

It is precisely this *being bothered* that is what Christians should feel when they neglect loving others. Feeling such guilt, this prompting of conscience, awakens us to how we should act in daily life. It is popular to claim that life is too busy just at the moment for charitable acts. These are mere excuses for a Christian when it comes to doing that which is done out of love whether it be someone you know or a stranger. Remember hospitality is love. (Matthew 5:16; 1 John 3:18; James 1:22–25; James 2:15–17)

---

[1] *Rule of St. Benedict*, Chapter 53:1 & 6

22 February — Feast of Saint Peter's Chair

 N THE APOSTLE Peter, we have wonderful examples of the love of Jesus. This is not just in the spiritual guardianship, *the keys of the kingdom of heaven,* that Jesus gave to Peter. (Matthew 16:18–19) Jesus showed us how we are like Apostle Peter in our weaknesses and strengthens. For example, in Peter's denial of him, Jesus shows us that with true regret our reconciliation with God is always possible. (Luke 22:59–62) So when we are weak, we are also strong. (2 Corinthians 12; 8–10)

These examples from Peter's life with Jesus should inspire us to return to the love of Christ and the will of God no matter how far away we may have fallen.

Let what Jesus told Peter make your faith ever strong: *I now say to you: You are Peter, and on this rock I will build my community. And the gates of the underworld can never overpower it. I will give you the keys to the kingdom of heaven: whatever you bind on earth shall be bound in heaven; whatever you loose on earth will be loosed in heaven.* (Matthew 16:13–19)

So if you should falter as a disciple of Christ, then turn again to the inspiration of Jesus' call to Peter and the authority he gave him in spite of Peter's human failings. Ask yourself if you are in need of such spiritual understanding today. Study the letters of Peter and meditate on what he tells you and understand your divine heritage is one that can never be spoilt or soiled or faded away. Be holy for that is your goal. (1 Peter 1:3 and both letters of Saint Peter)

23 February—Commemoration of Saint Polycarp of Smyrna

 E CAN DO no better than to study the examples of the many martyrs to our faith when we think about the perseverance necessary in following Christ. One such example of such a martyr was Saint Polycarp. From the moment of his conversion, he served Christ with an unwavering devotion.

As bishop of Smyrna in Turkey, he was a key leader in the Asian minor churches until the Romans demanded he renounce his faith when he was a very old man. Saint Polycarp when accused replied: *For eighty-six years I have served Christ and he has never wronged me. How can I renounce the King who has saved me?* Refusing to renounce his faith, he was ordered to be burned alive, but the flames did not touch him. In spite of this miracle taking place before their eyes, the Roman authorities were as if blind and finally ordered him to be killed with a dagger.

What Saint Polycarp said in his *Letter to the Philippians* gives us wise advice on how we should live as disciples of Christ. He wrote: *Stand fast, therefore ... and follow the example of the Lord, being firm and unchangeable in the faith, loving the brotherhood, and being attached to one another, joined together in the truth, exhibiting the meekness of the Lord in your intercourse with one another, and despising no one.*[2] (See 1 Peter 2:17 & 12; 1 Peter 5:5; Tobit 4:10 & 12:9)

How long has it been since you thought about the many Christians who have died martyrs and helped make it possible for you to live in your faith today? How often do you pray for those Christians who are prosecuted *now* and even face death because of their faith? Think how many have died and are still dying so you were free to follow Christ. Do not let them be martyrs in vain.

---

[2] St. Polycarp, *Letter to the Philippians.*

24 February — On the presumption of the wilful sinner

E ALL HAVE a natural desire for our own well-being. We need to feel safe. Such desire is natural for all living creatures, including humanity. However, many people indulge in the belief that this gives them control over their lives and that such control is within their own power. Such presuming people are arrogant and shallow. They foolishly believe they are in control no matter how often they fail, ending their days with a feeling of lack of achievement no matter how much they have succeeded in the eyes of the world. They meet with invisible and visible barriers that prevent them from reaching their goal of being in control of events in their life. Everything they run after turns into shadows. (Hosea 2:8–10)

Is it any surprise that such a person finds nothing but discontent and eventually sorrow? Can any thing be more foolish than to seek for good while turning one's back upon God, the source of everything good? (Luke 18:19; Mark 10–18)

Unless God wills it, nothing happens to any of us. We are never in control of our lives even if we have a choice between good and evil. We must trust in God, love others, and hope for the best.

25 February — On the vanities which people prefer instead of serving God

 OW VAIN ARE all those things, which so many people prefer before God. How they pursue the empty bubbles of longing, the toys and trifles of this world, the false promises of people and things, the fashions that are here one minute and gone the next, and all the other deceitful baits of desire that capture their souls. All these are pills of vanity concealing a poison deadly to the true self. They glitter with invitation, they entice with deluding dreams and the phantoms of ambition and materialism. Such vanities say, *More is good. Have a double serving* !

How often we fall into a preference for our comforts and amusements. Perhaps even adding regular church-going to our sense of belief that *all is right in the world,* when we know perfectly well that starvation, poverty, and need is not far way. How easy it is to forget the poor when our stomachs are full of good food, our bodies comfortable, our bank accounts plentiful and our homes safe havens. Charity cries out to us and is ignored.

Yet, all these vanities quickly disappear, bringing no lasting satisfaction and leave our hearts empty. This fool's paradise of an imaginary happiness given by the world can change in an instant from what appears so innocent into dreadful evils. An accident, a death, a war, a change in laws, an explosion and our comforts vanish. Millions of people have had just such experiences, so why shouldn't it happen to you?

If you are a person yearning for what is really just vanities, then ask yourself how long will your heart be closed and will you love what is futile and seek what is false? (Psalm 4:3)

Reflect upon those that have gone before you who have enjoyed the most of what this world could offer in honours, riches, and pleasures. Your local cemetery is full of people who thought the world could not do without them. If you could question them, what judgment now do you think they would make of their worldly values and their vanities? Will they cry out that in all these things they found nothing but futility, that all was chasing after the wind? Will they admit at last that there is nothing to be gained under the sun? (Ecclesiastes 2)

Surely then, let us decide today never to follow this wretched choice of worldly values and vanities that only bring disappointment and a forgetting of God. Instead, let us keep the Cross of Jesus in our mind whenever we feel we are succumbing to vanity, whenever fashion seems to dictate our life, and whenever our physical and mental comfort reigns over our choices in living. This will return us to the narrow road of Jesus.

26 February — What is God's wisdom?

ESUS ADDRESSED HIMSELF to God in these words: *I bless you, Father, Lord of heaven and earth, for hiding these things from the learned and the clever and revealing them to little children.* (Luke 10:21)

Many great truths of the Gospel have been hidden from those in the world who are thought wise by the world's standards, but they are revealed to the humble, many who may not know how to read or write and even those we think are not very bright. However, no matter what we may think, God does not hide his wisdom from such humble people, since they are able to receive such truths because their hearts are open through their kindness and innocence. If you have ever wondered why Jesus chose mostly ordinary and simple people to be his first apostles, then here is one answer.

If this is so, then why be impressed by the intellectual claims of worldly people, who say that they know the truth and the nature of things. False prophets like fake news are often hard to unmask. Why believe in the perceived wisdom of mere celebrities who come and go like wind in the trees or find belief in the most recent discoveries of science, which their history shows will be discarded as soon as a better discovery is made? There is no end to what men and women will profess to be the truth.

Yet, the truth of life and death remain in a locked casket to which only God and Jesus Christ have the key. This key has been held out to us again and again through our faith in the promises of God. When Jesus gave thanks to God, he invited us to come to him, offering us such a key, telling us: *Come to me all you who labour and are overburdened, and I will give you rest.* (Matthew 11:28) What does this mean except to show us that the key to life and death is ours if we have faith in God and follow the path of Jesus?

27 February—Remembering the judgments of God

 E DO NOT like to recall that God can be angry with us. Just think of the flood, which swept away all sinners on earth. (Matthew 24:39) Consider the judgment of fire on Sodom. (Genesis 19–21; Jude 1:7) Witness the many judgments on the rebel Israelites in the wilderness, particularly when the earth opened and swallowed up Koran and his companions and when the flames from the Lord destroyed in a flash over 14,000 of their supporters. (Ezekiel 20:13–14; Numbers 16:20–35) See how many flourishing cities and whole nations have been punished by wars, pestilences, famines, and earthquakes, all brought upon them by disobedience to God.

Knowing all this, who could not fear the wrath of God? So let us contemplate the judgments of God on sinners and learn to fear offending him. Our fear of God is the beginning of wisdom. (Proverbs 9:10)

28 February — The secret judgments of God

 LTHOUGH THE VISIBLE judgments of God upon unrepentant sinners are common and terrible, there is yet another kind of more secret judgments. These secret judgments are visited daily upon millions of men and women. These are far more terrible than you can possible imagine, because they bring a punishment of damnation during the person's life on earth. It is through such a person's abuse of grace and their obstinacy in sin that a blindness and hardness of heart so deep and so unmovable has come into them. They have arrived finally at a moment in their lives when they have no more fear or thought of God. They have cast aside all that Jesus Christ brought to the world and the promises of God. They have refused holy love.

It is then that God sets upon them his terrible judgment. He leaves them in a wilderness unlike any other where still unrepentant they add iniquity upon iniquity on their poor souls.

This fate is the very worst of all God's judgments. It was this he visited on the Israelites, darkening their eyes so that they could not see and bowing them down so that iniquity upon iniquity was poured upon them. (Romans 11:7–10, Psalm 68:24) He does this everyday with millions of habitual sinners who continue to resist his repeated call to repent and to be reconciled to the holy.

Now nature is over-generous in all its many earthly delights, but we know it can instantly change into devastation, destruction, and suffering. Earthquakes, floods, hurricanes wait in the wings of tonight or tomorrow and over-whelm us. Likewise, our sensual pleasures of eating or making love or our quest for wealth and power can end in unhappiness when we are over-whelmed by them. Such wild hungers, like dangerous changes in nature, drive us away from the embrace of God and into the progressive self-destruction of jealousy, anger, greed, vanity, self-concern, and bad habits. These destroy our peace of mind, the health of our body, and the hope that is in our spirit.

So it is also with those who take no notice of the warnings of God. (Proverbs 1: 24–31) They turn again and again to the idols of this world that bring them disappointment after disappointment. (Isaiah 2:8) We need to be like Mary, Peter and the Apostles and find a new and better life through Jesus. We need to be like Noah and set sail in an ark of hope on the sea of God's love.

29 February — On the happiness of serving God

 ONOURS, WEALTH, POWER and pleasure are the things on which the world sets the greatest value and considers blessings. These so-called blessings, however, are not what the prophet Isaiah was talking about when he said, *Blessed is the upright for he will feed on the fruit of his deeds.* (Isaiah 3:10–11) Our true blessing, which is what Isaiah was speaking about, is to do the will of God as though all riches were ours. (Psalm 118: *Beth* 14)

While worldly things are transient and swiftly pass in our short lives, to be a servant of God means we are blessed with ever-lasting gifts. We have contentment now and treasure in the life to come. (Matthew 13:44–45)

Meantime, while we await the fruits of eternal life, we are already blessed here on earth, because we are able to walk and talk with God. No matter who we are, God reads our hearts and knows all our anxieties, fears, needs, dreams, and hopes. When we draw near to God he draws near to us. (James 4:8)

How much more meaningful then to have your name blessed by heavenly enrolment in *The Book of Life* than in the books, papers, and records of the world around you, a world which needs always to reinvent itself and create what is so easily and quickly forgotten and turned to dust. (Exodus 32:32; Daniel 12:1; Luke 10:10–11; Philippians 4:3; Revelation 3:5, 13:8, 17:8, 20:12, and 20:15.)

Now, why should your name be inscribed in *The Book of Life* with all those from Adam to the last person in human history? The reason is that Jesus Christ died to pay for the sins of *every* member of the human race from its beginning to its ending. By this act of the greatest love all humanity was blessed. Let the guarding of such honour be the only object of your ambition.

THE SEASON OF LENT

Theme: Sharing the Cross of Jesus Christ

 WANT TO KNOW Christ and the power of his resurrection and partake of his sufferings by being moulded to the pattern of his death, striving towards the goal of resurrection from the dead. (Philippians 3:9–11) These few words sum up the essence of Lent.[1]

---

[1] A Carthusian, *From Advent to Pentecost: Carthusian Novice Conferences*, p. 67.

Ash Wednesday

OME BACK TO me, God declares. *Come back to me with all your heart, fasting, weeping, mourning. Tear your hearts and not your clothes, and come back to Yahweh your God.* (Joel 2:12–13)

You need to hear this call in the depths of your heart and answer it without delay. Do not leave God waiting. Instead, use this day of repentance to put yourself right with him. Nothing is so dear to God as when men and women turn to him with true sorrow for having forgotten his commandments.

We know that God holds such repentance dear to his heart, because Jesus told us that he had come not to call the righteous but sinners to repentance. (Luke 5:32) Since God knows even our most secret thoughts, there is no way we could ever claim not to be sinners. (Psalm 93, especially line 11) He has called us to be holy and there is no better time than right now at the beginning of the *Season of Lent* for you to promise God that you will keep his commands. (1 Thessalonians 4:6–7; Psalm 118: *Koph* 145–152) It is your chance for a new beginning.

As you leave the altar today with the mark of ash on your forehead, consider it's meaning for it is a symbol of your life: *For dust you are and to dust you shall return.* (Genesis 3:19) This truth will shadow your every moment whether you are asleep or awake, rich or famous, poor or forgotten. We may ignore its truth for most of our life but by accident, illness, age, or approaching death, we must finally acknowledge it.

So let those ashes on our forehead be the outward sign of our inner contrition. Let it be an emblem of humility, a remembrance of our frail composition, and the awareness of how short is life.

Let us make good use, then, of these forty days of penitence, this *Season of Lent*. Let us spare no pains in asking for God's mercy in the manner he has declared good for us and acceptable to him. Let us plead for his compassion through our fasting, mourning, and prayer. In this way, we prepare for the glory of the Cross that is the resurrection of Jesus Christ.

Thursday after Ash Wednesday — On fasting

 ASTING IS RECOMMENDED to us in the Old Testament and the New Testament and by the examples of Jesus and the Saints. (Joel 1:15–16; Jonah 3:5) We learn that the devil will not leave us except by prayer and such fasting. (Matthew 4:1–2; Mark 9:25–29) It is made clear that, while we fell from God's favour originally by disobedience, we return to him by fasting. The gratifying of our sensual appetite most often betrays us both to the flesh and to the Devil. In the discipline of fasting, we overcome them. In short, fasting for a Christian is never out of fashion.

However, fasting is often undertaken just because we want to look or feel better about how our body looks. But fasting for God is much more than that. It pleases the Holy Spirit, since the reason for our fasting is a desire to please God. A desire which, when acted upon, cleans up the soul — the palace in us where God lives.[2]

There are great advantages found in fasting. First, we know from Holy Scripture that it appeases God, because we acknowledge our guilt for having displeased him by choosing such fasting or denial of what legitimately pleases us. Even more, we take part in God's justice by such depriving ourselves. Fasting is *not* a form of self-punishment but is an act of homage. It is meant to give glory to God.

Another great advantage of fasting is that we are enabled by it to overcome unruly desires of our will, such as our pride, ambition, envy, and lust. When performed with a contrite and willing spirit, fasting humbles the person and, consequently, restrains such desires.

A third advantage of fasting is that it makes our spirit more lively and vigorous. This sets the spirit free from the restraints we put on it by our wayward self-will. We are able to turn away

---

[2]   St. Teresa of Avila, *Interior Castle*.

from worldly values and goals without fear. We are free to be ourselves and to hold high heavenly values and goals.

So set great value on fasting for God, but make sure it is accompanied with prayer and the study of Holy Scripture. In this way your fasting will be a true spiritual penitence and an act of love.

Friday after Ash Wednesday—On rules for fasting

T IS IMPORTANT to remember when you begin your fast that, while it means refraining from eating certain foods and eating less, it is essentially a spiritual discipline. It is a way of increasing awareness of the body and its appetites so that we are able to concentrate on more spiritual things. While fasting focuses your mind and turns it toward heavenly things, denying certain food whether plentiful or scarce or of any special kind, does *not* in itself bring you closer to God. (1 Corinthians 8:4–13) In fact, there is a danger that fasting for some people allows their false pride to grow, that is they feel more righteous.

While *fasting* and *abstinence* are related, they are different spiritual practices. Sometimes the two practices are confused. When we *fast*, we restrict the amount of food we eat and sometimes when we are to eat it. But *abstinence* is the avoidance of certain foods, such as not eating meat or chocolate.

As we know food in its self is not impure for a Christian and is to be considered a gift from God. Christ declared that it is not *food* that defiles, but it's the things that come from the heart that are more important. (Acts 10:15 and 11:5–10, Romans 14:14–15, Mark 7:18–23) For this reason, we ought always to treat any food with respect. Indeed, what is a prayer of before eating but a thanksgiving for the food we are about to received? When we abstain from a certain food, we are voluntarily giving up something that is good, so as to obtain a spiritual benefit, which is a greater good.

Outward observance of what we eat during Lent is not enough unless it brings us a deeper spiritual awareness. Such fasting is essentially penitential and implies a sorrow for when we have turned away from a life with Jesus Christ.

These feelings lead us to desire to return to God. Fasting and abstinence done in this spirit of penitence cannot fail to move God to mercy. However, let us remember that severe fasting and abstinence does not necessarily bring any greater sanctity or spiritual growth.

Try to better understand the spiritual reasons for these Lent endeavours, since they facilitate your reconciliation with God. In this way, you will find a refreshed spirit, ready for the glory of the resurrection celebration to come.

Saturday after Ash Wednesday—On the true fast of a Christian life

HE BEST FAST of anyone is to abstain from sin. This fast should be a life-long one. It obliges all sorts of persons, young and old, sick and healthy, at all times, and in all places to live in virtue and to love as Jesus did.

The true purpose of this great fast of abstaining from sin is made clear to us: Let the wicked abandon his way and the evil one his thoughts. Let him turn back to Yahweh who will take pity on him, to our God, for he is rich in forgiveness. (Isaiah 55:7)

Now to fast in public while still committing wilful sin in private is a mockery. Such mockery makes you a hypocrite, a liar who claims to follow the righteous path of God but does not. Remember how the Pharisees were not the better for their fasting, because they remained corrupted with pride, covetousness, malice, and hypocrisy? Did not God reject the fast of the Jews, because on the days of their fasting they continued to provoke him by their customary sins? (Isaiah 58:2–5) If we pretend to fast, but continue in sin, then we are as guilty and as displeasing to God as these people were in ancient days.

The life-long Christian fast should not only put a restraint upon the sensual appetites, for example in eating or sex, but also extend itself to a more general control of all the senses by which we are lead to excess. The eyes, the ears, the tongue, and all the rest of our body should fast, therefore, from curiosity, sensuality, vanity, carnal pleasures, idle conversations, and other worldly diversions and sensations. These are unbecoming to a serious Christian at most times, but especially in Lent.

Yet, this fasting from sin that we try to do during our lifetime is a fast from our own self-interest.

> Is not this the sort of fast that pleases me, says the Lord:
> to break unjust fetters, to undo the thongs of the yoke,

to let the oppressed go free, and to break all yokes? Is it not sharing your food with the hungry, and sheltering the homeless poor? If you see someone lacking clothes, to clothe him, and not to turn away from your own kin? Then your light will blaze out like the dawn and your wounds be quickly healed over. Saving justice will go ahead of you and Yahweh's glory come behind you. Then you will cry for help and Yahweh will answer; you will call and he will say, 'I am here.' (Isaiah 58:6–10)

Try to keep this greatest of all fasts that so please God. Resolve to break the bonds that hold you in the embrace of unworthy values and worldly aims. We can do this by acts of compassion and love to others. Such charity will distance us from self-love. We will be imitating Jesus and all will be well for us in this world and the next.

First Sunday in Lent—On the fast of Lent

ONSIDER HOW THE Lent fast of forty days has been recommended by the prophets and sanctified by the example of Christ himself. Moses fasted forty days when he spoke with God on the mountain and received the divine law. Then again, when the people had sinned, he returned to the Lord on the mountain, and fasted another forty days. (Exodus 24:18 and 34:28) After taking some food, Elias too fasted forty days in the wilderness before he came to the mountain of God, where he was favoured with the vision of God. (1 Kings 19:8–11) Before Jesus set out on his mission of preaching his Gospel, he retired into the wilderness where he spent forty days in prayer and fasting. (Matthew 4:2)

We cannot do better than to imitate these great examples of Jesus Christ, his Apostles and those of the people of the God who have gone before us. In this way our hope is to draw nearer to God by focusing on him through our fasting and prayers, our greater attention to the Word of God, and to a more frequent participation in the Sacraments of Confession and the Eucharist during this time.

In order to this, we need to withdraw more frequently to both exterior and interior silence and solitude as Christ did. We need less noise and distractions around us to help calm and focus ourselves. We need such interior solitude in order to examine more deeply how we really feel, to lessen our stress and anxieties, and to get more focused on heavenly matters. We need more peaceful time with God. In this way we can join our prayer and fasting to contemplation. Then with heart unlocked, we can make better use of this holy time in which mercy flows.

Now is the special time to seek our Lord while he may be found and call upon him when he is near. (Isaiah 55) We must remember that God is the name of the *Compassionate*, the *Merciful*. (Psalm 144:8; Exodus 34:6–7; and in *The Exordium* of *The Koran*)

Monday, Week 1 in Lent—On the aims of Lent

HE SEASON OF *Lent* gives us a wonderful opportunity to clean up our souls. It is so designed that we are lead little by little into devotion over the course of days. The beginning of Lent, *Ash Wednesday*, is meant to bring us to our senses about how short our life really is and how humble we must be if we are to follow Jesus. We are dust and to dust we will return. (Genesis 3:19) We are meant to be aware of our fate in judgment and to get reconciled to God *now*.

In our devotion built up during Lent, we should make the sufferings and death of Jesus the subject of our daily meditation. Even our most feeble meditation arises our awareness of God and we become sorry for any offense to him. This regret at our lack of obedience to God's rules is what Lent is suppose to do for us. It is a necessary readiness for participating in the divine mysteries of Easter. Otherwise, how else would we poor sinners be pure enough to celebrate the glory of the resurrection of Jesus? Lent has holy aims and, indeed, they are heaven-sent and very grand. It is a season of the healing of mind, body, and soul.

Along with our intentions, God already knows our desires and passions, we need to spread them out before us so we too can know them. Lent is a time to slow down and examine what and who we are in this life. We need to ask such questions of ourselves as these: *Am I pleasing to God? How do I stand in relation to God? How do I stand in relation to my neighbours? How do I stand in relation to my faith? Am I masking my offenses by a pretext of good intentions or wrapping them under the folds of a comfortable self-love?*

111

Tuesday, Week 1 in Lent—On the examination of our interior state

HINK HOW MANY people, who call themselves *Christians*, imagine they are in need of nothing and feel smug and proud with their wealth, comforts, and social status. They are proud of regular church going and, if asked, often brag of how faithful they are.

Yet in the sight of God, *they are wretched, and miserable, and poor, and blind, and naked.* (Revelation 3:17) This is so because all of us beguile ourselves from time to time and do not know our hidden feelings. We need to beg the Lord: *From hidden faults acquit me.* (Psalm 18:13)

Wednesday, Week 1 in Lent—A further examination of the soul

EW MEN AND women are ignorant of their carnal sins, even if they make excuses for them or otherwise try to deceive themselves. However, few people take much notice of their *spiritual* sins. While these are more interior and thought less scandalous in the eyes of men and women and often are not offensive to them, they remain deplorable to God. Such spiritual sins are very subtle and not easily discerned without a diligent search of the dark part of ourselves.

These spiritual sins are of these five kinds: *pride, covetousness, envy, secret malice,* and *spiritual sloth.* Examine these spiritual sins one by one. If our self-love will let us be impartial in our search, we probably will find we are guilty of more of these sins than we first thought.

As to *pride,* consider how fond we are of every thing that flatters us. How we presume to be in charge of ourselves and the events in our life as if we are in control of everything. How we are prone to compare ourselves to others and usually find we are somehow more favourable than them. How we usually give preference to what we want instead of giving preference to what others might like. How unwilling we are to suffer any reproof or criticism and are always ready to be indignant over every opposition we encounter. How much we are concerned at what the world will think or say about us. Finally, when we examine our daily life, is it not true that we usually have sought worldly approval rather than the approval of God? Now what are all these but the result of unending *pride*?

As to *covetousness,* the greatest miser does not think him or her self as guilty of such self-centred meanness, but the tree is to be known by its fruit. (Luke 6:43–45) In such a case, what is harvested is anxious worry and constant attention to the things of this world and neglect of spiritual duties. Thinking about money and acquiring it is a distraction from being with God. If we lock up your heart in our bank account, we will end by wanting yet more money and possessions. If we are afraid of losing worldly goods then we have already lost our way to heaven.

What about *envy*? What about secret *malice*? These feelings can remain buried deep in the heart. They are bad for happiness and displeasing to God. Do not indulge in them.

As to *spiritual sloth*, such laziness is an encumbrance to the soul, infinitely opposed to the love of God, to the spirit of prayer, and to a due care in frequenting the sacraments. Is this not a common spiritual sin, especially of all lukewarm Christians?

So we need to look well into our heart in this time of Lent. Do not succumb to spiritual sins nor think you are above them as if you were never guilty of them.

Thursday, Week 1 in Lent—On the sins of omission

 OW OFTEN WE notice sins we have done through our actions, but forget about those done through omission, those actions we know we should have taken but did not do. For example, how many times do we examine ourselves about the commandments of God and the precepts of the Church, but pass over the duties and obligations we may have in regard to carrying them out? Just thinking about them or keeping them in mind is not enough. For instance, we know we should love our neighbour as ourselves, but actually loving him or her is quite a different matter and we often neglect it. Such is a sin of omission.

Now, if the grand duty of every man and women is to consecrate themselves to the love and service of God, we must ask ourselves if our days are given to this goal. An omission of this obligation is usually the first sin that we fall into as adults. *The Season of Lent* is a time to right this wrong. It is a time in which to find no omission in our Christian duty and our personal call to serve God.

Friday, Week 1 in Lent—On exercising works of mercy

 ESUS TELLS US that in order to find mercy we must show mercy. *Blessed are the merciful,* he explains, *they shall have mercy shown them.* (Matthew 5:7) The Apostle James tells us those who show no mercy will be judged without mercy. (James 2:13)

So important is mercy that God himself expressly rejects the penitence fast of those that refuse to show mercy to their neighbour. He declares he will neither hear their prayers nor accept their sacrifices. (Proverbs 21:13; Isaiah 1:11 & 15–20)

If then, we desire at this Lent time to seek divine mercy in the forgiveness of our sins, see that your fasting and prayer is accompanied with your own acts of mercy to others. If you possess much, give abundantly. If you have little, take care even then to be willing to bestow something on others in their need. The charity that is almsgiving is essential to the Christian life. Indeed, it is an essential command for all the religions of the children of Abraham, because God himself is all merciful and all compassionate.

This is all the guidance you need when it comes to acts of mercy. (Tobit 4:7–11) An eternal kingdom in heaven is promised to all those who are diligent in this exercise and threatens with eternal damnation all those who are negligent. (Matthew 25) This encourages even the greatest sinners *by upright actions break with your sins, break with your crimes by showing mercy to the poor, and so live long and peacefully. (Daniel* 4:24) Christ considers what is done for those in need as if done for him and God will reward it accordingly. (Matthew 24:45)

Practice this virtue of mercy, but see that your intention is pure. Beware of losing the benefit of it by an insincere heart.

Saturday, Week 1 in Lent—On the spiritual works of mercy

F GOD IS pleased to reward the feeding of the hungry, the clothing of the naked, and such similar works of mercy, how much more will he reward those works of mercy by which men and women are helped to be drawn out of darkness and brought back to God. Holy Scripture tells us that whoever causes a sinner to be converted from the error of his or her ways will save themselves as well from eternal death. So great is the importance of this spiritual work of mercy that those who give it will shine as stars for all eternity. (James 5:20; Daniel 12:3)

Spiritual works of mercy are principally accomplished by reclaiming sinners from their unhappy ways, even ways so evil we hardly dare to think about them. But no one is beyond mercy for this is the arrow of love that changes all hearts and never wounds but always heals.

We can help such men and women to recover their dignity and favour with God. However, such mercy is not done by hectoring, arguing, or lecturing people. It is achieved by real tenderness, careful listening, great kindness, gentle corrections, quiet instruction, sharing friendship, studying Holy Scripture together, supporting them when they are tempted, and bearing all they say with patience, forgiveness, and prayer.

There are three basic ways to help others that anyone can do and from which no Christian can be excused. Firstly, we can set *an example of a holy life* by the way we live. Secondly, we can *pray*, because fervent prayer poured out to God on behalf of poor sinners is effective. Thirdly, we can *listen* to such people with an open and non-judgmental heart.

Acts of mercy are not optional for a Christian, but are a strict obligation. They apply to all who would follow Christ, because we are commanded to be concerned for our neighbour and this includes his or her eternal welfare. This is the practice of love.

Let us remember that the world abounds with men and women in need of the condolences of the Holy Spirit and the hope that is given by the promises of God. It does not matter if they are poor or rich, famous or unknown, powerful or without status. We can help them by seeing in each fallen person the living Christ in them. Nothing less will do. This is the perfect practice of love.

Second Sunday in Lent — On prayer

ASTING, ALMS, AND prayer are like three sisters going hand in hand. Each is different, yet all share the same father and belong to the same family. While necessary at all times, prayer is certainly indispensable at this holy time of Lent. *It will obtain for us from God all that we ask.*[3]

But what is prayer? It is a conversation with God. A rising up of our mind and heart to God, presenting him with our homage, adoration, praise, and thanksgiving. Once in his presence, we lay before him all our needs and those of the whole world as well. We ask for mercy, grace, and salvation at his hands for ourselves and for others. Doesn't this praying in some measure anticipate the joys of heaven? For what is heaven but to be with God?

Day or night, in freedom or prison, healthy or ill, poor or rich, the door to God is never shut for it is fashioned from mercy. Think what an honour this is. Would any king or ruler in this world give anyone such a constantly open invitation? Nothing could be sweeter, more profound, and more rewarding than this heavenly conversation. Why not take advantage of it and let your prayers unlock the floodgates of God's love for you.

---

[3]   Tertullian, *On Prayer;* also John 4:24.

Monday, Week 2 in Lent—On the necessity of prayer

E CAN DO nothing towards our salvation without the grace of God, but with his grace we can do all things. Now, prayer is the great means of obtaining this necessary grace: *Ask and it will be given to you, search, and you will find; knock and the door will be opened to you. (Matthew 7:7)*

Is God in need of our prayers? No, certainly not. He stands in no need of us, but we are continually in need of him. Therefore out of love for us, he often presses us to pray, because he knows that without frequent prayer we remain miserable. We need to talk to God.

Just consider the necessity of prayer in the warfare in which we fight against those three desperate enemies—the world, the flesh, and the devil. We are surrounded with dangers from every side. We walk in the midst of snares and temptations of all kinds. We live in a world that is wicked and cruel where greed rules. We are surrounded by deluded people who are strangers to the Gospel, people who encourage disobedience to God's commandments by their words and actions, who seek to drag us along with them into the self-destruction of self-love.

In addition, we must carry our flesh, this miraculous composition of ourselves we call the body. Although we cannot live without it, the body weighs us down with endless demands, passions and lusts. The flesh is made for joy with its necessary but mysterious functions. Yet it is also like a devil, adoring comfort and wanting never-ending physical beauty, but often forgetting God who gave it existence.

What shall we do? How can we escape all these dangers and overcome all these enemies? How do we love our body but still keep it under control? The first and, perhaps, the only thing we can do is to pray not to be tempted. Our prayers will engage God's attention. With him all our enemies will fall before us, because if God is with us it does not matter who is against us. (Mark 9:40; Luke 9:50; Romans 8:31; Psalm 118: *Aleph* 6) This includes the forbidden desires of our body.

Tuesday, Week 2 in Lent—On attention in prayer

N ESSENTIAL CONDITION of prayer is that we pay serious attention to what we are doing. We need to be completely focused. To pray in a state of distraction or with a nonchalant attitude is a mockery of the divine majesty to which we are addressing ourselves. *God himself said of such people that they honoured him with their lips but their hearts were far from him.* (Isaiah 29:13–14) If you are half-hearted like this when praying, then be quick to remedy such offense.

So in order to pray well, no distraction must interfere. Turn off mobile phones. Close the windows against outside noise. Shut the door against intrusions. Tell others who are home that you are not available for a little while. We need private space for our personal conversations with God. It does not matter where you pray. It can be in a church, a room, even in the bathroom. God does not care as long as our thoughts are fixed on him and not scattered here and there, thinking of a hundred different things and always dwelling on worldly matters. We must resist having a mind like a monkey that jumps here, there and everywhere. We need to listen to the wise man who told us: *Prepare yourself before making a vow and do not be like someone who tempts God.* (Ecclesiasticus 18:23)

Therefore, preparing the soul for prayer, which like a vow, consists in emptying the mind of all worldly thoughts and concerns as much as possible. It means paying close attention to what we are doing. We are in the process of untying our heart from all affections, worries, responsibilities, and the wanderings of the imagination. We are being mindful of God. As we reach out to him, so he reaches out to each of us. (Job 11:13; Deuteronomy 4:29; Psalm 16:6; Psalm 62:9; Malachi 3:1; John 6:44)

Wednesday, Week 2 in Lent—On other conditions of prayer

 ONSIDER THESE WORDS of the Apostle James: *It is because you do not pray that you do not receive; when you do pray and do not receive, it is because you prayed wrongly, wanting to indulge your passions.* (James 4:2–3)

These are strong words, but often true. When we are more concerned for the transitory things of this world than for the eternal welfare of our souls, and we make such things as these the principal subjects of our prayers, we must not be surprised if God chooses not to hear us.

What we need to do in our prayers is to seek first mercy and justice. As to other things we seek that might be good for us, God will give them as far as he sees them suitable. If at any time we pray for blessings or to be delivered from sufferings, we include in such requests a complete submission to God's will. Like Mary, we must hold his will with gladness, thanksgiving, and complete trust. No matter what is happening to us, our pray must include these words: *Let it be as you, not I, would have it.* Our prayer must always reflect that of Jesus himself when he prayed for God's *will to be done.* (Mark 14:36)

Thursday, Week 2 In Lent — On being eager in praying

 OW CAN WE expect God to take notice of our prayers if we present them with indifference? To be indifferent is to pray as if we did not care whether he heard us or not. Such lukewarm prayer as this instead of drawing down his blessings upon us is simply rude and disrespectful. It is doing the work of God negligently, which brings the worst consequences to a Christian.

Eagerness in prayer is commended to us by the great example of Jesus *who during his life on earth, he offered up prayers and entreaty, with loud cries and with tears.* (Hebrews 5:7)

Jesus teaches us that we should not be faint-hearted about praying. (Luke 18:1–8) This means we are not to be discouraged or to give up if we don't immediately get some effect from our prayers. We need to take the example of the poor widow seeking justice, who continued to prevail upon a judge and knock at the gate of heaven by her pleading for justice until God was pleased to answer her. (*Ibid.*)

Perseverance in prayer, then, is an essential part of our praying. We must imitate Our Lord.

Friday, Week 2 in Lent — On prayer without words

 t Teresa of Avila says that mental prayer is nothing else than an intimate friendship, a frequent heart-to-heart with Him by whom we know ourselves to be loved. The basic difference between meditation and contemplation is that meditation is a human mode of prayer whereas contemplation is divinely infused prayer. Such prayer does not depend on words or have any need of them, because this kind of prayer takes place in the secret palace of the heart — the place where your spirit finds God and is consumed by his presence.

This kind of prayer employs all the powers of the soul, the memory, the understanding, the rising of the unconscious into holy awareness, and the complete absorption of you in God. It is the divine school in which you learn to love God without reservation, a place where all is dissolved in the mystery and peace of God's unending love for you.

Although contemplation as a form of prayer is no more effective than any other kind in being with God, but the Holy Spirit goes where it will. So we must not set bounds or make rules about praying. The Holy Spirit reigns and God will advance us spiritually as is his will for us. (John 3:7–8) If he intends us to pray with words, that is what will happen and it is good. If he intends us to contain our prayer in our mind with silent lips that too is acceptable to him. If he leads us to contemplation then that is also good, since all prayer done in sincerity and faith pleases God.

Saturday, Week 2 in Lent — On diligence in praying

 ET NO FEARS about difficulties in praying discourage you from daily practice of it. If you continue resolutely in your endeavours, the grace of God will make it easy for you. Do not be frightened or think you have failed if you meet with nothing at first but dryness and distractions. Keep praying because God has not forgotten you nor are you doing something wrong in the way you pray. In his own time, God will let his light shine once again on you and he will take you to himself. By perseverance in prayer, we arrive at the presence of God. This moment will recompense you for all the dryness you may have suffered.

So what you must do is have great diligence in your praying. Keep at it. Never give up. Never be discouraged. Never think God has deserted you. Remember that when you call, God *will* answer. (Isaiah 58:9, 65:24; 1 John 5:14–15; Ephesians 6:18; 2 Chronicles 7:14)

Third Sunday in Lent — On devotion to the Passion of Christ

EDITATING ON THE sufferings and death of our Redeemer ought to be a principal part of our Christian devotion during the time of Lent, because the time is approaching when we join together in memory of our Lord's passion.

However, we should never forget the suffering and death of Jesus at any time of the year, even if we take this yearly time of Lent to especially remember it. His passion is an ever-flowing source of mercy, grace, and salvation to us, since all that is love flows from his Cross. The more we place ourselves near the Cross through our meditations on this event in his life, the more we partake of that mercy and grace.

Let us daily accompany the crucified Messiah by such meditations on his sufferings. Lent is the season for you to acclaim with Saint Paul: *I have been crucified with Christ.* (Galatians 2:20)

Monday, Week 3 in Lent—On the benefits of devotion to the Passion Of Christ

 T IS IN meditating on the *Passion of Jesus Christ* that we contemplate the great object of our faith and the reasons for our hope. This leads to repentance for our offenses against the commandments of God and the teachings of Jesus. We pray: *God, be merciful to me, a sinner.* (Luke 18:9–14)

As the belief of Jesus Christ crucified and resurrected is a fundamental understanding of the Christian's faith, so it has the greatest influence on all the other aspects of faith. According to the Apostle, *All have sinned and lack God's glory, and all are justified by the free gift of his grace through being set free in Christ Jesus.* (Romans. 3:21–26)

Conclude then to put yourself at the foot of the Cross and fill yourself with faith, repentance, hope, and love through the contemplation of the sufferings of the Messiah.

Tuesday, Week 3 in Lent — On the lessons Christ teaches in his Passion

 EVOTION TO THE Passion of our Lord brings with it other great advantages to our soul, because it teaches us many lessons for living according to his example. He gives us a perfect pattern of all the virtues for us to follow in the practice of our lives, so that we might always be holy according to God's intentions for us. (1 Peter 3 onwards)

While the life of Jesus is full of wonderful examples of all the virtues which love brings, yet nowhere do they shine more brightly than in his passion. Here at the Cross, he has drawn together all the great lessons of virtue he had taught in his life both by his words and his works. All virtue is summed up in his obedience to the will of God. From such obedience springs all other virtues, because this willing submission arises from love.

Thus, the *Passion of Christ* is the great school that Christians must frequent through our love for others, a preference for humility, a discarding of worldly values, and a freely chosen obedience to the will of God in everything. We must do all these if we desire to learn the virtues taught by Jesus and to follow the path of life that he showed us. (Hebrews 8:5; Philippians 2:5–11) The Cross is the pulpit from which Jesus most effectually preaches to us.

Wednesday, Week 3 in Lent—More lessons from Christ in his Passion

 E LEARN FROM Jesus during his ministry about the place of submission to God's will as well as the place of humility in our lives. (Matthew 11:29) On the Cross, he taught these lessons too. Isaiah foretells how Jesus will respond at the time of his death: The Lord God has opened my ear and I have not resisted, I have not turned away. (Isaiah 50: 4–9) The Apostle Peter explains we were given prophetic words as an example that we should follow the path of Jesus. He tells us that when Jesus was reviled, he did not revile; when he suffered he threatened not, but delivered himself to them that judged him unjustly.' (1 Peter 2:21–25)

Let us learn from this behaviour of Jesus to endure courageously in the midst of insults and injuries of all kinds. Here is the primary lesson in holy obedience and humility.

Thursday, Week 3 in Lent—On the love Christ has shown us in his Passion

 HINK ABOUT THESE words in Holy Scripture when it speaks of Jesus: *No one can have greater love than to lay down his life for his friends.* (John 15:12–17) History scarcely shows us any instances of a friendship so perfect as that one friend should be willing to lay down his life for another. How imperfect, then, is human friendship compared with the love we have been given by Jesus Christ? What love between people could ever bear the least resemblance to this divine charity? It reminds us that love is the foundation of our religion and that love itself is the reason for love.

Friday, Week 3 in Lent—Other considerations about Christ's love for us

 HE LOVE THAT Christ shows us in his passion does not content itself with words or professions of affection nor with passing sentiments of tenderness like we may imagine we have for him in our devotions. God's love for us gave us Jesus, the Messiah, so that we might be recalled to heaven and be reconciled to our father there.

To do this mission, Jesus divested himself of all his divine beauty and majesty so that he might become for us a human of flesh like every person we see around us except that he was without sin. (John 1:7–8) His incarnation in the flesh of humanity makes us aware of all his suffering, because as men and women of the flesh we understand the emotional and physical pain caused by others. We learn from Jesus Christ that we too are capable of forgiveness and love.

Bruised, beaten and wounded, Jesus endured all this suffering in willing love for God and all men and women. (Isaiah 2:17) In this way, he opened the fountain of salvation to us. He was the new Adam, giving us reconciliation with God.

But what does this reconciliation and his great sacrifice mean to us? Are we willing to renounce our own will, to mortify our inclinations and passions, to suffer and to bear our crosses for him as he did for us? Are we generous lovers willing to be with him on Mount Calvary as on Mount Tabor? Is his love the mirror by which we judge ourselves? Have we made love the meaning of our lives?

These are questions not just to ask during the Season of Lent, but every day in order to stay on the path of life that Jesus gave to us by his teaching, his death, his resurrection, and the sending of the Holy Spirit.

Saturday, Week 3 in Lent — The sufferings of Our Saviour before his Passion

 ow often in the psalms we hear echoes of the history of Jesus suffering in the course of his earthly life. For example, in *Psalm 34*: *They have hidden a net for me wantonly; they have dug a pit… Now that I am in trouble they gather, they gather and mock me…* (Psalm 34)

But all this hardship was nothing compared to what he suffered continually during his life from knowing the sins of men and women and the misery this caused them. He was aware of their malice, violence, injustices and cruelties, deceits and lies, greed, blasphemies, and licentiousness. He knew the pride, ambition, envy, and hypocrisy of so many of their priests, scribes, and Pharisees. He saw the oppression of the poor, the contempt of virtue, and the forgetfulness of God. How Jesus must have suffered from all those around him with their hardness of heart, those hearts that should have been holy but were not.

Yet, he did not turn away but reached out to all with concern for he knew they were created for joy and righteousness. He came to bring such sinners back to God, telling us that he had not come to call the righteous, but sinners to repentance. (Luke 5:32; Mark 2:17; 1 Timothy 1:15) By your sharing in his life and treating everyone as a brother and sister, the heavenly kingdom will await you.

Fourth Sunday in Lent — On Our Lord's Prayer in the garden

UR SAVIOUR'S PASSION began the night before his death. Having eaten the paschal lamb with his disciples, he humbly washed their feet. Then, he instituted the great Passover of the New Covenant. In remembrance of him, he gave them his body and blood through bread and wine. After this, Jesus went out with them to Mount Olivet to pray.

He went there on this last night to prepare himself for his passion. Here by his own example, Jesus tells us what we are to do when we face dire trouble and fear for the future. The answer is to pray to God, because remembrance of God heals the heart. (Psalm 33:18)

Resolve to follow this great example of Jesus in his prayer in the garden. Arm your self against all trials and temptations and tribulations by going to God. Learn that this is where the source of all your strength comes in the time of earthly and spiritual battles. Listen to what Our Lord said to his disciples upon this occasion: *Stay awake and pray not to be put to the test. The spirit is willing enough, but human nature is weak.* (Matthew 26:41)

Monday, Week 4 in Lent — On the agony of Jesus

HAT ANGUISH AND sorrow overwhelmed Jesus in his last night. Consider how he sweated and felt enormous pain. He endured such agony in mind, body and spirit. He was pierced by awareness of the sins of so many men and women around him. All these now came upon him as if they were his own and, like that scapegoat *of sacrifice who was once chosen to have the burden of our sins, Jesus was to be sacrificed for the sin of everyone. Reflect well on the words of Holy Scripture which foretell of this event: Aaron will then lay both of his hands on its head* (of the live goat), *and confess over it all the guilt of the Israelites and all their acts of rebellion and all their sins. Having thus laid them on the goat's head, he will send it out into the desert…and the goat will bear all their guilt away into some desolate place.* (Leviticus 16: 21–22)

But why are we told of all this agony in the garden before he was crucified? Surely his death on the cross was sufficient for our redemption? Why then are these sorrows of his last night, his trial, and his torture told to us in such awful detail? It was only so that we might deeply understand the love Jesus had for each of us and the resolution of his complete surrender to the will of God. There is no moment in his mission in which Jesus was not teaching us.

Tuesday, Week 4 in Lent — On the treason of Judas

E SEE IN the example of Judas that no life, no matter how holy, is safe from the danger of evil. This Apostle was called and taught by Jesus and empowered through God to cast out devils and work miracles. Nevertheless, Judas was tempted and fell so far from grace as to rise no more.

This example is a deadly warning. It teaches us to realize on what slippery ground we stand, even at the very moment we feel most secure in following Jesus. This means we must never trust ourselves but place our whole confidence in God at all times, even more so when we best feel we are pleasing to him.

But what was it that brought Judas to this terrible betrayal of Jesus? It was greed. The love of money was the vice that strangled his soul. He indulged his love of money at first in lesser things through carrying the common purse of the Apostles. But once greed and the love of money took root in him, it grew and grew until he sold the Messiah himself for a pocketful of silver.

The end result of any vice is always the death of the soul. Like Judas, we can so easily fall from small injustices into the betrayal of all that is good on earth and in heaven. While other vices wait to grow and destroy us, greed, especially the love of money, is first in line to tempt us and take root.

Yet, few Christians are willing to think themselves infected by this love of money. How often pretexts and pretences are used to cover this evil of wanton materialism. How many men and women make frauds, injustices, loans, and tax avoidance schemes with the excuse that others do the same or that *it is allowed*. Do we forget in our desire for more that what is perhaps allowed by the world may often be contrary to God's commandments?

Learn from the life of the Apostle Judas to mistrust yourself and your own judgment in all matters where your worldly honour, interest, or pleasure are concerned, because it is natural on these occasions for you to be biased to what is most agreeable to your self-love. None of us can be an impartial judge of ourselves.

So when temptation faces you, especially a love of money, remember Judas Iscariot and beware of the fatal trap of vice. Do not try to bend the law of God to your will, but bend your will to the law of God.

Wednesday, Week 4 in Lent—On being awake for Jesus

I T HELPS US to consider how Jesus went for the third time to his disciples. He had asked them to pray and watch with him, but found them asleep. Are we also like the Apostles and not with Jesus and fully awake to remembered sorrow and needed repentance?

When you gaze at the Cross know that the Christ is the one friend, the one lover, the one companion, the single person in this world who died for you and he did it out of love.

Thursday, Week 4 in Lent — Jesus appearing before Annas and Caiaphas

 ONSIDER HOW THE rabble having taken Jesus prisoner, dragged him into the city with loud shouts and cries, bringing him first before Annas, one of the chief priests, to give him the pleasure of seeing the prisoner and of exulting over him. Admire the courage and evenness of temper, Jesus displays. He shows us that true courage consists in bearing injuries and not in revenging them. Surely, nothing can be more honourable to a Christian than to imitate his Master.

Consider further how Jesus is hurried away with the shouts and insolences from Annas to the house of Caiaphas, the high priest. Here, the council was assembled, determined to destroy Jesus. What we should most admire on this occasion is the wonderful innocence of Our Lord, who took on the full weight of their unjust accusations in silence. Learn from this silence by Jesus not to be excessively sensitive regarding your own honour and, if you must defend your innocence, do it with calmness and modesty.

Learn from the great example of Jesus before Annas and Caiaphas that when you may be called to your own trial in this life, whatever form that trial takes, never to deny you are a Christian no matter what danger might be provoked by doing it.

Friday, Week 4 in Lent—On Our Saviour's treatment in the house of Caiaphas

 O SOONER WAS the condemnation of Jesus pronounced than all the people around him began to treat him with all kind of outrages. *They spit in his face and hit him. They blindfolded him and struck his face.* They mocked him and pulled out hair from his head and beard. (Matthew 26:67;Luke 23:36) Yet in all this, Jesus made no resistance, but gave up his body to those who tortured him. He did not try in any way to avoid their cruelty. (Isaiah 1:5–6)

Do you truly understand that Jesus willingly submitted to all this terrible treatment in order to save us from sin and hell? Do you feel unworthy of such great charity or do you remain arrogant, full of pride, and still hungry for power and possessions?

Saturday, Week 4 in Lent — On Peter's denial

MONG ALL THE sufferings of Jesus, nothing must have hurt him so much as the behaviour of his own Apostles. Just imagine how he felt when they abandoned him and when Peter, who had professed the greatest zeal and love for him, denied three times that he even knew him. Forsaken by all his friends, hear again the anguish of Jesus when he cries out with the writer of the psalm: *Look on my right and see- there is no one who takes my part. I have no means of escape, not one cares for my soul. Friend and neighbour you have taken away; my one companion is darkness.* (Psalms 141:5; Psalm 87:19)

But what was it that induced Peter to deny his Lord? Had not Peter boasted earlier that though all the rest should forsake Jesus, he, Peter, would never deny him? Yet, when a servant asked Peter if he knew Jesus and was his follower, this question filled Peter with such terror that he denied knowing the Messiah.

Learn from this of what men and women are capable and how fear can wipe out even holy faith. Beware of thinking you are stronger in faith than Peter.

Finally, Peter went into the company of the enemies of Jesus. Surrounded by them and hearing their talk, he was drawn into doubts. From this we see that we must avoid the corrupting influence of bad company. Indeed, we must run from any influence that is prejudicial to the good of our spirit, because our faith can be fragile at times. Like Peter, we can be too easily led away from God. From his sad example, we also learn the tongue can be an ignorant and cruel weapon of bad influence. (John 13:37–38; Proverbs 18:21) It shows us that the tongue can be an instrument of denial. The Apostle James warned us that the tongue is a whole wicked world: it infects the whole body; catching fire itself from hell, it sets fire to the whole wheel of creation. (James 3:5–8)

Always be on guard then. Be careful about what you say. Stay away from people who are bad influences. If we think we are strong in our faith, then we need to watch out that we are not about to fall as Peter did. Humility is our best insurance and regular prayer our best security.

Fifth Sunday in Lent—Passion Sunday—Jesus is taken to Pilate

 HE HIGH PRIEST convened the *Sanhedrim* or great council and declared Jesus guilty of blasphemy for which the sentence was death.

Now this decision was not about observance of religious law but stemmed from malice against Jesus. Such malice must always have fear as its root cause and easily gives rise to envy. In this case, Jesus' miracles and his ever-increasing number of followers threatened the council's position and authority.

How quickly the people who only a few hours before had held Jesus as a Prophet, now joined in condemning him. See how they insulted him. How his friends grew distant and ashamed of him. Where would you stand in such a moment? Whose side would you have been on if you had lived then and been part of that crowd of men and women? Would the crowd have persuaded you to turn against your beliefs and values? What would fear have done to your faith?

Such questions as these are as relevant today as they were then, because such things as homelessness, proxy wars and corruption may be done by your nation in your name as a citizen. In this way, these situations continue through our silence and inaction. Indeed, many feel not doing anything to correct injustice is to endorse it through silence. It is so easy to become part of a crowd who demands injustice—just like the crowd did when Jesus was condemned unjustly. Is this the way a Christian should behave?

Monday in Passion Week—Jesus is sent from Pilate to Herod

HEN PILATE INQUIRED what accusation they brought against Jesus, the people told him many lies, including that Jesus had raised up seditions, stirred the people to rebellion, forbid tribute to be paid to the emperor, and told everyone he was the king of the Jews. Under these slanders, Jesus showed a constant tranquillity. He kept silence to the great astonishment of the governor. He did not argue or proclaim his innocence. He did not get angry with his accusers. He did not cry out or plead for mercy or give any hint of fear. He remembered that the only fear we should have is a holy fear of God. (Psalm 18:10)

In this situation Jesus teaches us that we should learn to be patient. Jesus shows us that our calmness and humility will be a better proof and defence of our innocence than passion and rage or returning injury for injury.

See how Jesus is brought in bonds before Herod and treated with mockery and scorn. Yet, Jesus remains silent in the face of all this torment. We understand from this neither to worry about the judgment of the world nor to lament if people accuse us of foolishness and folly, because we should never expect better treatment than was given to Our Lord. Therefore, we need to remember these words: *Do you not realise that love for the world is hatred for God.* (James 4:4)

Tuesday in Passion Week—Barabbas and the scourging of Jesus

 HEN PILATE REALIZED the high priest and council were still bent on destroying Jesus and that no real evidence had proved him guilty, Pilate thought of a way to release him without giving offence to his accusers. As it was the privilege of the people to have their choice of a prisoner to be set free on the day of the paschal solemnity, celebrated in memory of their being delivered on that day from the bondage of Egypt, Pilate proposed to the people a choice between Jesus and Barabbas, who was a notorious thief and murderer. Unbelievably, they chose Barabbas and demanded Jesus be crucified.

Now think of your own life, because we often face such a choice between good and evil just like the people did when Pilate made his proposal. Have you ever preferred a Barabbas type person, situation or passion before the Lord of Glory?

If so, do not continue in arrogance. If guilty, we must prostrate ourselves at the foot of the Cross and cry out to God, *Have mercy on me, a sinner!* With our face to the floor, our eyes shut, our heart in regret at our neglect, we remember that Jesus the Messiah is the foundation stone of life. His people rejected him then and many people reject him now, even though God sent him to the world. (1 Peter 2:4–5 & 7–8)

Wednesday in Passion Week—Our Lord is crowned with thorns

OW PLEASED THE crowd was when the soldiers crowned Jesus as a king, pressing down on his head a wreath of sharp thorns and calling this his crown. See how Jesus still stands like a wounded lamb in the midst of wolves, his wounded body red with blood. Picture how the soldiers thrust a reed into his hands as if it were a sceptre. How they knelt at his feet and pretended to pay him homage, scornfully shouting *Hail, King of the Jews!* Then they spat in his face.

Yet, Jesus bore all this insult and pain in patience and silence for the love of obedience to faith in God. Surely none of us would have serenity in such a situation. Even holy saints have groaned and cried out at the moment of their martyrdom. To know this is to be reminded of the hope that Jesus gives us by his great sacrifice, this salvation of love for the sake of all men and women.

By hearing the terrible details of his suffering and humiliation, we can truly understand at what cost Jesus purchased our redemption. Has anyone else ever been willing to die for you? Have you ever been so loved?

Thursday in Passion Week—The wounded Jesus is exhibited to the people

 ILATE, STILL HOPING that the Jews would no longer insist on Jesus's death, has him lead out with his crown of thorns upon his head and his body wounded and shows him to the people. Pilate imagined the sight of so much innocent blood would extinguish their thirst of anger, whereas it made them even more eager for Jesus' death. As we all know, anger can quickly get out of control and rages, like a storm at sea, uncontrollable and devouring everything in its way. This is what happened when the people saw the wounded Jesus.

How foolish Pilate was to expect that men and women's passions could be abated by just giving them a little of what they wanted. Is it possible we sometimes make the same mistake as Pilate by trying to rid ourselves of some troublesome situation by making a kind of compromise and giving in to it just a little? Have you ever sipped at such a cup of passion, thinking only to have a little drink and found yourself unsatisfied until you had drunk the cup empty? Sin in any form has a thirst that is never quenched until it has tasted the last drop of virtue in us.

Therefore, let us find charity in all we do in imitation of God himself, because God, the fountain of all charity, knows no boundaries.[4]

---

4   Pope Saint Leo the Great, *Sermon 10 on Lent*.

Friday in Passion Week — On the suffering of Mary

 ROM THE TIME she heard that prophetic prediction addressed to her by Simeon that a sword would pierce her soul, Mary knew that she would suffer more than ordinary anguish in her life. (Luke 2:34–35) She was to suffer the loss of her child, the deepest wound and the most unforgettable pain of any mother and father. A pain that pierces not just the mind and memory but forever breaks the heart. Surely, the loss of a child is the heaviest cross our earthly pilgrimage has to offer.

Think for a moment of your own experience of grief over the loss of someone you loved. Recall those you have known who have lost a child. Then, you will truly appreciate the suffering of Mary.

We can only imagine how Mary must have felt at Simeon's prediction, even more so because the love she bore Jesus was not just as her child, but also as the presence of someone on this earth from God himself. Mary could never forget those mysterious and wonderful words the Angel Gabriel spoke to her: *The Holy Spirit will come upon you, and the power of the Most High will cover you with its shadow. And so the child will be holy and will be called Son of God.* (Luke 1:35)

Dare you hold Mary's hand as she follows Jesus on his last journey to Calvary and share what she had to watch? Can you be that strong, that brave, that loving? Can you be with her as she watches Jesus struggling to bear his cross on his bleeding shoulders? Can you watch with her as her beloved child is hoisted in the air and then hear the nails being driven into him, as she must have heard them? Can you weep with her as she then cries out with the prophet: *All you who pass this way, look and see: is any sorrow like the sorrow inflicted on me, with which Yahweh struck me on the day of his burning anger?* (Lament 1: Lamed 12 & read also Mem 13)

This is why the deep grief of Mary is unique on this earth. It is an unimaginable sorrow for those fatal wounds suffered by her son, Jesus the Messiah, the *Man of sorrows*. But *he will grow great, will rise to great heights*. (Isaiah 52:13; 53 all)

Saturday in Passion Week—Jesus is condemned to the cross

ERCEIVING THAT PILATE wanted to release Jesus, the crowd told him that, if he did so, he was no friend of the emperor, because anyone who made himself a king opposed Caesar. (John 18:12)

So it was that Pilate's resolution to somehow save Jesus disappeared in the face of losing favour with his emperor. Like so many of us, Pilate put fear of losing favour with worldly powers before what his heart told him was a grave injustice.

From this we understand how human respect for other people's power and position are capable of producing evil and how sad it is to fear anything more than God. Have we never had a share in this kind of such guilt? Has fear or the apprehension of what our neighbours, friends, or family would think too often influenced us to turn away from standing up for what we know to be right and just? Do we use vain excuses to wash our guilt just like Pilate did?

Palm Sunday—The triumphant entrance of Jesus into Jerusalem

N BIBLICAL TIMES, the local custom called for kings and powerful nobility arriving in procession to ride on the back of a donkey, because this animal was a symbol of peace. Hence, those who rode on a donkey were proclaiming their peaceful intentions. The laying of palm branches and the spreading of cloaks on the road indicated that the king or dignitary was arriving in victory or triumph. So it was for Jesus when he rode into Jerusalem. This fulfilled the prophecy of Zechariah: *Rejoice heart and soul, daughter of Zion! Shout for joy, daughter of Jerusalem! Look, your king is approaching, he is vindicated and victorious, humble and riding on a donkey.* (Zechariah 9:9)

Although we are ready to join in this triumphal procession by celebrating the coming victory of your Lord over death, many may wonder why this day looks back on the life of Jesus just as we enter Holy Week and we are already deep into the story of his condemnation.

Perhaps this contrast between triumph and crucifixion is to remind us how easily men and women are swayed by mob action from honouring a hero to hating him. Palm Sunday shows us how hard it is to stand up for our faith and not succumb to what the crowd may say and do.

When we wave our green branches around in celebration at church and then take them blessed into our homes, we should remember how easily we fall from grace into sin.

Monday in Holy Week—Jesus carries his Cross

 HO CAN CONCEIVE the feelings with which Jesus carried his cross, this cross destined to be the instrument of our redemption. What are your feelings with regard to it as you journey through the Season of Lent?

We know that we must embrace this cross with him if we want to reign with him. So, when you next look on Christ crucified, bow down in worship. (Psalm 95:5–6)

Tuesday in Holy Week—Our Saviour is nailed to the Cross

MAGINE JESUS ARRIVING at Mount Calvary, his enemies still pursuing him. The crowds gathered around him full of excitement, forgetting why this innocent man was being crucified. Indeed most of them then as now are thrilled by the prospect of death as long as it is someone else who is dying. Just recall how recent it is that crowds of men, women, and children gathered together to watch a hanging or a beheading. But then, we know the innocent are always dying. Just this morning someone innocent somewhere in our world died by the hand, the gun, the bomb, or the stone, killed in anger, revenge, or cruelty and all done under the pretence of offense against some political, religious or other law made up by men and women.

We must beware for the anger of God at injustice and murder is the same today as it has always been and his vengeance is swift. (Ezekiel 25:17; Deuteronomy 32–43; Psalms 149:7; 59:10; 98:8)

After being nailed to his cross, the charity of Jesus for others does not lessen. He forgives the poor thief and cries out for God's mercy on everyone in the crowd. (Luke 23:34, 39–43 & 46; Matthew 27:50) Here is the example of the love we should follow, a love that holds no expectations, a love offered in spite of everything, a love that is unending. This is the meaning of mercy and compassion.

Wednesday in Holy Week — On the sufferings of Jesus on the Cross

 RAW NEAR BROTHER and sister in Christ and sit down under the shadow of your true lover's cross. Do not hesitate or turn away from his agony and the terrible details of his wounding and torments. Instead yearn to be his student in this school of love for that is what you find in the Cross, a school of love, a teaching of obedience, and God acting in Divine Providence.

Commit yourself to remember and meditate on our Saviour and the goodness of God in sending him. Dwell on the meaning of his death. Ask for forgiveness and fulfil the obligations of Lent.

Holy Thursday—On Jesus preaching from the Cross

HE WHOLE LIFE and doctrine of Jesus was a continual lesson to his followers to renounce self-love with its three branches. These are the love of the flesh; the lust of the eyes, that is, the love for the material goods of this world; and the pride of life that is the lust for power, privilege, prestige and honours from other people.

In the end, all these aspects of self-love leave us unhappy, because they draw us away from God. If we satisfy all these worldly goals and values, we have exchanged our allegiance to God, the fountain of life, for mere puddles that can never satisfy our thirst for the meaning and purpose of our life.

With the passing of time we naturally lose all our beauty that brought us satisfaction in the desires of our flesh. Eventually, we become so old that no one desires us anymore. Even if we have all the money in the world, all this wealth is useless, because when having everything we are left bored or restless, still not contented and still seeking *more*, but not knowing what that *more* is.

Like youth, our power, privilege and prestige pass away. We are like the wild flowers here today, gone tomorrow, and eventually remembered by no one save the crumbing monument over our grave where our name may remain after we are forgotten by the living. Our cemeteries are full of people now forgotten, ignored, and waiting in silence for that final judgment. (Psalm 102:15–16; Matthew 6:25–34; 1 Peter 1:24)

The sermon that Jesus preaches from the cross is about love. He speaks few words from this pulpit of his Cross, but in those few words and by his behaviour he condemns self-love and the false values of this world. By example, he teaches us that we are to throw out self-love and follow him in true love, the kind that knows no bounds, holds out forgiveness to everyone, and comes from God, the fountain of life itself, the being in all things.

If we desire to be holy, we must learn from our dying Saviour to make this offering of ourselves to God. It is our act of greatest love and in doing it, we join our offering of unselfish love with his eternal love. We must make such an offering everyday of our lives and not just in the *Season of Lent* or at the times of other great seasons in the life of the church. We follow a religion of love and need to remember this foundation of our life.

Good Friday—On Our Saviour's death

Now is the darkest hour. Now is the time we must wait on God. Now is the day of sadness and regret. The hour approaches when the light will leave this world. A time when the feasting will end and joy will be taken from us. (Matthew 9:15)

The shadow of death descends on Jesus as he cries out in willing submission to God's plan for him.

Jesus dies to consummate the great sacrifice of the redemption of the world. Be astonished in contemplation of this mystery that the source of light should die so we can be delivered from death and given eternal life. (Psalm 27:7; Luke 23:46)

Holy Saturday—On Our Saviour's burial

FTER JESUS DIED, Joseph of Arimathea was given permission to take away his body for decent burial. Jesus is then shut away in a burial cave of darkness like anyone dead forever and forsaken by the living. (Psalm 87) But let us stay with Jesus and guard him in prayer. Let us weep over him with tears of compassion for his sufferings. Let us wait with tender love for him. Let us keep watch.

Resolve *to* keep near to Jesus the Christ by daily meditating on his life and death, because he is near us in our life and in our death. He is our friend and our teacher, always beside us in good times and bad.

EXTRA FESTIVE DAYS FOR MARCH

17 March—Feast of St Patrick, Apostle of Ireland

 ONSIDER THE ZEAL for God's Word through which Saint Patrick converted a whole nation of people. He wrapped himself in the armour of Christ and went into the world as a warrior for God. (Ephesians 6:11) It is said that the word of God in his mouth was like a fire, which breaking forth from the great furnace of the divine love which possessed him, communicated its flames of truth to the hearts of all who heard him and won them over to Christ.

Every man and woman without exception can achieve a true zeal for God by a profound humility, a spirit of prayer, and a heart burning with charity. It is hard work but these are the means by which like Saint Patrick, we help others toward God.

19 March — Solemnity of St Joseph

OSEPH, A COURAGEOUS and faithful man, was chosen by God to be the guardian of Jesus while he grew up. He acted out of love as every father, stepfather, foster-father or any guardian of a child should act.

There is little recorded about Joseph in the *New Testament*, but what is there tells us what it takes to be a righteous man. In fulfilling the holy task of raising Jesus as if his own son, Joseph shows us how faith and actions work together and the absolute necessity of completely trusting in God.

Most of all Joseph shows us that love and trust of God must be the deciding factors in all our decisions and that the opinions or values of this world are a poor second place. In particular, we learn how potential or current suspicions and gossip by others must not influence us in our decisions about people. Joseph shows us that we must leave judgment about other people as the privilege of God alone. (Matthew 7)

Saint Joseph gave real love to Jesus. This love included, as it always should with the raising of every child: an awareness of the presence of the Holy Spirit in ordinary life; charity to his mother and elders; diligence in whatever hardships might be put on him as in the case of their flight into Egypt; patience under afflictions and disappointments; honest work necessary to support his family; a lack of any prejudice in justice; and attention to God by regular participation in the duties of his religion. These are the obligations of every guardian of a child.

In all of this, Saint Joseph shows us exactly what is demanded of every man, whether a father, a foster-father, or a stepfather. This exercise of the duties of love should be also the expectation of every mother as to how a man should behave who assumes the role of a father in helping raise a child.

Since these are the expectations of God, why shouldn't they be the expectations of every mother for the man in her life? Indeed, they should be the expectations of any man who would be a father to a child. Should not every man have the dignity and respect that goes with such honour?

We see in Joseph's life that a holy life may be found even in the midst of the distractions of a worldly calling to be part of a community and to work. If we encounter difficulties in this, it is not the fault of our situation in life, but of our not having responded fully to divine grace. Indeed, sanctity is not inconsistent with doing the labours of making a living in this world.

If God has blessed you with children or you are a step-parent or foster parent, take care to instil into each child the love of God. Show them the error of self-love and the happiness that virtue brings *by the way you act and live yourself*. The way in which we act ourselves is the best witness to the glory of God. We need equally to keep a balance between the attention you devote to their minds, bodies, and spirit. Never neglect one aspect in favour of the other, because every person was created by God as one person, a union of mind, body and spirit. Make certain that each child in your care is healthy, safe, respected and loved. Honour all your obligations to provide for them whether those are material or emotional needs.

All these duties, those obligations of love and the qualities we must show a child, are hard to do on a daily basis. Everyone knows this who is a guardian of a child. But in these ways, like Saint Joseph, we may nurture all that is good in these little ones, because we do not know if the child we help today may grow up to be a saint of heaven and a chosen one of God.

25 March — Solemnity of the Annunciation of the Lord

 HIS SOLEMNITY COMMEMORATES the moment when God commanded Jesus to be in the womb of the Virgin Mary. God said, *Be!* And Jesus was made flesh. (Genesis 1–28 Matthew 1:18–20; Luke 1:35, John 1:14) Today in church readings and ceremonies we focus on this event from Mary's perspective.

At this glorious moment, the first lesson from Mary centres on her obedience to the will of God. In this she shows us that we must cast aside what society may think of us when we chose to be obedient to the holy plan of God. We must fear nothing but God and wisdom will be our possession. (Job 28:28; Psalm 110:10; Proverbs 1:7; Proverbs 10:13; Ecclesiastes 2:26; James 1:5)

By her obedience, Mary replaces the disobedience of the first Eve. As the second or New Eve, Mary once again opens the way of virtue for all women and all men. No one is excluded. Mary shows us that we must trust in God. We must possess unwavering faith in his promises and unfailing belief in his mercy for us. With Mary's consent to the divine plan, the incarnation happens. The Word is made flesh. We have been given the Messiah. The light of the world triumphs.

Saint Luke tells us of the song of Mary, *The Magnificat*, which is the glory of her obedience. (Luke 1:46–38) So sing her song to heaven as often as possible, because it is a prayer pleasing to God:

> My soul glorifies the Lord,
> my spirit rejoices in God, my Saviour.
> He looks on his servant in her lowliness;
> henceforth all ages will call me blessed.
> The Almighty works marvels for me.
> Holy his name!
> His mercy is from age to age,

on those who fear him.
He puts forth his arm in strength
and scatters the proud-hearted.
He casts the mighty from their thrones
and raises the lowly.
He fills the starving with good things,
sends the rich away empty.
He protects Israel, his servant,
remembering his mercy,
the mercy promised to our fathers,
to Abraham and his sons for ever.

THE SEASON OF EASTER

Theme: The glory of Salvation

I know that my Saviour lives and at the end he will stand on this earth. My flesh may be destroyed, yet from this body I will see God.
Job 19:25–26

Solemnity of Easter Sunday—On the resurrection of Jesus Christ

HIS IS THE day of our greatest joy, because we have been saved through love. (Ephesians 1:4–5) It is a wonderful moment in the history of God and humanity. It is a miraculous event in this world. It shows us for all time that God is All Merciful, All Compassionate.

How glorious was Christ's triumph over all the powers of darkness. In his resurrection, he showed how vain are the attempts of men and women when they try to go against the decrees of God, since nothing can defeat him. (Proverbs 21:30) Yet, love has saved us and showered us with the wonderful promises of God.

Everyone should rejoice on this holy day, because as St. Maximus of Turin pointed out:

> No one should separate himself from the general rejoicing because he or she has sins on his conscience; no one should refuse to take part in the public worship because of the burden of his misdeeds. However great a sinner he or she may be, on this day he should not despair of pardon, for the privileges granted on this day are great. If a thief was thought worthy of paradise, why should not a Christian be thought worthy of forgiveness?[1]

St. Augustine has this to add:

> Be glad wherever you are today, because no matter how long we are on earth God, Christ and the Holy Spirit are with us. So do not be anxious nor ever lose hope.[2]

Indeed, this is the day that the Lord has made. A day to sing out our praise. A day to fall on our knees in thanksgiving. A

---

[1] St. Maximus of Turin, *Sermon 53*, 1–2 & 4.

[2] St. Augustine, *Sermon 171*.

day to rejoice with great happiness of mind, body and spirit. (Psalm 117) Rejoice and be glad! *Rejoice!*

Easter Monday—The Resurrection of Jesus Christ

CCORDING TO THE Apostle, Christ was our Lord Jesus who was handed over to death for our sins and raised to life for our justification. (Romans 4:25) His rising from the dead was designed to be a model of our own resurrection from the death of sin to the life of grace. But in what way does our resurrection imitate that of Christ?

First, we should imitate him by truly rising up to a new life in Christ and not just do this by outward appearances. Just think how many people pretend to rise again with Christ by going to Confession and Communion and, yet, they deceive themselves, because the efforts they make are half-hearted. They renounce their sins for the day or even for the whole of Lent and the season of Easter, but their hearts are not in it. Their making a new life in Christ is but a phantom for such people return to their passions, desires, and the values of the world as soon as they leave church. They are still dead. (Colossians 3)

When Christ rose from the dead, he left his tomb and his burial sheet behind him, retaining nothing of the symbols of death. This teaches us that if we would rise with Christ, we too must leave behind all the elements and signs of death, that is to say we must leave behind all that displeases God and is against his instructions.

We can do this by renouncing bad habits, keeping our passions under control, and avoiding situations or people that we know would make us fall into the ways of the world. We should do this until no symptoms of death remain in us. (Romans 6:9–11)

In order to walk in this newness of life, we must try as much as we can to walk with God by an inward solitude and a spiritual recollection. Frequent prayer helps to keep open this gateway to God and the glory of Easter reminds us to seek things that are heavenly, not the things on earth. These are the feelings we need to possess to make our joy complete and lasting, because Christ defeated death that we might truly live in God. (Colossians 3)

Always ask to be given the strength to pursue that which gives honour to God and his Messiah. In this way, the resurrection of Jesus and his return to God will live in us not just in the Easter Season but also in everyday of our life. (1 Peter 1:3–4; Luke 24; Matthew 28:5–7; John 20:27–29; John 3: 16–17 Romans 10:9–10; Job 19:25–26; Psalm 49:15; Revelation 1:17–18; 1 Corinthians 15:12–20)

Easter Tuesday—On Jesus Christ after his Resurrection

HE RESURRECTION TEACHES us that the way of Jesus means we must receive God's blessings with joy and his wounding with a peacefulness of heart, because both joy and suffering are within God's plan for our lives. Acceptance of everything that happens to us, both good and bad, is the meaning of obedience to God. If we accept blessings, then we must accept the wounds too.

Remember the women who came first to Jesus's tomb? They carried sweet spices and fragrant ointments to perfume the body of their beloved Master. But when they arrived, the great stone blocking the tomb had been moved away. Suddenly, angels appeared and then Jesus himself. How astounded and confused they were, even at first not recognizing him. But the joy of his resurrection would very soon fill their hearts and replace their sorrow.

What can we to learn from these events at the tomb? Firstly, we learn to go in quest of Christ with the perfume of desire for him to be in our life. Secondly, we learn to be constant in our good resolutions, since God will help us by his grace to overcome all difficulties that may arise. So keep your faith strong and alive like those women who came first to Jesus' tomb.

Consider Mary Magdalene, who came to the tomb. She had been constant in her love of Christ from the time of her conversion. She followed him to the Cross. She waited there in grief, not sparing herself from witnessing his terrible sufferings. She saw his body laid out in the tomb. She was the first after the Sabbath day to go to him. Searching for him, she was full of sorrow. Then she saw an angel, the messenger of God, and shortly after Jesus himself appeared.

This holy woman, Mary Magdalene, showed us that love should never cease and that perseverance must accompany love through all the events in our life. If you should so love and persevere in seeking Christ like Mary Magdalene, then be assured you will surely find him. His tomb may be empty, but you will find Jesus alive and waiting in your heart. Do not forget that even if your sins and misdeeds are as red as scarlet, they will be made as white as snow by God, *because love* is the shortest way to forgiveness and to all other virtues. (Isaiah 1:16, Psalm 52:3)

Easter Wednesday — The mystery of the Resurrection

HAT IS A miracle? It is an event that seems beyond anything we know. It is inexplicable. When we think about a miracle, it becomes a true enigma, a mystery, something that never can be fully understood. Try as we might with our science and studies, we cannot explain a miracle. It transcends what we understand about how our world works. But miracles serve a holy purpose, because they call us to a place where God exists and, thus, where all is possible. (Luke 18:27) In this way, all miracles by their inexplicable nature serve to draw us toward God.

The Scriptures are full of miracles. For example, God parting the Red Sea in Exodus or the story of Moses, and Elijah on Mount Carmel calling down fire from Heaven. We learn about the miracles of Jesus. How he walked on water and healed the wounded and sick. The blind saw again. The lame could walk again. He fed some 5,000 people with two fishes and five loaves of bread. At the wedding at Cana, he turned water into wine. He returned the dead to life. Credit for such holy powers came from God in all these miracles. (Acts 2:22) These are just some of the miracles we know about, but there must have been others not recorded by the Prophets, Apostles and the various authors of the Old and New Testaments.

In truth, we are surrounded by mystery. Just think how little we understand our dog or cat, the trees in our garden, the star we see at night or the earth beneath our feet. In miracles we are shown the divine and cannot explain it away. Where our rational thinking and logic ends, our faith takes command, because nothing is too difficult for God. (Jeremiah 31:24)

Yet, most of us still have a corner of our mind that remains sceptical, a small whisper that asks: Did the miracles actually occur or are they simply a way of speaking about God? The only way we can satisfactorily answer this is by returning to Scripture, where all four Gospel accounts of Jesus's life refer to him as a miracle worker. (Matthew 11:10–11 & 12:17; John 11:25) Jewish authorities during the first century acknowledged the miracles of Jesus and Islam teaches that God gave Jesus the power to perform miracles. (John 3:2–3; *The Quran*, Surah 2 & Surah 43)

To prove or disprove anything, science depends on verifiably repeatable experiments. Miracles are *not* repeatable. They suspend or transcend the order and laws of nature and the universe as we understand them. While useful for studying nature and phenomenon, this scientific method is not a way of understanding that which is super-natural. God has and will continue to transcend the laws of nature and the universe to accomplish his purposes whenever he wishes. Remember that what is impossible for humanity is possible for God, who only needs to say *Be!* And it is. (Luke 18:27; *The Quran*, Surah 19:30–35)

So it is best to dismiss any scepticism we find in ourselves. It will only trouble us and bring unease into our life, weakening our faith and fogging up our vision in trying to follow the teachings of Jesus. Endless curiosity and the questioning of the mysteries of God can become human conceits that lead to discontent and may destroy the meaning of life in us.

The greatest mystery of all was the resurrection of Christ. This was the conquering of death and the transcending of Jesus to be with God. In a few words, Jesus told how all the miracles of God were possible and, therefore, not mysterious if we have faith. We have been told by angels and Jesus himself: For nothing is impossible to God. (Luke 1:37, 18: 27; Matthew 19:26)

So let us sing out with the psalmist: *How many, O Lord my God, are the wonders and designs that you have worked for us; you have no equal!* (Psalm 40:6)

Easter Thursday — On the dead being raised up

 T IS ESSENTIAL to our faith is that we join Jesus in a full resurrection of ourselves. This means that those who died in Christ will be raised up with him on the final day and those who are alive at his holy return will be changed and receive new and glorified bodies. (1 Thessalonians 4:13–18)

How can it be possible that each and every one of us will rise again in his or her body? Some of us will have turned into dust, others eaten by worms or by wild beasts or by birds. Some will have been burned up and the wind taken their ashes far away. Once beautiful flesh and fine bones will disintegrate in dark places. How then can it happen that angels will call forth each of these once human forms to come to judgment and be raised up again in their own original flesh? (St. Francis de Sales, *Sermons for Lent 1622*; 1 Corinthians 15:53)

This is the miracle and mystery that awaits us to be done by the power of God. As it was easy for God to produce our body in the first place by picking up a handful of dust and creating Adam, so it will not be any more difficult for him to produce a body again. (Genesis 2:7) As we belong to God, he does not let us go from himself either in life or death and the promise of salvation is that we will one day be with him as Jesus the Christ is with him now, fully risen in all ways.

Knowing this is our destiny, fear nothing for God is with us always. (Isaiah 58:11; Deuteronomy 31:8)

Easter Friday — On Christ showing himself going to Emmaus

IMAGINE THE TWO disciples walking along the road to Emmaus on the same day as Jesus' resurrection. While they discussed the meaning and truth of his death and teachings, the risen Christ becomes present. He speaks with them about their doubts and their slowness in accepting the truth. He explains the meaning in the Scriptures that related to his passion and resurrection. His words rekindle the fire of devotion in their hearts. Suddenly they know this was no stranger but Jesus himself, alive and well and resurrected as foretold. (Luke 24)

Here is a wonderful example of how our conversation when it takes Christ for its subject, draws him into our lives. We are like these two men on a road to Emmaus, when we may be suddenly aware of Christ's presence in our lives. The Holy Spirit descends. Jesus is present to us. Isn't this the meaning of what Jesus tells us when he says, *For where two or three meet in my name, I am there among you.* (Matthew 18:19–20)

What a pity then that there should be so little mention of God and Jesus Christ in the conversation of most Christians.

Here are some questions we need to answer about ourselves: When was the last time you spoke of God or Jesus Christ with a fellow Christian? When was the last time someone spoke to you about God? How often is the holy name of Jesus included in your words to others? When was the last time you heard someone in church, outside of the service, speaking of God? When was the last time someone invoked the blessing of God by greeting you with these words: Peace be with you!

How can this forgetfulness of God be reconciled with our loving him? It is natural for us to take delight in speaking of what we love for when an abundance of love fills the heart, it spills over into the words of our mouth. (Luke 6:45; Matthew 12:33–37) For example, think how often we speak lovingly of our children and grandchildren. So how can we flatter ourselves that the love of God is master of our hearts, when we seldom care to speak of him?

Reflect further on this Emmaus story, because there are more lessons to be learned from this first appearance of Christ than we may think at first. For example, the two men did not immediately recognize Jesus as present, because their faith in him was weak and imperfect. If we have such weakness of faith or our church going at best is *once in a while* or *mostly on christenings, weddings and funerals*, these could be reasons why Christ does not manifest himself to us in our life? If we are to have a strong faith, we must practice it like Mary.

We need also to let Christ know that we want his presence in our lives. We need to actively seek his company and acknowledge his presence in our conversation Above all else, we must be faithful in following his way, because his is the *School of Divine Love* where faith is strengthened and hearts opened. Such is the law of God in all its fullness. (Romans 13:10) To acknowledge God and to know him by obedience to him is indeed the perfect virtue. (Wisdom 15:1–3)

Easter Saturday — On Christ appearing to all the Apostles

 N THE EVENING of the same day as our Lord's resurrection, the disciples gathered together, carefully barring the doors to the room for fear of the authorities. Suddenly, Christ stood in the midst of them, and said to them: *Peace be with you!* (Luke 24:36) He showed them his body—the wounds of his hands, feet, and side and those from the thorns on his head. By these testimonies of his body and blood, he confirmed their faith in him and inflamed their love. (Luke 24:37–44; John 20: 19–29)

We have this same glorious resurrected body and blood in the Eucharist. Although we may not see him with our eyes nor feel his wounds with our hands, our faith and our hope brings such inner vision, a vision which assures us that Christ is present. In this way, each time we receive such nourishment at the altar, we join the Apostles in having our faith confirmed and our hearts set aflame with love of God. Unlike the Apostle Thomas, we have not seen and believed by the outward senses of our eyes and hands, but believe by our faith and, thus, we are blessed. (John 20:29)

Remember that Christ is always with you even to the end of the world. (Matthew 28:19–20)

Solemnity of Easter Sunday of Divine Mercy — On the peace of a Christian

HE NIGHT BEFORE his passion Jesus bequeathed his peace to his disciples saying, *Peace I bequeath to you, my own peace I give you, a peace which the world cannot give, this is my gift to you*. Then after his resurrection, he wished them his peace more times, saying, *Peace be with you*. (John 14:20, 27 & 28)

But what kind of peace is this that Jesus so earnestly wants to impart to the Apostles and through them to us?

It is not the peace the world pretends to give. This peace never lasts for long and always contains what is false and deceitful although it may be hidden at first and we do not see it. Nation after nation, political leader after political leader, society after society says, *Peace! Peace!* But there is no peace. (Ezekiel 13:16) Wars, needless famine, forced migrations of millions, torture, injustice, and the greed for power and wealth around the world continue today just as they have for thousands of years. We have not yet learned to love as God commanded.

To receive the peace that Christ offers is to receive the peace that is lasting, but we must reach out to God for it. This peace from God is totally different from anything the world has to offer, because holy peace passes all understanding. It dwells deeply within us and endures. (Philip. 4:6–7)

The peace from God is three-fold: A peace of the heart and soul with God. A peace within us that rises above self-will and self-love. Finally, a peace with everyone no matter his or her race, religion or nationality.

It is the duty of every Christian to maintain this kind of holy peace. This means not allowing our wilful self-regard and worldly passions to be at war with what God wants and expects from us. No person can fight God's will and his commandments and still expect to have peace. (Job 9:4) But be warned never to forget that the wicked are like a raging sea, never resting, never truly still and quiet, always making waves that cast up debris and filth, poisoning the waters, and eventual destroying all life including us. Indeed, there is never peace for the wicked. (Isaiah 57:20–21)

Consider further that no Christian can maintain this holy peace with God unless he or she is at peace with all other men and women, because no one can say that they are at peace with God if they do not love their neighbour. (Hebrews 12:14–17; Romans 12:18; 1 John 4:7–13)

So we must ask if you have truly renounced all animosity and rancour, all discord and contention, all malice and envy, and whatsoever else is opposite to charity? Have we learned to be tolerant and to forbear others with patience? Are we at peace in our relationships? Are we at peace with mother, father, brothers and sisters? Are we at peace with our wife or husband? Are we at peace with our children? Are we at such holy peace with the man across the street and the woman next to us at work?

Search until we find that person we should have loved but did not and give love to that person. Without such charity there cannot be love and without love the peace of God and his Christ will be not be with us.

Monday, Week 2 of Easter—On the Sacrament of Baptism

 HROUGH BAPTISM WE are incorporated into Christ and Christ comes into us. We are made living members of his mystical body, which is his church. We have *become the people of God; you are a chosen generation, a kingdom of priests, a holy nation, a people to be a personal possession to sing the praises of God who called you out of the darkness into his wonderful light.* (1 Peter 2: 9–10)

What a happy dedication this is! Yet, how often we forget this great reception of us by God. Why is it that so many of us when we grow up, do not remember that our life is meant to be holy? (1 Peter 13–16)

Tuesday, Week 2 of Easter—On the Sacrament of Baptism

 ONSIDER THE GREAT dignity that has been bestowed on us by our life being consecrated to God through our baptism. In consequence of it, no matter who or where we are now our life is more than a mere clog in the wheel of the world and all its commerce. Each of us is a holy person through this consecration and dedication of our baptism. It does not matter whether this took place when we were an infant, a growing child or an adult. Our real consent in baptism is always the will of God for our life.

We are reborn in baptism, and become like Christ himself. We are risen up as a holy vessel of God. Our life *is* important no matter who we are, because by our baptism we are brought to the Holy Spirit and introduces us to all that is good. It becomes the means by which we are brought to the table of Christ and share in the bread of life. We are made entirely new in a new beginning. (Titus 4:5–7; Ephesians 4:22–23) We are able to say with the Apostle: *I have been crucified with Christ and yet I am live; yet it is no longer I, but Christ living in me.* (Galatians 2:20 & 3:27–29)

Wednesday, Week 2 of Easter — On the covenant of baptism

 N BAPTISM WE make or our parents and godparents make for us like Mary did with Jesus, a solemn covenant with God by which he gives us an unquestionable right to the inheritance of his everlasting kingdom. We promise a strict observance of God's law, especially the greatest commandment to love him with our whole heart, our whole soul, and with all of our strength. We also promise to extend such love to our neighbours just as we would want such love shown to us. (Luke 10:27)

Fulfilling God's law and commandments means being obedient to him. This is a profound challenge. When we stumble, as surely we will, we must ask forgiveness and mercy. But what supports us as we try to follow Jesus is the Holy Spirit.

We saw this help as a dove descending upon him when Jesus was baptised. This sign of the Holy Spirit also descends on us when we are baptized. As surely as a cape rests on our shoulders when we wear it, so the Holy Spirit cloaks us with heavenly help. This is why we must never make the Holy Spirit sad or act as if it was not our abiding companion and the sign of God dwelling with us.

Thursday, Week 2 of Easter—The virtues of faith, hope and love

INCE GOD IS the supreme spirit of all being and the sovereign truth, we must worship him in spirit and truth. (John 4:24) Our external praise, prayer, and sacrifice finds its wellspring in the three internal divine virtues of faith, hope, and love, all of which dwell in our heart. Where these virtues are daily exercised all is well for then God dwells in us, but where any one of these is lacking all goes wrong for us. The Holy Spirit becomes sad as eventually we too become sad, because without virtue we are lost and find no peace.

Faith believes in God as the sovereign truth and obliges us to give unreserved acceptance to all the truths revealed by him, because he neither can deceive nor be deceived. This truth about God brings *hope* and allows us to worship him as the inexhaustible source of all that is good. *Hope* raises up in each of us an expectation of mercy, grace, and salvation from God, a salvation founded on his eternal power, goodness, promises, mercy and the blood of his Messiah. *Hope* destroys all our loneliness, because in hope is Christ and since Christ is the very essence of love, we realize we are loved. This *love* overwhelms all our negative feelings and turns our heart toward heaven.

Therefore, the brightest jewel in the crown of virtue is your love of God and your charity to others. Love worships without limit or expectation in complete freedom, because such holy virtue loves God for his own sake and for his own goodness and loves all men and women because they are made in his image. (Genesis 1:27)

183

Friday, Week 2 of Easter—On faith

ONSIDER HOW *impossible it is to please God without faith,* because faith is the foundation of all our obedience to God. (Hebrews 11:6) Here is where we must begin the fulfilment of our salvation.

But what is this faith of which we so often speak? It is not with a confidence that their sins will be forgiven no matter what they do as many Christians vainly imagine or presume. This is just vanity otherwise Hell surely would be empty. The faith of a Christian is a firm and insistent belief in all that God has revealed or promised. Such a faith allows no doubts or divisions of the heart. It does not matter how much or how little we understand or even whether we can read and write, because such faith is beyond our explaining. Such faith remains a mystery.

What is important is that our faith stands as the real substance of all the things we hope for in God. It is evidence of a confidence in the things that are not seen. (Hebrews 11:1) The good things we hope for and the truths we believe may be unseen, but they are spiritually visible to us. The whole conduct of our life is lived according to this gift of God that is faith.

In this way we become the fruit of the vine that is nourished by the living waters about which Jesus told the Samaritan women at Jacob's Well. (John 4:10) So it is that we pray to God that he will harvest this vine for he is the one who planted it. (Psalm 79:15)

Saturday, Week 2 of Easter—On the effect of faith

 AITH HAS THE effect of vanquishing the pride of men and women. It does this by captivating their whole being—mind, body and spirit. It obliges them to believe what they cannot see, to adore what they cannot understand, and to submit to truths that they cannot comprehend by their intellect or their science or any other means at human disposal.

Such faith sacrifices what is dear to our pride, that kind of personal liberty of which we are so fond and which the world promotes. This liberty is most often an illusion that rulers, politicians and commercialism like us to believe we possess, but only if using it profits them. It is liberty or *right* understood by most people as meaning they can please themselves in all matters. Such thinking leads not just to this illusion of freedom but unhappily it most often leads to thinking we are in control of our life instead of knowing it is in the will of God. Faith defeats such unrewarding self-love.

If you hope to build a spiritual palace within yourself in which God may choose to dwell, make certain to lay a strong foundation of faith. To build upon any other foundation is to build upon sand, which the waters of worldly life will quickly wash away. Remember we will *never* understand what God is planning for us. We can try as hard as we like. You can be the smartest, the wealthiest, the most powerful person in the world, but you still will never find out what God has in mind for you. Many men and women may claim to understand God's plans, but they don't. (Ecclesiastes 8:17) Have faith and you will find contentment in this life.

Third Sunday of Easter—On hope for the Christian

 E MAY THINK we are in a situation where hope is gone from us, but this is not true. When we feel this way we need to remember that hope belongs to everyone. Even if we give up on God, he does not give up on us. Thus, hope always arises in us for it is part of our thanks for just being alive. It is a grace from God and leads us to realize that no one, regardless of our situation, can take our spirit from us. Others may damaged our body, insult our reputation, imprison us, threaten us with death, lead us to the torturer, or make our minds confused, forgetful and full of false thoughts, but no one, absolutely no one, can take away our spirit. Every prisoner, every holocaust victim, every demonstrator for human justice knows this.

Therefore, hope is the blessing for which we should pray when we wake, thanking God for another day of life. We should declare, *I am alive! Alleluia!* This is a serious statement, not made in a superficial jest, because none of us know the hour of our death. Remembering this fact should make us truly thankful for the time we have been given to live, never mind whether the conditions of that life are unjust and cruel or comfortable and pleasant. Such awakening of our consciousness of God raises up hope in us that today will be better than yesterday.

Hope lifts the dark curtain of depression and despair. Hope brings light into those imprisoned. Hope spurs on those who are weary with pain and illness. It gives a new vision to those who are struggling whether with relationships, unemployment, or poverty. Hope is the flame of youth and the comfort of the old.

Hope, of course, may in itself solve none of our problems, such as freeing us from prison or saving us from being wounded by bombs, but it does have a positive effect on the mind and body. Hope stimulates those elements in the body, which bring positive effects for good health. Since the body and mind do not exist without influencing each other, the mind too becomes stimulated and our thinking more positive.

Thus, hope generates in us a vision beyond the immediate and gives wisdom even to the fool, reminding us that God never deserts us. This fortifies and supports us. Hope is always a sure sign of the presence of the Holy Spirit. We have refuge under his wings and are freed from the snares of this world. (Psalm 90)

Monday, Week 3 of Easter—On hope as the promise of God

S WONDERFUL AND positive as all these various effects of hope are, there is a more profound meaning of hope for the Christian. This is that hope given to us through the sacrifice of Jesus with its promise of salvation and our resurrection at the end of all time. Such hope is a bright promise in our heart, lifting our spirit, and reminding us that nothing in this life is hopeless as long as we hold onto God.

God has given us many promises. Perhaps some of these promises may seem less magnificent and astounding than that of our eventual resurrection, but these seemingly minor *promises enable you to share his holy nature and escape the world's corruption caused by human desires.* (2 Peter 1:4; John 3:16) God promises he has plans for each of us so as to give us hope and a future. (Jeremiah 29:11)

Listen again to that voice of revelation: *Behold, the dwelling place of God is with man. He will dwell with them, and they will be his people, and God himself will be with them as their God. He will wipe away every tear from their eyes, and death shall be no more, neither shall there be mourning, nor crying, nor pain anymore, for the former things have passed away.* And he who was seated on the throne said, *Look, I am making the whole of creation new.* (Revelation 21:1–27)

In this present time we wait for the one prepared for us at the end of all time. This is to be reborn into a new life in Christ, believing that whoever believes in God and is obedient to him will not perish but have eternal life. (John 3:16)

Hold this hope as a precious gift of God. This will keep your eyes turned heavenward, your heart ready, and your souls a royal palace where God may dwell. (Psalm 56:3 & 107:2–3)[3]

---

[3]   See St. Teresa of Avila *The Interior Castle.*

So sing out in thanksgiving and give praise for God, because he has given you the greatest of all gifts—the hope of eternal life in the house of God where you will live forever. (Psalm 94:1–2; Psalm 54:15; 2 Corinthians 5:1) Answer Christ's call, *Come to me!* (Matthew 11:28–30)

Tuesday, Week 3 of Easter—On the Lord's Prayer

N A FEW words the prayer that Jesus gave us, the *Lord's Prayer*, comprises all our hopes. In this prayer, are all the virtues of faith, hope, love of God, conformity to his blessed will, charity for our neighbours, forgiveness of injuries, and repentance for our sins. What a pity then that Christians in general should say this prayer out of habit and routine with so little sense of what they are actually praying.

Let us think about what we are doing when we say the *Lord's Prayer*. Consider what we say at the very beginning when we address God directly by calling him, *Our Father.* Pause there and be astonished at this high honour in being a child of God. Next we say: *who is in heaven.* This should focus us on holy things and clear our mind of worldly affections and worries. In these very first words, *Our Father, who is in heaven,* we go to be with God. What a wonderful beginning with which to greet God.

Conclude then to use the *Lord's Prayer* with serious attention, fully aware of what you are saying and that God is listening, because you have called him. Let us remember that Jesus himself gave the very words we are saying to us.

Wednesday, Week 3 of Easter—Hallowed Be Thy Name

HE FIRST PETITION of the *Lord's Prayer* is contained in these words, *Hallowed be thy name*. When we say this we are declaring that God's name should be praised and glorified. This petition comes first in the *Lord's Prayer*, because the first duty of a Christian is to love his God with his whole heart. Therefore, the first thing we pray for is the glory of God.

In praying for such glory of God, we are in effect asking for the glory of the whole world. This means we are praying that the knowledge of God may spread over all the earth so that all nations may serve him, all tongues praise him, and all hearts love him. By this sanctification we are asking that all men and women may all be united in the glory of God not merely by their prayers and religious duties, but much more by their lives since it is in the way we live our life that is the most perfect way of glorifying the name of God.

Thursday, Week 3 of Easter — Thy Kingdom Come

HE BIBLE TELLS us that the kingdom of God is to be understood in three different ways. Firstly, it is as the eternal kingdom of God in heaven. Secondly, it is as the spiritual kingdom of Christ in his church, which is in the body of Christ composed of his people. Thirdly, as the mystical kingdom of God in our souls just as Jesus told us when he said, *Look, the kingdom of God is within you.* (Luke 17:21) So in this second petition of *The Lord's Prayer*, when we say *Thy kingdom come*, we are asking that all these three aspects of God's kingdom should come into being.

Should we not be astonished that as poor humans created from dust we should be authorised to aspire after a holy kingdom of God to reign for endless ages? Yet, this is what Jesus himself taught us to ask for when we pray, *Thy kingdom come.* These three words contain the grandest act of divine hope, because they profess faith in all the promises of God and of his Word. By these few words, we also pray that God's kingdom may be victorious over the entire world and in relation to all men and women so that they may be may be faithful subjects to the one God. Thus, we are praying for the happiness of all people. Such a prayer for others is to love our neighbour as ourselves.

Friday, Week 3 of Easter –Thy will be done on earth as it is in heaven

 N THIS THIRD petition, *Thy will be done on earth as it is in heaven,* we ask to embrace the holy will of God. These words of willing obedience spring from our free will, because such obedience to God must be freely given. It is an act of love. As such, it includes charity to your self and to your neighbours by desiring for them and your self the great blessing of a willing conformity to the will of God.

This will of God is for God himself to be in charge of our life. This is what we are asking God when we pray, *Thy will be done on earth as it is in heaven.*

Saturday, Week 3 of Easter—*Give us this day our daily bread*

 N THE FIRST three petitions of the *Lord's Prayer*, we pray for the glory of the name of God, the spreading of his kingdom, and the execution of his will on earth as in heaven. But when we pray for *our daily bread*, we pray for God to help us survive by providing us with the necessary nourishment we need to sustain us.

But nourishment of our body, even that which helps our mind, is not enough to sustain us in life, because our spirit must have nourishment as well and this too must come from God. Such provision must include the grace of God and the Word of God for without these we would be lost from the path of life that Jesus taught and God promised would bring us to him.

The means to help us has been given to us by Jesus himself when we celebrate his life and resurrection in which is, indeed, *our daily bread*. This *daily bread* is not only the food we need to live in body and mind, but is the nourishment of the sacred body and blood of Christ himself, who declared, *I am the living bread which came down from heaven. Anyone that eats this bread will live forever and the bread that I shall give is my flesh, for the life of the world.* (John 6:51)

Fourth Sunday of Easter—Forgive us our trespasses, as we forgive those that trespass against us

 OT A DAY goes by in which we do not in some way fall into an offense against God's glory. (James 3:2) Temptation, like the prowling lion, is always waiting to grab us. (Isaiah 5:29; 1 Peter 5:8–9; Psalm 9:8–11) We forget to guard our mouth, our eyes, and especially our hearts. For example, as Jesus Christ told us, if we lust we have already committed adultery. (Matthew 5:28)

Therefore, we need frequently to ask God's forgiveness of our sins while at the same time we must exercise love by forgiving anyone who has given us offense.

So those words of petition, *Forgive us our trespasses, as we forgive them that trespass against us,* remind us that we must not look for forgiveness of our offences if we do not forgive the offences our neighbours have commit against us.

Monday, Week 4 of Easter—Lead us not into temptation

 EMPTATION ARISES IN the heart and it is from there in a person that evil thoughts begin in a person. For example, murder, adultery, sexual immorality, theft, false testimony, and slander. (Matthew 15:19) When this happens a person may forget virtue and succumb to making such thoughts a reality. The thought of stealing something, for example, becomes irresistible for some people and so theft is committed. Temptation has triumphed. So it is that when evil thoughts have been conceived in the heart, they can give birth to sin and when sin is fully grown, it gives birth to death. (James 1:14–5) Temptations exist in many forms, some are good, many are very bad. So we need to examine each one to see if it is tempting us into sin or is one of virtue that takes us closer to God.

Therefore, when we pray *Lead us not into temptation*, we are asking God to help us overcome the temptations of our unworthy thoughts and to help us remain faithful to him when he sends trials to tempt us away from belief in his promises.

Tuesday, Week 4 of Easter—Deliver us from evil

 N THIS PETITION we pray to be delivered from all evil, past, present, or to come. We ask God to deliver us from all the consequences of sin and from the tyranny of evil.

In these few words, *Deliver us from evil,* we ask God to protect us from everything that may hurt us in body, mind and spirit. We are declaring to God that we are nothing and that he is all-powerful. We need no more words than these few to petition for our safety.

Wednesday, Week 4 of Easter—Feast of Saint Mark, Evangelist

 HE GOSPEL OF Mark tells us of the history of Christ's life. Often considered the earliest gospel to have been written, it shows us the actions and his authority of Jesus. For example in his forgiving sins and defeating demons. Mark, who was a follower of Peter and was with Paul and Barnabas on their first missionary journey, is important in establishing our understanding of Jesus as the Messiah of God.

Mark's gospel opens with the glorious proclamation of John the Baptist which was written by Isaiah the prophet of God: *Look, I am going to send my messenger in front of you to prepare your way before you. A voice of one that cries in the desert: Prepare a way for the Lord, make his paths straight.* (Isaiah 40:3)

That *Lord* of which Isaiah speaks is the one whose history of life, death and resurrection is recorded for you by the Evangelist Mark and he is *Jesus the Messiah,* who was sent by God to save us.

Thursday, Week 4 of Easter—On The Divine Office

 HRISTIANS HAVE PRAYED *The Divine Office*, formally organised in the *Liturgy of the Hours according to the Roman Rite*, for many centuries, especially every day by men and women in religious life, priests, and hermits. It is not optional for them to say these prayers that include all the psalms spread over the days, but a requirement. This requirement is in keeping with vows of charity and obedience and helps to keep close to God.

It is commended to all Christians to acquaint themselves with these books of prayer, called *The Divine Office*, because in them inspiration will be found from the great treasure of Christian life that belongs to all men and woman. It is a holy patrimony, like the psalms themselves, and an inheritance belonging to every person. These prayers are often called *the way of beauty* for they are for all people when they are in the household of God. (Isaiah 56:7)

This *Divine Office* or *Liturgy of the Hours* contains the Word of God, the study of the Old and New Testaments, and the inspired thoughts and sermons of saints and unknown but holy men and women of God. As such, it fulfils the command of our Lord to pray without ceasing.

You do not have to be a priest, a hermit, a nun nor a monk to use this liturgy. You need only be a man or woman who yearns for God in all things, a person who desires to be a servant of God and who fulfils the teachings of Jesus the Messiah by living a life of love in obedience to God. In short, you need only be any man or woman of prayer who believes in God, his prophets and messengers and who tries to live a life of love without expectations.

If you have not done so before, then acquaint yourself with this holy guide. *The Divine Office* is there to help you celebrate

God and to nourish your spirit. Here you will find the psalms, those prayers, which glorify God and give thanksgiving for his Creation. Indeed, it is *the way of beauty*.

Friday, Week 4 of Easter — On the habit of Prayer

HERE ARE THREE occasions each day when we should say our prayers. This is the morning, the evening, and when we take food, because these are basic prayers of thanksgiving to God for the blessings of nourishment for body, mind and spirit. These prayers are available in little books based on the *Divine Office*.

In the morning we are thankful for the blessing of awakening to a new day of life. When we eat, we thank God for the food we have been given to sustain that life. Finally, we pray at the close of our day in thanksgiving for the day we have lived, the present moment in which we are, and for the life to come whether on earth or heaven.

Then, in the final moments of our day, when we fall asleep in the guardianship of the Holy Spirit our last words should be simple, direct and without fear like that of a child: If I should die before I wake, may God my soul to keep.

Perhaps God will whisper back to you: *Peace be with you, good and faithful servant.* (Matthew 25)

Saturday, Week 4 of Easter—On beginning a new day

 VERY SERVANT OF God ought to begin the day with the worship of God and give his or her heart to him (Ecclesiasticus 39:6) Indeed, the royal prophet who wrote the psalms says, *My soul clings to you; your right hand holds me fast.* (Psalm 62) Never neglect this worship at the beginning of a new day, because it may let the devil run away with your first thoughts into the world where vice and wrong virtues are waiting to trap you. But give your first thoughts to God and all will be well.

If your first thoughts are worries about your day, anxiety about your work or duties, fear about what might happened to you, impatience and anger about your health or a thousand other common first thoughts that people have when they wake up in the morning, then vanquish them by thinking first of God and more spiritual matters. This will help you, because remembrance of God is the healing of the heart in every way. (Revelation 21:3–4; Psalm 33:18; Psalm 146:3)

A good beginning of the day is of great importance. Start with God and keep going with God through the day. In this way, your body will be patient and accepting in obedience to God's plan for you, your mind will be at peace through Jesus Christ, and your spirit will be made content by your love for others.

Fifth Sunday of Easter — On Morning Prayer

HEN YOU WAKE in the morning before you think of anything else or even do your Morning Prayer, go to God with these simple words: Thank you God for my life!

Now, we may think that God likes our spontaneous prayers or prayers that come from the Gospels. For example, the *Song of Mary* or prayers our church has developed over the years for us to use. All these certainly must please God. But our first thoughts in the morning should be of thanksgiving to God for life itself. This is recognising his glory.

Monday, Week 5 of Easter—How to make a formal morning prayer

 F YOU ARE in doubt or do not know how to make a more formal morning prayer or do not have *The Divine Office* or a similar book to guide you, then here are some petitions a morning prayer could include.

1. Adoration of God by saying The Lord's Prayer
2. Thanksgiving for all his blessings.
3. An act of contrition for past sins with a resolution to renouncing them.
4. An offering of all thoughts, words, and actions of the day to God
5. A humble asking for the blessings of God for everyone in need.
6. Conclude with acts of charity, especially those who are ill.

It is not the length of the prayer or the number of words in a prayer that counts, but what the heart renders to God that is true and acceptable. It does not matter whether your prayers are spoken, thought or you remain still in contemplation. All of these are being with God. In any case, fix the following words in your mind and repeat them silently or aloud as you go about your day: *God have mercy on me, a sinner.*

Tuesday, Week 5 of Easter (1 May) — Optional Memorial of Saint Joseph the worker

 AINT JOSEPH SHOWS everyone an outstanding example of love, especially as a husband, a father, and a worker. As a husband, Joseph stood by Mary. He did not desert her nor look around for another woman. He was faithful to his marriage and honoured his wife by his loving care for her. Here is an example for every husband.

As a father, Joseph cared for Jesus and other children in his family. He was dependable, stable, and provided them with loving care in their need for shelter, food, and all the things that children need. Here is an example for every father, stepfather, and foster father.

As a worker, Joseph spent his days as a carpenter, content with working to provide for the needs of his family. He worked out of love for them. In this way, he honoured God as well as his family. What kind of work we do does not matter to God. What matters to God is how we do our work and what we do with the results and payments for that work. Here is an example for every worker.

Saint Joseph stands as an example for all who care for children in any capacity. Remember that all children are very special to God. As Jesus said, *Let the little children alone. And do not stop them from coming to me, for it is to such as these that the kingdom of Heaven belongs.* (Matthew 19:14–15)

Wednesday, Week 5 of Easter—On Evening Prayer

 s God is our first beginning so he is also our last end. Therefore, just as we ought to begin the day with him by Morning Prayer, so we ought to finish the day in his company by our evening prayer. Morning and evening prayer are like two daily meals for the soul. They should not be neglected, since the soul might grow weak without this nourishment.

One of the most important things at Evening Prayer is an examination of our conscience, which is what we have done during the day that pleases and displeases God.

As to that which displeases God, we should not just remember our wrong acts, those of *commission*, but also those of *omission* of the things and actions we did not do that we know we should do as Christians. On the other hand, we should recall the acts and things we have done that please God, remembering that God meant us to have a life of joy. The following is helpful in such an examination. This exploration of our conscience is the process of repentance and reconciliation with God.

1. Give thanks to God for all he has done that day for you.

2. God already knows everything about you, so ask for his help in this review of your day.

3. Try to call to mind how you actually spent your day. Try to discover how you have discharged your duties as a disciple of Christ and a servant of God. Do not seek to hide or forget your failings and unwanted passions. God knows them anyway but here you are trying to join him in such awareness.

4. Make a humble confession of all you find in this examination of your conscience and be sorry for when you have displeased God.

5. Resolve to amend your life in accord with God's commandments and teaching.

Conclude never to neglect Night Prayer for an examination of your conscience brings reconciliation and this brings joy. You will sleep better. Your mind will be at rest. (Psalm 4:9)

Thursday, Week 5 of Easter (3 May)—Feast of Philip and James, Apostles

HE APOSTLE PHILIP had no sooner met Jesus than he brought his friend Nathaniel to meet him, because he wanted his friend to have the same happiness that he, Philip, had found in Jesus. This act of friendship was true charity.

As followers of Christ we too should bring our friends to meet Jesus. But we need to do this without giving offense, because many people have doubts about the existence of God or a divided heart about the spiritual life. They judge themselves to be atheist or agnostic or the best judge of moral behaviour. In any case, they do not want anyone preaching to them about God or religion. Among such people are many who do not like churches or other places of religious practice. They are often put on the defensive or easily offended by too many strong words about the place of the spiritual and religion in their lives.

The best thing to do in all such cases is for us to make our life an example of what Christianity and the meeting of Jesus, has done for us and to tell the other person what difference all this has made to our own life. We need to witness Jesus in our lives.

Yet, few Christians realize this is their duty. But then, how infrequently we suggest going on a retreat to our friends and how there in a new space and time when everyday living is put to one side, they may find an awareness of the role of the spiritual in life or by suggesting that the regular practice of meditation or even by joining others in a prayer group may hold healing? In fact, how many of us tell others we follow *a religion of love*?

To speak of love to our friends is charity, even if the action of the Holy Spirit in them meeting Jesus is up to the gift and grace of God as it always must be.

Friday, Week 5 of Easter—On praying always

 E ARE CALLED upon in the Word of God to *pray without ceasing and never lose heart in seeking the Lord.* (Luke 18:1; 1 Thessalonians 5:16–18; Psalm 104:4) Since love always seeks the company and conversation of its beloved, a person truly loving God will never bear to spend all day without thinking of him and speaking to him. Now it is by the means of our prayer that we come into this company and conversation with God, our greatest love.

Yet, many Christians pass the whole day without thinking about this love, without talking to God and without his companionship. So it is that we need to pray continually. In this way, God will be present with us all the time no matter what we are doing. Whether we are in church or washing the dishes, God is present.

Saturday, Week 5 of Easter—On praying continually

 OW THEN DO we *pray continually*? This kind of praying does not require that we should be always on our knees in supplication nor always have a prayer book in our hands nor always be reciting a special form of prayer. To pray continuously does not disrupt our work or what we are doing. It does not hinder us even in our conversations and recreations, because to pray this way is simply to stay in the presence of God by continually conversing with him.[4]

For example, in the beginning of every action you should turn to God by offering up to his honour and glory what you are going to do and call for his assistance by short ejaculatory prayers, such as *Alleluia!* or *God is great!* or *Glory be to God!* or *Forgive me Lord!* or *Blessed be God!* Whatever of praise comes to your lips, let them speak the words, perhaps aloud, perhaps silently, perhaps only in a whisper. No matter how and when you praise him, God will hear you. These short remembrances of God are prayers and help to keep you in his presence. They re-centre your heart on God. Once again, it is worth remembering that your praise and keeping in the presence of God does not depend on what you are doing. The lay friar, Brother Lawrence of the Resurrection (1605–1691), claimed that even in making an omelette you could, like the ancient patriarchs of old, walk with God and in his sight. (Genesis 5:24; 2 Corinthians 5:7; Micah 6:8; 1 John 2:6)

So praying continually is possible no matter what you are doing. No matter if you are at home, work or out having some fun.

> The trouble with all of us is that we fail to live in close,
> intimate and living contact with the source of the only

---

[4] See *The Practice of the Presence of God,* Letters of Br. Lawrence of the Resurrection.

true life, God himself, Our sorrows come from that. Our helplessness discourages us, because we forget the all-powerfulness of God, who is always ready to come to our aid. The evil in others as well as ourselves, and the sad state of our times, these all affect us only because we do not know how to keep ourselves in the presence of God.[5]

Brother Lawrence of the Resurrection wrote this about continual prayer:

There is not in the world a kind of life more sweet and delightful, than that of a continual conversation with God; those only can comprehend it who practice and experience it.[6]

---

[5]   A Carthusian, *They Speak by Silences*.

[6]   *Ibid*.

Sixth Sunday of Easter—On the great pattern of charity

 E KEEP THE light of Christ shining in our lives through the practice of love by which we have been commanded to live. By such love, a great pattern of charity is spread from us to our neighbours and, indeed, throughout the world. We may not realize this greater effect of our love, but small acts of charity come together in a great pattern of charity.

Our love is like a stone thrown into water. It makes first one small circle, then a larger one, then many rings, each bigger than the last So it is when we show love, because, like the stone thrown into the water, our act of charity has a rippling effect and spreads to others effecting the lives of many people.

This is the great pattern of charity, because its effect is bigger than its first action. In charity, we love and by such love we help build up that peace for which all men and women yearn.

Yet, we can be so easily discouraged when we see and hear so much about destruction and war. All this cruelty and killing makes us often wonder how our own short and seemingly powerless lives can help achieve peace. It makes us wonder if it matters what we do in our lives, because peace in this world does not seem to happen and even when peace does come, it does not usually last very long. Destruction and war seems always to be with us.

We look around at our own community to find if peace reigns there. We most often find yet another disappointment, because we see how little peace there is between our own community and another even if they share the same culture, religion and language.

The need to belong to a particular culture, religion, society and the belief that somehow we are better, more just, or more civilized has always caused injustice and often wars and ruin.

Finally, we turn to our family in a last hope that here charity must surely triumph and with it peace at last. But what we find are disputes, disappointments, resentments, unfulfilled expectations, and anger.

It is all very discouraging and makes us feel that getting and keeping peace is a hopeless goal, because men and women show such little charity to one another. We forget that what is impossible for us is possible for God. (Luke 18:27)

In spite of all this environment of cruelty and lack of love, we must not turn away from trying to make peace. Even if everything seems to be against peace, we still must make our lives an example of charity, because even with death Christ did not turn away from this ultimate of all virtues. He showed us that peace comes through charity. As his disciples, we must keep the light of the Holy Spirit bright and welcoming to all others.

Let us not forget in our disappointments about the peace that Christ gave us. He said, *Peace I bequeath to you, my own peace I give you, a peace which the world cannot give, this is my gift to you.* (John 14:27 & 16:33)

If we have such peace waiting to work for peace in this world, then our first action is to look deeply inside ourselves, because we must have charity for ourselves before we can love others. So to make peace in this world, we must first make peace with ourselves. To do this, we must put aside our anger. We must forgive those who have offended us. We must forget bad memories and remember the blessings in our life, those good memories. We must be present to this moment in our lives.

This reassessment of our selves and living in the present moment helps us to see this world and eternity in the timeless grandeur that it is. So do not be afraid to persist in trying to make peace, whether in yourself, with your family and friends or in the wider world, because you have been assured that wherever you go God will be with you. (Isaiah 65:1)

Monday, Week 6 of Easter—On the oil of gladness

 OD ANOINTED JESUS with the oil of gladness. (Hebrews 1:9) This was nothing less than the anointing with the Holy Spirit, because the oil of gladness *is* the presence of the Holy Spirit. This anointing gave Jesus the ability and power to carry out his great mission to bring us to God. Long before the Messiah appeared on earth, the prophets foretold of such anointing and we are told about it in the New Testament. (Isaiah 61:183; Exodus 29:7; Hebrews 1:8–9)

When a shared love of Jesus unites us as brothers and sisters, an invisible oil of gladness covers us, because the Holy Spirit holds us in the embrace of love. Such a moment of holy affection came for Jesus when a woman poured precious oils on his head, anointing him with love, the oil of gladness.

Each time we do an act of charity, each time we feel brotherly love for another person because Christ lives in them, love binds us together and God is present. Indeed, we are anointed with the oil of gladness. (Psalm 44:8; Hebrews 1:9)

Tuesday, Week 6 of Easter—On looking beyond this earthly life

F YOU WANT have any part with God in his eternal kingdom, start now to be humble here on earth. Throw pride out of your life. Let your little vanities go. Turn away from the conceits of your self-will and the passing attractions of this world so that God may not sentence you like the barren tree to be cut down and cast into the fire. With humility, you will discover the joy that comes after the sorrow of your exile from God. The more you practice humility, the more God will lift you up and exalt you.

We should remember as Christians not to confine the scope of our faith to boundaries of doctrine and dogma, good and true as these may be, and so limit our vision of life. God's dominion knows no boundaries and, as we have been told, the Holy Spirit is like the wind, going where it pleases. (Isaiah 57.15; Ecclesiastes 11:5; John 3:8) Christians must have a freedom of vision that encompasses the universe and sees everything on earth as one, the single creation of God united in every other creation. This vision of the union of everything as one interconnected whole is a vision that is true, because in Creation nothing is separate from another. Everything in this world is held in union by *being*, that is by God who is *being* itself.

Wednesday, Week 6 of Easter—On having expectations of God

MANY MEN AND women are disappointed in God when they have been diligent in all their religious practices, because their lives are filled with tragedy or the loss of a loved one or other sad events. This has caused many Christians to turn against God and his Christ and going to church. They refuse to carry the Cross.

If they do not refuse God through personal sufferings, then they look at the world around them. All they see is cruelty, injustice and wars. They wonder how the God of love with the power to change anything he so wishes, could possibly allow all this to happen. They have expectations of God and when these are not fulfilled, they turn away from him, forgetting that we must willing receive wounds as well as blessings from the hands of God. In our arrogance, we have tried to judge God's plan for this world, forgetting to leave cruelty of the world to the justice of God.

But God acts in his own time and his time is measured in a different way than our time. To him a thousand years are but a few seconds as we understand time. (2 Peter 3:8) God will deal in his own time and in his own way with the enemies of faith, hope, peace and love and all those who defy him by their sins. (1 Peter 4:5)

Trust in God no matter what happens to you or in this world. (Psalm 18; Psalm 26:1–12)

Thursday, Week 6 of Easter—Solemnity of the Ascension of the Lord

 HE LORD GOD Almighty has told us everything we need to know about him: *I am the Alpha and the Omega, who is, who was, and who is to come, the Almighty* (Revelation 1:8) Accept this mystery without question. Act on it as Jesus taught. Celebrate today that the Christ has ascended and is at the right hand side of God. The Holy Spirit has descended upon us all. Be holy for you have been blessed by a great gift of heaven.

Here is a reading from the sermon of Saint Augustine on the Ascension of the Lord:

> Today Jesus Christ our Lord went up to heaven: let our hearts go up with him. Listen to the words of Saint Paul: "If you have been raised with Christ, seek the things that are above, where Christ is, seated at the right hand of God. Set your minds on the things that are above, not on things that are on earth." Just as he ascended without leaving us, so too we are already with him in heaven, although his promises have not yet been fulfilled in our bodies. Christ is now raised above the heavens; but he still experiences on earth whatever sufferings we his members feel. Why then do we not exert ourselves on earth so as to be happy with him already in heaven through the faith, hope, and charity that unite us with him?[7]

---

7   See St. Augustine, *Sermon 98 on the Ascension of the Lord*, 1–7. See also Colossians3:1.

Friday, Week 6 of Easter — On the happiness given by the Holy Spirit

 ONSIDER THE HAPPY benefits that the presence of the Holy Spirit produces in us: *the fruit of the Spirit is love, joy, peace, patience, kindness, goodness, trustfulness, gentleness, and self-control.* (Galatians 5:22–24)

Love is *charity* for the love of God for his own infinite goodness and the love of every neighbour. This endowment of grace is remarkable. For example, the first Christians on receiving the Holy Spirit were so united in love of God that they had *but one heart and one soul.* (Acts 4:31–35)

Joy, arising from a clear conscience and from the sense of the presence of God.

Peace with God, our neighbours and ourselves. Such a peace is not granted to the wicked. (Isaiah 48:22)

Patience in supporting our sufferings which the Holy Spirit helps to make easier.

Kindness in helping people and listening to them without making judgments about them.

Goodness or a willingness to impart all that is good to every neighbour, no matter how they act or irritate us. This includes wife, husband, children, father, mother, friend and stranger.

Trustfulness is the liberty that innocence of the heart gives a person. It includes an abiding faith in the promises of God.

Gentleness arises from restraining our anger and bearing injuries without reprisal.

Self-control is when we resist evil, banishing inappropriate desires and passions from mind and body. Self-control means we should be modest in all ways from our appearance to the words we say. It means we maintain a guardianship of the eyes, the lips, the flesh, and the mind in a way that is pleasing to the commandments of God.

How happy is the man or woman in which the spirit of God gives all these gifts!

Saturday, Week 6 of Easter—On more gifts of the Holy Spirit

 ONSIDER WHAT PRECIOUS gifts the Holy Spirit imparts to us. The prophet Isaiah mentions seven gifts, The Spirit of wisdom and of understanding, the Spirit of counsel and of fortitude, the Spirit of knowledge and of godliness, and the Spirit of the fear of the Lord. (Isaiah 11: 1–9)

The gift of spiritual wisdom is not the wisdom of this world, which is mere folly in the sight of God, but that wisdom which consists in the love of God and seeks to find him in all things.

The gift of spiritual understanding convinces a person that nothing is truly great or worthy of affection but that which leads to eternal life.

As we make the best of our way through the midst of difficulties and dangers, God comes to our assistance with the spiritual gift of counsel to show us the snares and schemes of our enemies and to guide us safe through all dangers.

The gift of spiritual fortitude is the courage and strength to help us over-come all opposition from the world, the flesh, and the devil.

The gift of spiritual godliness makes the soul perfectly willing to be a servant of God.

Lastly, the spiritual gift of the fear of the Lord that Scripture calls the beginning of wisdom. It is a fear restraining a person from doing anything that may offend God. (Proverbs 9:10)

These are seven precious treasures indeed, so guard them well.

Sunday of the Seventh Week of Easter—On keeping the Holy Spirit in your life

 F WE DESIRE to keep the Holy Spirit active in our life, then we must take care to live in a manner pleasing to God. If we take little or no notice of this heavenly presence, if we easily turn away to every amusement that offers itself, and if we do not frequently use the gifts that the Holy Spirit gives us, then we make this Spirit of God sad.

The question every Christian must ask themselves about their faith, whether of the Cross, the Resurrection or the presence of the Holy Spirit is this: *Do I have a divided heart?*

A divided heart has no place in the Christian life, because such a heart is clothed in doubts and questions and leaves no room for the works and gifts of the Holy Spirit. God claims our whole heart and will have all of it or none.

Since the Holy Spirit lives in the temple of your inner self, that is the kingdom of God, we must go to this temple frequently. This is the true way to engage the Holy Spirit to stay with us and to make us the palace of his rest. But take great care to stay on the path that Jesus taught you *for if any man or woman violates the temple of God, God will destroy him or her.* (1 Corinthians 3:17)

Monday, Week 7 of Easter (14 May)– Feast of Saint Matthias, Apostle

AINT MATTHIAS REPLACED Judas Iscariot after he betrayed Jesus. Details about St. Matthias have not been given to us in Holy Scripture. This explains why we cannot draw lessons from his life as we do with the other Apostles. What we know, however, is that Matthias would not have been chosen under the leadership of Saint Peter if he had not been a worthy disciple of Jesus. St. Matthias fulfilled the qualifications that St. Peter insisted upon when he declared to the remaining apostles when they were to chose a successor to Judas: *Out of the men who have been with us the whole time that the Lord Jesus was living with us, from the time when John was baptising until the day when he was taken up from us, one must be appointed to serve with us as a witness to his resurrection.* (Acts 1:21–22)

We know that the gifts God gives can be visible or invisible, public or private, but all such gifts are always full of hope and holy healing. Perhaps it is for this reason that Matthias, whose name in Hebrew means *Gift from God,* is the patron saint of all people who need hope and healing of body, mind and spirit as they struggle with any kind of addiction.

Tuesday, Week 7 of Easter—On the Holy Spirit being in you

 HE SPIRIT OF God is never idle. He is a holy fire that is always active, always in motion, always a flame in the direction of heaven. The marks or fruits of this divine vine growing in us are charity, joy, peace, and patience. If we have none of these fruits, then the Holy Spirit is not with us.

So ask yourself: What is the state of your faith? Is it solid? Is it lively? Or is it rather dull and almost dead? Does it show itself in the practice of your life? Do you live by faith? What is your hope? What is your sense of the things of eternity? What is your love for your neighbour? What is your hidden vanity? When you pray and converse with God do you listen to others or are you so occupied by self-love you do not hear anything except about yourself? Are you making a daily progress in the way of God or just too busy with the worries and duties of this world to give any time to him, except perhaps on a Sunday? Is your devotion as a Christian occasional or consistent? Are you a person of charity, joy, peace, and patience?

Your answers to such questions will tell you if the fruits of the Holy Spirit abide in you or not.

Wednesday, Week 7 of Easter—On being thankful for our food

 N THE PAST, families ate their main meal together. In many cases, a prayer of thanksgiving was said before eating. Times have changed. Coming together as a family to eat a meal is mainly reserved for holidays and celebrations like birthdays in many countries. Even if we go to church on Sunday, it does not mean a day of rest, especially as in many households time is spent shopping, catching up on domestic chores, watching television and checking-out electronic messages and information.

But all this current change about taking meals together does not mean that the relationships built up by sharing food has changed. It is still valuable for us as family and friends.

Remembering that millions go hungry while we are feasting should make us thankful for our food.

Thursday, Week 7 of Easter—On drawing near to the Cross of Jesus

 HO IS IT that hangs there dead on the cross before your eyes? It is the *Word of God* and the Saviour of all men and women then and now. Jesus, crucified for the love of us, is the foretold and promised Messiah, the gift sent by God. He is our teacher, our friend, our consolation, our joy.

All that happened to Jesus from his conception to his resurrection showed us that the law and all prophecies had been accomplished and the gates of heaven opened for us. Jesus said, *When I am lifted up from the earth, I shall draw all people to myself.* (John 12:32)

Let your heart share in this mystery by drawing near to the Cross. Repose yourself in these dark hours of Good Friday. Be still. Be silent. Be empty of all thoughts except those of love for God and Jesus the Christ.

Friday, Week 7 of Easter—Good Friday

 EE HOW THERE is nothing but bruises and wounds from his feet to his head as Jesus hangs from his cross. *(Isaiah 1:6)* We dare not touch the sharp thorns of the crown, which pierces his young head. We cannot administer salve to any of the wounds on his face nor stench the flow of blood from his side. We cannot ease his pain nor comfort his dying.

Yet, we are not helpless, because what we can do is make his gift of our salvation the goal of our life through our love and obedience to the will of God.

Saturday, Week 7 of Easter—How our life mocks or honours Jesus

 HILE WE DETEST the great shame and cruelty visited on Jesus, we remember that we hammer yet another nail into him on the Cross each time we give into temptation by deserting virtue and forgetting to love. By such disobedience to God and our forgetfulness of his commandments, we have shown no mercy to ourselves or to others. So do not share in crucifying Jesus and making a mockery of him. (Hebrews 6:4–8) Instead, honour our Lord by living as he taught us and as God commanded.

Solemnity of Pentecost—On the Holy Spirit descending on the world

 N PENTECOST THE disciples were all assembled together when suddenly there came from heaven a sound as of a violent wind coming, which filled the entire house in which they were sitting, and there appeared to them tongues as of fire; these separated and came to rest on the head of each of them. They were filled with the Holy Spirit, and they began to speak different languages as the Spirit gave them power to express themselves. (Acts 2:1–4) In that moment the Apostles and disciples received the promised Holy Spirit just as Jesus Christ had foretold.

However, this coming of the Holy Spirit, who is often called the *Paraclete*, was promised not only to the Apostles nor to the first Christians nor confined just to that time, but was sent as a blessing for all men and women throughout all ages. Jesus said, *I shall ask the Father and he will give you another Paraclete to be with you forever, the Spirit of truth.* (John 14:16–21)

What a happiness to have the Spirit of God with us! Celebrate with great joy this day of Pentecost for we have received the best of blessings.

AFTER PENTECOST TO END OF MAY

Theme: Gifts and obligations of faith

Your deeds, O Lord, have made me glad;
For the work of your hands I shout for joy.
Psalm 91–5

Monday after Pentecost—On the value of patience

 F WE ARE to endure with humility, we must have patience. This is a necessary attribute if we are to be content in this life, because none of us are without personal crosses and sufferings. Patience both sweetens and sanctifies all our sufferings and, as the Apostle James points out, patience is a perfect work, because in it we find perfected faith and will not fail in anything. (James 1:3–4)

Now this virtue of patience is best learned by observing the multitude and variety of Jesus' sufferings and how he endured them. In considering this, how can we complain or think much of any sufferings we have in this life when we have in mind this far greater suffering of Jesus, a suffering he endured with a patience formed and sustained by obedience to God?

If we want to imitate Jesus Christ, we need to learn how to handle the wounds as well as the blessings that come from the hand of God. This calls us to endure with patience. Therefore, pray to God to help us to bear the burden of the day and to accept his will without complaint.[8]

---

8   *Midday Prayer, The Divine Office III*, p. 127.

Tuesday after Pentecost — On the value of humility

 N ADDITION TO the endurance that patience brings, nothing contributes more to making our prayers effective than a profound humility, because God never despises a contrite and humble heart. *The prayer of the humble pierces the clouds.* (Ecclesiasticus 35:17)

Conclude to pray with eagerness, fervour, endurance, humility, and a powerful strength of spirit in order that right at the beginning of your prayers you put yourself in the presence of God. Be calm. Be still. Have patience. Listen with your heart to what God says.

Wednesday after Pentecost — On spiritual labour

VERY GARDENER KNOWS no plant will flourish unless the ground is cleared of weeds. The roots of brambles and thorny plants are deep. They cling to the soil with determination just like our bad habits cling to us. If the grace of God waiting in the holy seed of faith given to us, is to be planted and flourish, we must first dig up such weeds as grow in the ground of our life. We must root out harmful affections, our liking for worldly distractions, and our desires for sensual pleasures that hold vice and not virtue. As long as these persist in us, no holy seed of faith will bear fruit.

Every Christian must be a good gardener. At the first sign of thorny regrowth in the garden of his or her soul, it must be dug it out. In this way, the grace of God remains in everlasting flower within us. Such perfection always mirrors the life of Jesus.

Thursday after Pentecost—On God not asking us to bear more than we are able to do

RUE DEVOTION IS not always sensible. It does not necessarily consist in a certain uplifting tenderness that people may experience in prayer or in sacred music or in the study of Scripture.

In fact, spiritual experiences are of many different kinds. There are many who experience nothing for a long time in their devotions but the dryness and desolation of the desert. Think of the years that Saint Teresa of Avila was so affected. Remember Saint John of the Cross writing of the dark night of the soul. Even the most holy of men and women can experience a desolation of the spirit and feel God has deserted them. They feel forgotten by heaven and that their prayers are unheard and useless. But the difference between the saints and most men and women is that saints like Saint Teresa and Saint John persisted in their prayers. They never gave up on their faith in the promises of God. They continued to be servants of God even when they felt God had deserted them. In short, they endured.

Such a situation should remind us of the many Christians who shrink under every suffering that comes their way, forgetting that God does not ask us to bear more than we are able and that his help is always at hand if we will simply turn to him. (1 Corinthians 10:13) Their faith is not strong enough, their self-love too great, and their love of God too weak. So they turn away and find no strength to persist and continue to pray and serve God as best they can. They refuse to endure.

Even for the most devout among us, a complete submission to trust in God is difficult, because our self-love blocks our faith and demands attention. We want God to take notice of us. We despair when we suffer. We nurse our wounds as undeserved and unfair instead of feeling such wounds are a form of blessing in God's plan for us. Our prayers are pleads for our self, forgetting to ask for mercy and help for others. Even with the Cross of Jesus before us, we cannot abide our own suffering. We have lost our trust in God. We do not endure.

To avoid this we need to be like the saints so that our faith endures in spite of everything that happens to us. Otherwise, we remain a slave to our passions, always accepting what we want and rejecting anything God sends that does not fulfil our expectations or desires. This is a denial of charity and faith without which no one can please God. (Hebrews 11:6)

Conclude then to be wary of any false appearances and phantoms of devotion and to take no account of any feeling, like dryness in praying, that is not accompanied with charity, humility, and conformity to the will of God. We need to keep believing in the truth that God never asks us to bear more than we are able to do. (1 Corinthians 10:13)

Friday after Pentecost—On the prudence of the wise Christian

 EVER PLAY UPON the brink of a spiritual cliff with the sword of divine judgment hanging over your head as it did with King David. God may instruct an angel at any time to let the sword fall on you. (1 Chronicles 21:15)

For example, no prudent person would refuse to be immediately reconciled to a person he had offended, if such a person had the power to condemn him to death for his offence. How much less should the sinner put off reconciliation with an offended God, who can cast him or her into death in an instant.

Resolve now to remedy this situation by not playing brinkmanship at a spiritual cliff and tempting God. (Matthew 4:7; Luke 4:12) Satisfy the demands of conscience so that your life is pleasing to God. Be alert! Be wakeful! (Mark 13.33–37) Accept God's invitation to be called and always hope to be chosen. (Matthew 22:14)

Saturday after Pentecost—On not having a hard heart

I F OUR RESOLUTION to change by following the way of Jesus is superficial and we are easily overcome by the first temptation or difficulty that we face, then our heart is like a rock and has not yet softened. A hard heart pleases no one and it does not succeed with God. But a soft heart is a heart that always turns finally to what love demands. Such a heart is both pleasing to God and a weapon we need in fighting temptation.

While our good resolutions are welcomed by God, they are not enough in themselves. It is often said that the way to Hell is paved with good intentions. We must change ourselves. Everyone knows old habits are hard to change. So this changing ourselves is very difficult.

The only answer that works is determined prayer and the continual acknowledgement of the presence of God and Christ in our life. Here is the support we need to fulfil our desire to change. Here is the breaking down of the rock that is our heart. The living waters of God will soon flow, nourishing the holy seed planted in us.

Solemnity of Trinity Sunday—Mysteries and teachings of our faith

CRIPTURE IN THE Old Testament declares, *Listen, Israel: Yahweh our God is one, the only Yahweh.* (Deuteronomy 6:4) and the early Christians had to try to understand how all this was to be understood after Pentecost and the descent of the Holy Spirit. This was especially so when Jesus told the Apostles and all Christians to go out and make disciples of all nations, baptizing them in the name of the Father and of the Son and of the Holy Spirit. (Matthew 28:19) They found all these events and instructions confusing and argued about it. If there was only *one* God, then what could it mean to say, *the Father, the Son, and the Holy Spirit* at a baptism?

There were many disagreements among Christians for years about this confusion over these questions of doctrine raised by the *New Testament*, including by leading bishops of the time. Finally in 325 CE at the Council of Nicaea, the church leaders agreed the doctrine of one holy essence in three persons, God the Father, Christ the Son, and The Holy Spirit. This settled the issue of the doctrine of the *Holy Trinity*, which we know today as the *Nicene Creed*.

Every Sunday in the year might be called *Trinity Sunday*, because every Sunday is set aside for the worship of this Trinity of three in one. The great celebration that is offered daily on millions of altars throughout the world is principally designed to give adoration, homage, praise, and glory to this Holy Trinity. However, this Sunday is set aside today to honour the chief doctrine of our religion in a more special manner.

Monday after Trinity Sunday — On the manna from heaven and the bread of Elias

HE MANNA WITH which God fed the children of Israel for forty years in the wilderness was a prophetic emblem of the true bread of heaven that we receive in the Eucharist. *Moses did not give you bread from heaven,* Jesus told the Jews, *but my Father gives you the true bread from heaven — I am the living bread which came down from heaven. If any man eats of this bread he shall live forever and the bread that I will give is my flesh for the life of the world. As the living Father has sent me, and I live by the Father, so he that eats me shall live by me. This is the bread that came down from heaven, not as your fathers ate manna and are dead. Anyone who eats this bread will live forever.* (John 6: verses 32,51,57, & 58)

The prophet Elias in the wilderness was also fed heavenly food by an angel when he was fleeing from the persecution of Jezebel. *Get up and eat,* said the angel to him, *or the journey will be too long for you.* (1 Kings 19:7–8) In the strength given by this food, Elias walked forty days and forty nights to Mount Horeb where he was favoured with a vision of God, as far as a human is capable of seeing God in this life.

Both the food given to the Jews and to Elias reminds us that in order to make our pilgrimage to God, we need to be supported by God for our long journey through the wilderness of temptation on our way to eternal life. The bread of heaven is Jesus himself, the Messiah sent to show us love and bring us salvation. Eat often of this heavenly bread and you will find the spiritual nourishment you need.

Tuesday after Trinity Sunday—On Christ inviting us to his heavenly banquet

 ONSIDER THESE WORDS of the parable in Luke's gospel: *There was a man who gave a great banquet, and he invited a large number of people.* (Luke 14:16) Did not Jesus do the same thing? Reflect how he also prepared a great banquet for us in the institution of the Eucharist. To this heavenly banquet Jesus invites all the faithful in the most loving manner. *Come to me*, says Jesus Christ, *all you that labour, and are overburdened, and I will give you rest.* (Matthew 11:28)

Have you ever had such a sweet invitation? An invitation to a banquet that would nourish your mind and spirit as well as your body? A banquet that is not just a one time only feast, but one which is available for our whole life and may be attended as frequently as we need it? Let us, therefore, do our best to come to this heavenly banquet as often as possible and nourish ourselves there with Jesus the Christ.

Wednesday after Trinity Sunday—On devotion before Communion

 VERY CHRISTIAN DESIRES to make a proper palace for God in their hearts. *The task is great,* declared King David, *because this palace is not for any human being but for Yahweh God.* (1 Chronicles 29:1) This is especially true when we share in the celebration of the Blessed Sacrament. The death and passion of Jesus Christ that we commemorate is an incomprehensible mystery of love itself, which will continue to astonish men and women for all eternity.

Preparation for this event must be by a lively faith and a realisation of whom it is that we are to receive. It must be accompanied by asking God to help us prepare for this feast, since he knows only too well our poverty of sin. We need his help to make ourselves a fit palace to receive Christ.

31 May after Trinity Sunday—Feast of the Visitation of Mary to Elizabeth

 HEN MARY HEARD that her cousin Elizabeth was to bear a child, Mary made the journey to visit her in spite of being heavily pregnant herself. As soon as Elizabeth heard Mary's greeting, the child in Elizabeth's womb leaped for joy. Filled with the Holy Spirit, Elizabeth cried out to Mary, *Of all women you are the most blessed and blessed is the fruit of your womb! Blessed is she who believed that the promise made to her by God would be fulfilled.* (Luke 1:39–45)

We learn many lessons from this visit to Elizabeth by Mary. For example, we realize that Mary made this journey out of love even when it was not physically easy for her. This tells us that sometimes loving someone calls for physical as well as emotional struggles, but that we must go ahead and do it anyway. Like Mary we must make the effort. We learn also that in the recognition of the sacred presence in Mary, the Holy Spirit filled Elizabeth just as it fills us when we are in the presence of God. Finally, we understand that keeping faith in the promises of God, as Mary did, will be honoured by such promises being fulfilled.

JUNE

Theme: *On being together in Jesus Christ*

For as many of you as were baptized into Christ you have put on Christ.

Galatians 3:27

1 June—On the presumption, folly, and madness of the wilful sinner

HAT YOU WOULD think if a garden snail was presumptuous enough to try attacking the gardener, who has the power of life and death over such an arrogant creature? What could this silly snail expect from making an enemy of such a powerful person, but sheer misery, even death itself. What hope has this poor snail?

Yet, the folly of this imaginary snail is often a reality in the lives of men and women, because they battle against God, the Master Gardener, and by acts of wilful sin they separate themselves from him, the being who has the power of life, death, and final judgment over them. Is it possible to conceive a greater madness than this?

In the great *Garden of Creation* is where we are living. It is a place where no creature, no matter how little or fragile, is insignificant. Every one of these creatures including the garden snail, have a natural desire for their own well-being. Each has a will to live.[1] But as far as we know a snail does not enjoy the same kind of free will that men and women possess and goes happily along its way content with its state of life. On the other hand, men and women since Adam and Eve, do not like to be forbidden anything and, since they have free will, they tend to use it and often in the wrong way. Some apple of desire is always hanging around to tempt them.

The trouble with such wilful sinners is that they indulge in the belief that everything about their life from birth to final destiny is within their own power. In vain they search for happiness and success in ways that always lead to disappointment, because rewards of any kind are the privilege of God to bestow. All others are transient and pass quickly away.

---

1   Albert Schweitzer,*The concept of reverence for life,* c.1915.

Is it any wonder then that such a person meets with an unexpected discontent and uneasiness and wonders about the meaning of life? Can any thing be more crazy than to seek for any good while turning one's back upon the source of all that is good? Are you, like the imaginary snail, a wilful sinner by your fighting against God's commands and his plan for your life?

We do well to remember that when sinners turn away from God every thing they run after turns into shadows. God always blocks the way. (Hosea 2:8–10) So conclude to be a contented creature in the great *Garden of Creation,* which is this earth, and to always please the Master Gardener with love and service. So leave the forbidden fruit of sin uneaten.

2 June — On the vanity of all those things that keep people from the service of God

 OW VAIN ARE those things that worldly people prefer before God. How they pursue empty bubbles of longing, toys and trifles, false appearances, fashions that quickly change, the deceitful baits of all manner of passions that hooked their souls, and the deluding dreams of ambition and materialism. All these vanities quickly vanish and leave both hands and hearts empty.

This imagined happiness, this false dream that *more is better*, could turn in an instant from what appears innocent into serious sin. For example, just consider how fast this desire for more can turn into greed and envy.

Reflect for moment on those that have died who enjoyed the most of what this world could afford in honours, riches, and power. Look around at how every cemetery is full of people who thought the world could not do without them. Sadly, it is too late for them to discover that *there is nothing to be gained under the sun.* (Ecclesiastes 2:11)

So take a close look at worldly idols and values, those phantoms of honours, possessions, and consuming pleasures. See how much hard work and stress they require and how often people who pursue these things are stressed or depressed and emotionally fragmented. They become like perverted children, always demanding, never satisfied. (Isaiah 1:4) See how they have to be on guard once they possess such things and how quickly this need for safety and security turns into anxiety and fear. We need to understand how easily these possessions and power can be lost. In such a pursuit of worldly values, people are commonly exposed to ill health, the loss of time with loved ones, and all that tenderness that should be the first response of their hearts.

The great cry of such people is *I don't have time!* No time for family and friends and, certainly, no time for God.

Do we live to work like such people, instead of working to live, because we serve false values that are not heaven-sent, but arise only from temptations that God has forbidden? Do we often claim like them: *I don't have time!*

On top of all this, such people are exposed to the devastating probability that they will fail in their pursuit of such vanities. Where then in such failure is self-esteem? Where then is the sense of their life having meaning? Where then can they find liberty from a life that is no more than slavery to values that end by proving themselves inconstant, false, and deceitful?

With failure to achieve their worldly goals, such people often become bitter and inflict their failure not only on themselves but also on those nearest to them at home and at work. In this way, they spread their distress to innocent others like a contagious disease.

How wretched the life that is spent in weaving these cobwebs whose prey is themselves, in running after fancy butterflies of possessions, in catching at shadows of real living, in silly amusements that soon become boring, in the wasted time of idle conversation, in concerns for passing fashions, or in failed attempts to look young forever.

Surely such living in pursuit of worldly values must become tedious. It is devoid of contentment in this life and of all prospect of happiness in the next. Such people are like a field of grass without water. When all is dried out and dead, a single spark will set it on fire and there will be no one to put out the fire. (Isaiah 1: 29–31) It is as if they were sitting day and night on the eggs of poisonous snakes that when they hatch would bring them spiritual death. (Isaiah 59:5–8)

If you are such a person, then how long will your heart be closed and will you love what is futile and seek what is false? (Psalm 4:3)

3 June—Solemnity of Corpus Christi

 ODAY, WE CELEBRATE the institution of the Eucharist-the commemoration of Jesus the Christ. It is nourishment that keeps us going in life and in faith. Consider how Jesus gave us these precious gifts as a legacy of his love. These were given to unite us with him in such a manner as that we should abide in him and he in us. (John 6:56; Luke 1:68–75)

4 June—On the mysteries contained in the Eucharist

ll SACRAMENTS ARE mysterious signs and symbols of divine grace and truth. These graces and truths are concealed under various outward appearances, but they are there to be discovered and to be understood by us in their sacred sense. It is through these symbols and signs, enacted in our rituals of the Sacraments, that our holy devotion, our renewal of faith, and our reconciliation with God are conveyed to us.

Now the Eucharist is a great mystery. Just as sin and death came to us originally by eating of the forbidden fruit, so in this Sacrament we are nourished by the fruit of the tree of life that Jesus gave us under the form of bread, a basic food expressing his real and his mystical body. John in his gospel tells us what Jesus said, *I am the living bread which has come down from heaven. Anyone who eats this bread will live forever; and the bread that I shall give is my flesh, for the life of the world.* (John 6:51) Just as with the ordinary bread that men and women eat for daily sustenance, so this bread of life is spiritual nourishment for our soul.

It expresses as well the mystical body of Christ through which the church as his people are united. In this union of concord and charity all its members, like so many grains of corn, are brought together in harmony and peace, because these disciples of Christ become one bread through a shared celebration uniting the Messiah with all the people of God. We, although there are many of us, are one single body, for we all share in the one loaf. (1 Corinthians 10:17)

5 June—On devotion after Communion

UST AS WE prepare ourselves before receiving Holy Communion, so we need to take equal care after receiving it. As we welcome his presence in us, we must let Christ take complete possession of us. It is the moment of such union that we need to echo this song of King Solomon: *I caught him, would not let him go.* (The Song of Songs 3:4)

6 June—On the judgments of God on sin

 HERE ARE MANY convincing events of how much God hates sin. While it is true that God is a god of love and mercy, we learn in biblical history that he does not necessarily have endless patience with those who persist in disobedience. (Romans 11:10, Psalm 68:23–24)

Just think of the flood that swept away all sinners on earth. (Matthew 24:39) Consider the judgement of fire on Sodom. (Matthew 10:15, Jude 1:7) Witness the many judgments on the rebel Israelites in the wilderness, particularly when the earth swallowed up Kore and his companions and when flames from the Lord destroyed in a flash over 14,000 of their supporters. (Ezekiel 20:13–14, Psalm 94:10, Numbers 16:20–21) Think how many flourishing cities and whole nations have been punished by pestilences, famines, and earthquakes, all brought upon people by their sins.

In spite of knowing about these judgments, how often we take no notice of our spirit, like those ancient Israelites, and continue catering for the forbidden vanities and desires of our bodies and minds. (Proverbs 1:24–33) So do not tempt God's fury by continuing to pursue these wild hungers. Before it is too late, resolve to return to obedience to God.

7 June—Beware of your passions

HOSE CONDEMNING JESUS to the Cross had scruples about body uncleanliness, but they were not afraid of polluting their souls by unjustly condemning Jesus to death. Injustice triumphed. This shows us what people are capable of when confusion over the dictates of their faith leads them to join in mob hysteria. This happens today, just as it did in the time of Jesus.

Yet, the providence of God arose in the case of the crucifying of Jesus, because heavenly plans for this world are always carried out. Without knowing it, this confused mob were instruments in bringing about the designs of God for the redemption of the world through the sacrifice of the true Paschal Lamb, Jesus the Christ. Divine Providence, often draws the greatest good out of the greatest evil, because God is all-powerful and everything evolves to the greater good of his will.[2]

---

[2]   St. Thomas Aquinas, *Commentary on Romans* and *Summa Contra Gentiles*.

8 June—Solemnity of the Sacred Heart of Jesus

HAT WOULD THE world think of a prince who had such friendship for one of his servants that he offers himself to die just to rescue this servant from the justified punishment of his crimes? Would not everyone be amazed at such an extraordinary love? Even more so if the crime for which this servant had been condemned to die were no less than for a treasonable conspiracy against this very same prince.

For Christians this is but a faint resemblance of that love that Jesus showed in giving his life to rescue us from a death of eternal torment. Jesus is the eternal prince of the most sacred heart, the heart that loves so completely that it sacrifices its own life for the sake of others. He is that prince of such friendship.

9 June—On the virtues of Faith, Hope, and Charity

 T DOES NO good to just talk about these virtues without putting them into practice. For example, Faith often fades into just a habit of going to church on Sundays or becomes a virtue we profess on high days like church feasts, weddings, baptisms, and funerals. Faith seems so often to fall by the wayside as we continue judging ourselves by worldly standards. There is no better encouragement to a strong faith than to study Scripture, because the Word of God feeds the mind, body and spirit.

The foundation of all Hope is the hope in the promises of God. Even if our body is in chains and our minds constrained by others, hope secures the freedom of our spirit. Here is the liberty every man and woman needs.

As for the virtue of Charity, it is like a fire that never goes out. It may die away and grow cold if not kept alive through frequent use. Like coals in a fire, charity can diminish to a low glow, but once stirred can spring into flame again.

As the righteous man or woman lives by faith, so he or she must also live by hope and by charity. (Romans 1:17–24; Galatians 3:11–12; Hebrews 10:38) In this way, the whole life of a Christian ought to be continually influenced by the three virtues of faith, hope, and charity, none of which can be kept alive in us without frequent practice.

10 June—Why we should beware of too much curiosity

URIOSITY, THE CONSTANT seeking of reasons and information to explain things, may seem a delight. We may call it *science* and claim it as progress, but does this over-whelming *need to know* enlighten us or make us afraid of the future? Does it bring us closer to truth or simply perplex us? Does such curiosity help us to understand miracles or does it make us turn away from the supernatural to seek explanations in chemistry, neurology or psychology or whatever? Does it acknowledge our ignorance of the human spirit and make us forget that what is impossible for humanity is possible for God? (Luke 18.27; Matthew 19.26)

When at least ten dimensions are recognized as existing by science and technology even though we can only see three of them, like in a chair, ask yourself why do so many people discount the possibility of the resurrection? Have you really thought about what Jesus meant when he said, *Blessed are those who have not seen and yet believe.* (John 20:29)

11 June—Memorial of the Apostle Barnabas

 AINT BARNABAS IS justly remembered with this special day for the important part he played in the development and spreading of Christianity outside the Jewish communities. With Paul, he brought the *Word of God* to the gentiles. Saint Barnabas taught that all people were saved through Christ. As Christians are we like this Apostle in spreading the *Good News* or do we keep our mouths shut in deference to social politeness?

12 June — On the Sacrament of Confirmation

 ONFIRMATION IS THE Sacrament by which the faithful receive the Holy Spirit together in order to help them be strong in faith. While the Apostles were confirmed by the Holy Spirit coming down visibly upon them, the faithful, after the Apostles had died, are confirmed by their successors, who are our bishops, by *receiving the Holy Spirit through the laying on of hands and by prayers.* (Acts 8:16–17 & 19:6)

The special grace of the Sacrament of Confirmation gives a spiritual strength, valour, and courage in order to maintain the cause of God against the visible and invisible enemies of our faith. By this Sacrament we are made soldiers of Christ and put ourselves under his banner, receiving the mark of his cross on our foreheads. In this commanding post Jesus the Christ gives his soldiers nothing less than himself. Even if you have to die, keep faithful, and he will give you the crown of life for your prize. (Revelation 2:10)

Conclude then to show in every respect that you are a soldier of Christ through your faith and your virtue.

13 June — On the obligations of Confirmation

 OUR SPIRIT BY the Sacrament of Confirmation has been sanctified and consecrated to God. As a result, we are obliged to be faithful and holy, dedicated as his soldier in Christ and as his temple.

Therefore, always try to live up to the sacred character of Confirmation and Baptism. If you have been ordained to God as a priest, then this too lasts a lifetime. If you are a bishop, beware of falling into any temptation, because you are leading the faithful of God. If you are a religious persevere in your vows. If you are a layperson, remember that you are one of the people of God, his church. But no matter who you are in this life, do not be terrified at the prospect of the conflicts you must sustain or the crosses and hardships you will have to go through in this warfare of living in the world as a soldier of Jesus Christ and a servant of God. Remember that the angel of temptations does not care about either worldly or spiritual rank.

Yet in every case, no matter whether you are rich or poor, layperson or priest or bishop, nun or monk the peace of God which is beyond our understanding will guard your hearts and your thoughts in Christ Jesus. (Philippians 4:4–7; 1 Corinthians 13)

14 June — On the Eucharist as a sacrifice

 HE EUCHARIST IS not only a *Sacrament* in which we receive the body and blood of Christ for the nourishment of our souls, but it is also a *sacrifice* offered up to God in remembrance of the death and passion of Christ. In this way, we offer glory to God, give thanks for all his benefits, and ask his pardon for our sins. Such a *sacrifice* is an act of worship for God, because it testifies that he is the master of life and death, our first beginning and our last end. It is a sacrifice in which the Christ himself is both priest and victim. (Hebrews 10:5–7; Micah 5:1–3)

This holy commemoration is a gift to the well being of our mind, body, and spirit and the greatest help to our happiness and contentment in life. So celebrate and take part in the Eucharistic service as often as possible.

15 June—On the excellence of the Eucharistic Sacrifice

 OMING TO THE altar of the great high priest, Jesus Christ, each of us is called to be sanctified. Even as we stand with many others to share in the holy bread and wine, we remain in a one-to-one relationship to the Messiah and God. It is a moment of repentance and reconciliation, a moment in which all the mysteries of the visible and invisible result in our renewal. While the fear of God is, indeed, the beginning of wisdom, we must never be afraid at the altar for this is the place God wants us to be and in the state of the healed soul he wishes for us. (Proverbs 9:10)

16 June — On the Eucharist as adoration and praise

T IS NATURAL for us to pay homage to God by adoration and praise. For this reason, the psalms were composed, musical instruments played, and voices raised in song to accompany the sacrifices offered in the temple of God. Psalm 150 tells us how to worship God: *Alleluia! Praise God in his holy place; praise him in his mighty heavens. Praise him for his powerful deeds; praise his surpassing greatness. Oh, praise him with sound of trumpet; praise him with lute and harp. Praise him with timbrel and dance; praise him with strings and pipes. Praise him with resounding cymbals; praise him with clashing of cymbals. Let everything that lives and that breathes give praise to the Lord. Alleluia!* (Psalm 150:1–6)

We are told how King David danced before the altar, joyful in his adoration and wild with love for God. Ancient servants of God, like David, had a zeal for giving God the best homage they could and we ought to do no less. Many people wonder if perhaps we were created just for this purpose of praising God. This is a question about which many still ponder. Maybe we too are like the angel sent from heaven to Tobias with a mission of holiness, which in our case is to praise God through celebration and prayer. (Psalm 149:3; Psalm 150:1–6; Tobit 5 *The Fish* & 12 *The Revelation*)

Consider how little it is that any man or woman can offer to God compared to what God has given to them. The majesty of God is so infinite that the whole of creation is but one great offering for his glory. The sun, the moon, the stars, the rivers and seas, the mountains, all creatures and everything visible and invisible bow down in his honour. (Psalm 148) The trees in the wood shout for joy. (Psalm 95:12) Even the stones bask in his sunshine. Night and day his voice is heard and the universe answers, singing to God, each in its own holy form, each connected to the other from stone to star. (Psalm 18) Yet, even as such a multitude in all their forms of Creation may rise up in praise, our voices must always be among them.

So sing out when the organ strikes up a hymn or the choir begins to give voice, clap your hands in joy, even dance for God like King David or shake your tambourine in noisy celebration if you feel like it. (Psalm 56:8–9) On the other hand, you may decide to sit quietly in a silent celebration of thanksgiving. That can be just as joyous as when King David decided to dance. However we celebrate God, let it be with a great joy in our heart.

17 June—On the Eucharist as thanksgiving

OW WONDERFUL THAT God has given us a way to render him a regular and worthy means of thanksgiving through the Eucharistic sacrifice that is individual as well as communal. The thanksgiving offerings in the time of Moses fell short of answering in a complete manner the obligation on all men and women to give thanks to God. Therefore, the Messiah was sent. He came to tell us of that moral perfection in which God wanted us to live and to make him, Jesus Christ, our high priest and to offer him on our behalf as the worthy sacrifice of thanksgiving. In this commemoration all heaven and earth are united, so that there is a thanksgiving for God's mercy and a continuous celebration of the life, death and resurrection of his Christ at the same time. Nothing less will be equal to the debt we owe to God. Such an offering answers completely our obligation to give thanks to God.

18 June—On the Eucharist as a sacrifice of propitiation

HAT IS MEANT by the word *propitiation*? It is a word we rarely use in our conversations, but it is important to our understanding of the Eucharist. *Propitiation* includes meanings such as atonement, conciliatory action, the pleasing of someone we have angered, appeasement, averting being condemned by what we have done, seeking to amend by a offering in religious terms.

In other words, *propitiation* means mending a relationship, which we have broken and in which we have deeply offended the other person, which in this case means God himself. The Eucharistic sacrifice is a means of making such *propitiation* to God. In the context of Holy Scripture, this means we know God can be angry with us. The reason for his anger is our sin, which disgraces God's holy name and insults his glorious love for us. (Romans 3:23)

Our way to make amends is to stop wilful sinning, live in obedience to God's commandments, and to offer our atonement through the sacrifice of the body and blood of Christ that is the Eucharistic celebration. This is our propitiation for obtaining mercy and pardon for our sins. Jesus Christ substituted a new victim, himself, in the place of what was sacrificed in the time of Moses and the other ancient prophets. Like King David, we are keeping watch over our thoughts, our tongues, and our actions, careful to avoid any further offense to God so that our offering is lasting in our reconciliation with him. (Psalm 39)

19 June — Optional Memorial of Saint Romuald, Abbot

 AINT ROMUALD (950–1027) was founder of the Camaldolese, the oldest hermit order of the Western Church. He considered it better to say one Our Father prayer devoutly than to offer a thousand prayers with no devotion and full of distraction.[3]

It may come as a surprise for many Christians to discover that the hermit life is thriving today. Not only do the Camaldolese have a number of actively growing communities and an ever-increasing membership of oblates, but the number of men and women choosing to live a solitary life of prayer and a seeking for God as either a lay hermit or under a bishop, continues to grow around the world.[4]

Being a hermit is a vocation to which some people are called by God, so it is worthwhile understanding this solitary life for God as just one of the ways in which men and women are chosen to serve God.

When we think of hermits we often turn to the lives of saints like Julian of Norwich, Paul the hermit and Saint Anthony when he went to the desert. But let us consider the eremitical life not of long ago but of today. Contemporary research shows that in general those who chose this life display a balanced and integrated personality and are not anti-social or pious fanatics. At first those called to this hermit life usually opt out of the usual influences of society such as customs, idols, values and so forth, because they seek a wholeness of self and can only find this by transcending the society in which they live.

But after awhile such people in most cases begin some service to others, while at the same time maintaining their

---

[3] A saying attributed to St. Edmund 841–869.

[4] *CIC* 603.

individual life-style as a hermit. Such service is usually through prayer or helping others through spiritual guidance, but some hermits do give time to organisations that help others. So in general, hermits begin by an inward journey to God through a singular and often difficult exploration of their true selves and the building of a life alone, dedicated to God with prayer, contemplation, and study of Holy Scripture. However, this eventually results in an outgoing love for others in obedience to God's commandment to love.

Being a hermit or solitary is an inward journey *from* the world that returns the hermit or solitary *to* that world through the process of love, but leaving behind certain aspects of the world, which do not please God or are not suitable for the solitary life. In short, hermits and solitaries are *in* the world, but not *of* it.

From the very beginning of our Christian history, there have been those who follow the way of Martha and are active in good deeds and others who find holy fulfilment in the contemplative way of Mary. (Luke 10:38–42; John 11:20–27; 1 Corinthians 7:1–7) Many Christians, for example the religious, try to live a more holy perfection through vows of poverty, chastity, and obedience. Others, like St. Romauld, withdraw to being alone with God in prayer and contemplation. Perhaps worldly temptations may seem more frequent for those who live in the world and less for those who live a solitary life but this is not so, because the temptations that arise from within us take the same courage to resist as those that confront us in the world.[5]

We all need time alone with God of course, even though we may never feel called to serve him as a hermit. A more thorough examination of Saint Romauld helps to do this. After all, Jesus sought solitude for his praying and often went to a private place alone to pray and, for example, he spent forty days alone in the desert. So being alone with God is an

---

[5]   Reading from Saint Anthony of Egypt.

example set out by Jesus himself and mirrored in the life of saints and by all who pray as he instructed us. As Jesus said, *When you pray, go into your private room, shut the door, and pray to your Father who is in secret. And your Father who sees in secret will reward you.* (Matthew 6:6 & 26:32 & 41; Mark 1:32–34 & 6:46; Luke 6:12)

Whether we are a hermit or a Christian living in the world, St. Alphonsus Liguori (1696–1787) gives this wise advice: *Were you to ask, what are the means of overcoming temptations? I would answer: The first means is prayer; the second is prayer; the third is prayer; and should you ask me a thousand times, I would repeat the same.*[6]

---

[6] From Divine Office, Thursday, Week 17, Memorial of St. Alphonsus Liguori.

20 June — On making time with God

 E ALL NEED the time and space to converse with God. We all need time with God no matter how fulfilled and contented we are with our life, no matter how faithfully we may follow the path of Jesus, and no matter how great our obedience to the commandments of God or our faith in his promises. We need this time with God alone and in private without distractions of the world around us.

Saint Romauld instructed his monks how to achieve this desired situation with some rules. He told them first of all:

> Sit in your cell as in paradise. Put the whole world behind you and forget it. We should do the same when we pray to God, because our true cell is ourselves, our interior self. It is the inner space where only God and we may enter. The walls of our cell are those silent moments with God when we become attentive listeners with the ear of our heart.[7] The furnishings of our cell are the articles of faith we profess, the words of prayer we speak or sing, and our contemplation of heavenly things. This cell, which is our inner self, is a mansion of God built by love. It is a true palace where we invite God to live with us.[8]

St. Romauld's brief rule about what we should do when in this cell is a wise guide for every Christians. He says we should do the following:

1. Sit in the cell as in paradise.
2. Cast all memory of the world behind you.
3. Watch your thoughts as a good fisherman watches fish.
4. Do not abandon the psalms. Use them. If you cannot understand everything, strive to pray them with an understanding of spirit and mind now here, now there.

---

[7] *Rule of St. Benedict*, The Prologue.

[8] St. Teresa of Avila, *Interior Castle*.

When you begin to wander while reading, do not stop, but hurry to correct yourself by concentrating.

5. Above all, place yourself in the presence of God with fear and trembling, like someone who stands in the sight of a great king who holds the power of life and death over you.

6. Destroy your self-love by completely emptying yourself of all worries, anxieties, duties and other concerns.

7. Sit like a chick, content with the grace of God, because unless its mother gives it something, it tastes nothing and has nothing to eat.

21 June—On the practice of contemplation

 N STRIVING FOR a more holy life, practice may not bring perfection, but practice can bring increased skill just as with sport, arts, hobbies or cooking. The same is true with contemplation. So these suggestions may help in your contemplation:

1. Consider your posture and the place where you are. Embrace solitude. Be at peace. Breathe gently but deeply.

2. Detachment yourself from worldly worries, concerns and duties so you can concentrate. Still your mind from jumping from one thought to another like a monkey jumping from tree to tree.

3. Examine yourself and confess to God your desires and passions as well as the disobedience and temptations into which you may have fallen.

4. Ask for mercy at not loving enough.

5. Resolve to overcome all faults that displease God and that do not keep you on the narrow path of Jesus.

6. Concentrate on praying the Psalms, because these are seeds of reflection for us as well as prayers. Let them flourish in you until they flower with the presence of God.

7. Let humility fill you. Be joyous.

These suggestions for contemplation, like the rules of Saint Romauld, do not change over time, because the heavenly aspects of God and his commandments remain eternal. Being at peace with God and contemplating him, talking with him, and thinking about the meaning of life is the help we all need.

22 June — On the Eucharist as a sacrifice of prayer and supplication

HE EUCHARIST AS a sacrifice fulfils the intentions of the *burnt offerings, thankfulness offerings,* and *sin offerings* of the Old Testament. In being offered up by us in thanksgiving to God for all his blessings and for the remission of sin, the Eucharist is this *peace offering* of the ancients. Here we approach God with Christ as both our high priest and our beloved victim. We should never fear to make such a supplication, because God's favour is always waiting us.

In this Eucharistic sacrifice our Lord has provided us with an inexhaustible fund of grace, flowing endlessly from that *fountain of living waters that is God.* (Revelation 3:17–22; Isaiah. 12:3) This answers all our necessities, heals our infirmities, guards us against all dangers, and redresses our miseries. So then, avail yourself of the Eucharist as often as possible, thus serving *God without fear in holiness and justice all the days of your life.* (Luke 1:74 -75; John 7:37–39)

23 June—On the devotion with which we are to assist at the Eucharist

 INCE JESUS THE Christ as priest and victim is truly before us at the altar, we should give this celebration great devotion. Think how vital the covenant God has made with us through his Messiah now present on the altar before us, not veiled by cloth nor hidden as in ancient times, but presented openly to us in all its mystery.

Go in this spirit of reverence to the altar of God. Bow and bend low before it. Kneel before the God who made us. (Psalm 94:6) Make your intentions the same as his intentions. Go as if you were mounting Calvary to share in the salvation given to every man and woman by the sacrifice of his beloved Jesus. Here is your devotion.

24 June—Solemnity of the birth of Saint John the Baptist

 OHN WAS A saint from birth, wholly dedicating to the love and service of God. (Luke 1:13–14) To this end he retired while still very young to the wilderness, fleeing from the corruptions and distractions of the world. There he stayed *until the day of his manifestation to Israel, strengthened in spirit by God for the destiny he was born to fulfil.* (Luke 1:80)

Let us consider how God graced the life of John the Baptist in all these aspects of service. John was a martyr in laying down his life for justice and truth, a hermit in retiring into the desert to consecrate himself to prayer and self-denial, a zealous preacher of penance to reclaim sinners from their evil ways, and the herald announcing Christ and preparing people for his coming. Jesus himself said there had not been a greater man born of women than John and called him a burning and shining light in the world. (Matthew 11:11; John 5:35–36)

Above all else, we honour John the Baptist for being sent from God to bear witness to Jesus the Messiah that all men and woman might believe in him. *(John 1: 6–7)* Here was the dawning of the new day that God was bringing to us. Here was the daystar for which the world had been waiting. Until that moment of divine light, we were in darkness and the shadow of death. Therefore, we have the best of reasons to celebrate with joy the birth of John the Baptist as the prelude to our redemption.

25 June — On the lessons we learn from St. John the Baptist

HE KEEPING OF the festivals of the saints is to honour God by giving thanks for the grace bestowed upon these holy men and women and to encourage the faithful to an imitation of their virtues. The hope is that we might arrive one day in their blessed company by walking in their footsteps during our earthly life. If we desire to keep the festival of Saint John in a suitable manner, we must endeavour then to learn the lessons he teaches by his great example.

His life in the desert was one of prayer and mortification in keeping with the calling by God to the eremitical life. Here are lessons that all Christians in some measure must learn. If our daily occupations and human fragility does not allow us to maintain that continual attention to God that John possessed then at least we can aspire after him. For example, we can have a daily time set aside for prayer.

If we cannot bring ourselves to such a sparse diet and poverty as John lead, then at least we can give up over-indulgence in eating, drinking, sleeping, fashion and the abundance of other comforting and amusing but unnecessary diversions in which we currently engage. We may no longer mortify the flesh like many saints in the past. Indeed, the church does not encourage such extravagant self-punishment today, but we can mortify our vanity, curiosity, and sensuality.

Finally, we can learn from Saint John the Baptist to renounce our own will on many occasions, giving up our determination to have our own way. We can oppose unproductive inclinations to self-love. Instead of falling into the trap of temptation, we can look to the will of God, bowing down to the plan of heaven for our life.

When Saint John said he was only a voice crying in the wilderness, he was professing humility. (Mark 1:3; John 1:23;

Isaiah 40:3) Humility is pleasing to God for all other virtues are grounded in it. It is the foundation of the life of every saint. Make it so for your own life, because humility will bring you to Christ and be pleasing to God.

26 June—The motives of repentance

 T IS IN our nature to want to return to the favour of God who first gave us life on this wondrous earth. He put in us a spirit that yearns for him. However, our sin is always a rebellion against the sovereign good of God and his commandments. It denies us the presence of God. Thus, sin is odious to him, because it destroys the meaning of life itself and reduces us to depression, anger, dissatisfaction, and a life where joy and peace cannot thrive. When you consider the effects of sin and how we are made to yearn for God, can there be better motives for repentance and reconciliation with God? (Mark 9:43–50)

27 June—Love conquers all

 EMEMBER WHAT JESUS said of the sinful woman when he dined with the Pharisees: *I tell you that her sins, many as they are, have been forgiven her, because she has shown such great love.* (Luke 7:47) Go then like the sinful woman and kneel at the feet of your Saviour, because you love him so much and he will pronounce the same sentence on you as he did the sinful woman.

28 June— On sincerity in Confession

 HUMBLE CONFESSION GIVES glory to God. It affords joy to the whole church of the people of God. As to your confessor, he should see the hand of God in the humility and sincerity of your confession and rejoice in this happy change. A confession should also give the confessor a strengthening of faith and a hope in his own future.

Making a confession of having offended God is not just some church ritual or some habit of regular churchgoers. If you are not sincere in confessing and joyful of heart in receiving the mercy of reconciliation, then the judgment of God will be terrible, because you will have lied to the Holy Spirit. (Acts 5) Any hypocrisy is deceitful. (Jeremiah 17:9–10)

Equally, the confessor must bring to his part that quality of listening and attentiveness that love demands and Jesus himself would have shown a sinner. A confessor must never forget the privilege of the great power that has been passed to him through Jesus, because at the moment when his lips open to the signs and words of forgiveness, the Holy Spirit speaks. As to the one confessing, you are God's treasured possession, a chosen race.(1 Peter 2:9; Deuteronomy 7:6, 14:2, 26:11) Have no fear!

29 June—Solemnity of Saints Peter and Paul

EFLECT WHAT THESE two glorious saints were before being called by Jesus Christ. Peter was a humble fisherman and Paul was a Jewish zealot who fought against the new Christian community. When we consider these facts, we have before you examples of the wonder and mystery of God.

Scripture tells us how Peter was chosen to be the master-builder of the community of the people of God under the guidance of Jesus Christ and how he became the foundation of it. See how God raised him up to be the first minister of this kingdom of God on earth. (Matthew 16:18–19; John 21) In Peter's history we understand that God chooses those who are seemingly unimportant by human standards. Indeed, God often chooses those men and women who may count for nothing by worldly values and reduces to nothing of much importance those people that believed they counted for something important in this world. God does this in order that no human might feel boastful before God. (1 Corinthians 1: 27–31) In choosing Peter for the holy work of God, divine wisdom is set before us as a lesson for our life.

Let us next consider Paul, another instance of the wisdom of the ways of God. Although he was a devoted Pharisee, Paul was also a fiery zealot, a bloody persecutor intent on destroying the followers of Christ. Yet, he was made a vessel to bring Jesus the Christ before nations, kings and gentiles. In an instant, God changes him from a killing zealot into one of the flock of Christ. Such is the power of God.

Therefore, we should prepare ourselves before any confession of our sins by listening with the ear of our heart to what these two Apostles of Christ and Scripture have to say to us.[9] In this reflection, we recognize that God has called

---

9   *Rule of St. Benedict*, The Prologue, 1; Psalm 102:20.

each of us to a life through Christ for the glory of God just as he did with Peter and Paul. Learn then from these Apostles the practice of love.

30 June—On the seven gifts of God

 ONSIDER THE INFINITE goodness of God. Not content with giving us the *Sacrament of Baptism*, God then gave us the *Sacrament of Confirmation*. This dedication and declaration brings us the Holy Spirit to make us strong Disciples of Christ and good servants of God.

Yet in his generosity, this was still not enough for God gave us the *Sacrament of the Eucharist* to feed and nourish our souls to everlasting life, the *Sacrament of Reconciliation* so we could be reconciled to God and enjoy happiness, the *Sacrament of Anointing* of the sick and dying so that our final earthly existence might be one of mercy, and the *Sacrament of Marriage* so that we might have those unions of companionship, intimacy, and pleasure which bring contentment and fulfilment to our lives. Finally, he gave us the *Sacrament of Holy Orders* so that we might have dedicated shepherds to help us on our journey to eternal life.

These are the gifts of God and together with our penance give us reunion with God.

JULY

*Theme: **On being holy for God.***

Be holy in all you do,
since it is the Holy One who has called you,
and scripture says: Be holy, for I am holy.

1 Peter 1:15–16

1 July — On time and how we use it

OW PRECIOUS TIME is! The past gone. The present is disappearing. Tomorrow may never arrive. Each of us dances with time in a different way. Some live in the past, believing yesterday was always better than today. Others always seem to be living in the future, making excuses for postponing until tomorrow what they should do today. Many worry about the future so much that their present life slips away, wasted in needless fretting and anxiousness about what tomorrow may bring. Few of us live in the present moment. Meanwhile, the clock ticks away for all these different people. Youth passes into old age. When we may least expect it, the clock stops. Our time on earth is up.

But how does God desire that we spend the earthly time allotted to us? We are told to live joyously in the present, since our past is gone and our future unknown. (Matthew 6:31–34) In other words, drop the baggage from the past. Let it go. We can only do this *letting go* through God's help, because we are fragile creatures with minds jumping around like a monkey and struggling with our ups and downs while trying our best to find happiness and avoid lots of temptations.

The faith we need must rest on hope and our hope is in the salvation given to us by Jesus. This hope is always taking place now in this very moment and not just two thousand years ago when Jesus lived, because Christ is resurrected in each of us *now*, not just yesterday. Our prayers to God are *now*, not in what we prayed yesterday or might pray tomorrow. Our love of others must be *now*, not something we will do tomorrow. The joy in this moment of our life is *now* and joy is what God wants for us.

We finally learn that time, as we usually understand it, is no longer a measure for us, because we have a vision that is eternal and goes beyond our time on earth.[1] . Like flowers in the field, we no longer worry. (Matthew 6:28–34) We live in this moment, whether we are at prayer or cooking a little omelette or out walking the dog or engaged in some other activity, because no matter what we are doing God is present.[2]

Even with modern medicine and a healthy lifestyle, the majority of us still have only the biblical seventy years or eighty for the strong. (Psalm 89:10) But do not count on even this span of time for you had no control over your creation and there will be none over the time of your dying. The present moment is all you can call your own and only God knows how long it will last.

So employ every hour to the best advantage for pleasing God and achieving contentment with your dearest friend, Jesus the Christ.

---

1   St. Augustine, *Confessions*, Book XI; 2 Peter 3:8.
2   Br. Lawrence of the Resurrection, *The Practice of the Presence of God*.

2 July — The illusions of time

OW QUICKLY THE glories of this world pass away. How soon the natural grandeur around us disappears when winter strips the leaves from trees and fields lay bare. How certain it is that worldly pride and human pomp and all the riches and pleasures of life will be gone too after their brief celebrity in our lives. Just as we must die, so will all our vanities disappear just like the splendour of the seasons when this happens to us. (Ecclesiastes 3:1–9)

To avoid this truth, we dress time in wonderful illusions, because this pushes thoughts of death further from our minds. It seems one day we are young, the next old. After that what is left of us but dust? How true it is, then, that all is vanity except to love God and to serve him alone. (Ecclesiastes 1: 2 & 20; Deuteronomy 6:13 & 17) Is this the holy wisdom and understanding by which we live? Have we understood time in God's sense of it or are we still dressing up time in illusions?

We need to recognize time for what it is and what it is not. Let us discard illusions then and make the time we have left serve the needs of our spirit in its pilgrimage toward heaven.

3 July—Feast of Saint Thomas Apostle

 CRIPTURE TELLS US that Thomas doubted it was really Jesus when the other apostles told him that Jesus had risen from the dead. Thomas told them unless he saw the wounds of the crucifixion nails and could touch the wound of the spear in Jesus' side, he would not believe. (John 20: 25) Suddenly, Jesus appeared before him and commanded he do just those actions. Thomas, seeing and touching Jesus, cried out, *My Lord and My God!*

What happened to Thomas teaches all Christians that faith in Jesus Christ is possible without seeing him and that, although invisible to our eyes, he is present in our lives and fully visible to our hearts. As Jesus said to Thomas, so he says to all of us: *You believe because you can see me. Blessed are those who have not seen and yet believe.* (John 20:29)

Pope Benedict XVI explained that Thomas is important to us for at least three reasons:

> First, because it comforts us in our insecurity; second, because it shows us that every doubt can lead to an outcome brighter than any uncertainty; and, lastly, because the words that Jesus addressed to him remind us of the true meaning of mature faith and encourage us to persevere, despite the difficulty, along our journey of following him.[3]

The Pope added that Thomas's readiness to stand by Jesus shows us that we must never for any reason distance ourselves from Christ. (John 11:16)

Finally, Pope Benedict draws our attention to the *Last Supper* when Thomas by his questions prompts Jesus to explain: *I am the Way, and the Truth and the Life.* (John 14:5–6) *Every time we hear or read these words*, says Pope Benedict, *we*

---

[3] Pope Benedict XVI, *Discourse at General Audience*, 2006.

can stand beside Thomas in spirit and imagine that the Lord is also speaking to us, just as he spoke to him.[4]

We must listen to the ancient biblical patriarchs when they tell us our faith is the confidence of things hoped for and the conviction of things we do not see. (Hebrews 11:1) Indeed, blessed are those who have not seen and yet believe. (John 20:29)

---

[4]   *Ibid.*

4 July — On the good employment of time

 O DEMONSTRATE THANKSGIVING through a sensible use of time does not mean using it to gain worldly power, prestige and riches. It does not mean being so busy with the things and attractions of this world that you have no time for the next. It does not mean frequently exclaiming, *I have no time.* Such people need to ask themselves why they are so busy with the world?

As a Christian do not be deceived in thinking that the wasting of so much of the precious gift of time will not be judged. If you are to be accountable for every word and choice you have made in this life, how much more will you be accountable for how you spent every hour and day?

5 July — *On remembering your time will end*

EATH IS A subject of fear to most people and to discuss or think about it is avoided if at all possible. Yet the end of life, our death, is the very thing that will help us to remember we have an eternal goal. Thinking and talking about death can keep us on the path of Jesus Christ as we head toward eternity. Never forget that lust and pride can never bear the vision of death, because death puts an end to all temptations including these. (1 John 2:16–17) We need to remember in such a moment of truth that our spirit will return to God who gave it. (Ecclesiastes 12:7)

Remember what we have been told about the time we are allotted: *For by grace you have been saved through faith. And this is not your own doing; it is the gift of God.* (Ephesians 2:8; Proverbs 3:6–16)

6 July—On the certainty of death

HERE IS NOTHING more certain than that we will die, *but this is not the end of us because after earthly death comes judgment.* (Hebrews 9: 14) Such judgment is for all the descendants of Adam. (Ecclesiasticus 41:3–4) No one may escape. Every moment brings us nearer to it. Yet, most of us refuse to acknowledge that death is a natural part of living.

We usually never think about death until we are quite old or faced with a terminal disease. Generally, we view it as something distant and best not thought about or discussed. We tell ourselves it will happen to us later as if we had the power to postpone our dying or arrange the time and place of it. We are like a frightened ostrich putting its head in the sand. We stay in our daily round of duties, worries, and pleasures and try to forget death.

How can any of us fool ourselves, as millions do, about our length of life when we cannot even be sure of it from one day to the next?[5] It is never too early or too late to become aware of your end, because the love and power of God is waiting for you. (Acts 2:38; 2 Corinthians 12:9–10)

So why not learn now that this is our fate while time is still on our side? Why not return to that path of life that Jesus showed us? (Psalm 15:11; Job 23:11) Why not face the certainty of death by living now as we should want to die? (Psalm 118:17)

---

5   Thomas à Kempis, *The Imitation of Christ,* 57, 40:6.

7 July—On the time and manner of our death

F WE DIE without repentance for our errors and omissions in loving others and without reconciliation with God, then we die with much fear of the unknown. In the moment of death depends our eternal life. But when will this moment come? When will we die? Will it be tonight or tomorrow? Shall it be a week, a month, or years from now? All we can know is that it will come, like a thief in the night when we least expect it. (Luke 23–36)

Not only are we ignorant of the time of our death, but also we have not the slightest idea as to the circumstances of it. We neither know the place where we will die nor the manner of it nor whether our death will be violent or natural, gentle or painful, quick or lingering, at home or abroad. Will our health be good or bad? All these things are hidden from us and no wisdom on earth can help anyone in knowing about these things. (Matthew 24:36) We cannot know anything about the future except what God himself has told us.

It helps us to face this realty about life ending, if we are brave enough to ask ourselves such questions as these: What is the state of my present life if death comes to me in the next hour? Have I weighed up the good and the bad of the ways in which I live? Am I pleasing to God? Am I at least *trying* to please God? (Romans 12:1–2; 2 Corinthians 13:11; 1 Thessalonians 4:1–2; Hebrews 11:6)

When we examine ourselves by such questions, we must never forget that God is at work in us *so as to fulfil his good purpose for each of us.* (Philippians 2:13) No matter how much we may fail to please him, God never deserts us.

Since there is such uncertainty about our death, we should always be prepared for it. This is the responsibility of our faith, so we must not postpone nor ignore it.

8 July—On preparing for death

 E CAME INTO this world as pilgrims to make our way toward an everlasting paradise. The great business of our life is to secure this happy eternity. Nothing else can secure it but a good death.

A good death means that we are always prepared for it though our reconciliation with God. Even though we often stumble on our journey to him by succumbing to temptation, we must get up again, ask for forgiveness, and continue on our way. In our reconciliation with God we know he is our protection, the apple of his eye. (Psalm 16:8) We must try again and again and yet again to follow Christ, even if we fall into the trap of sin many times. (Ephesians 6:10–17) There is no giving up for a Christian.

A good death, then, must necessarily be in the very foundation of our lives, but not as the end of it but as our new beginning, a new life. Such a foundation must be solid and enduring, one that will weather the storms and temptations of this worldly life. This foundation is Jesus himself and we are the temple built upon it, a temple that is the dwelling place of God where the Holy Spirit lives. (Ephesians 2:22; Psalm 90:1–2; Revelation 21:3–4; John 2:19–22; especially read 1 Corinthians 3:16–17)

The general error of men and women is that they are most devoted and filled with contrition when they are sick and the fear of death overtakes them. Suddenly, they are pious. They have deceived themselves by such superficial behaviour. If we want a good death, then we must never tempt God by living in sin and thinking somehow we will die in grace expecting at the last minute to be embraced by our heavenly king. God is not to be mocked in this manner. (Galatians 6:7)

9 July — On the emotions felt at the hour of our death

IN GENERAL THERE are five stages of grief by someone who is dying. First is a state of denial and feelings of isolation. The dying person thinks that this cannot be happening to them and they feel terribly alone. Then, comes anger in which the person usually cries out, *How dare God do this to me!* After this, the person begins to bargain with God. For example, the person asks God to let them live to see a daughter or son married or asking to be spared by promising to take better care of an old mother or father or some other obligation which they have neglected.

When none of this bargaining seems to work, depression sets in. This just makes the illness worse. Often the person thinks they cannot face going through any more of the process of dying. They often exclaim, *I cannot put my family through this! Just let me die!*

These stages of denial, feeling isolated and anger, bargaining with God, and eventual depression are natural. For most of us, we progress through these stages quickly or slowly or sometimes not at all, because we have, like all God's creatures, an over-powering *will to live*.

This *will to live* is the presence of the Holy Spirit. From the insect in the grass beneath your feet to the person nearest you at this moment, God imbues everything that lives with this *will to live*.[6] This is God's gift of life, the *being* of all Creation *in* and *of* everything. It is the centre of your existence and in the centre of all the living, because it is the place where God himself resides in the glory of his Creation.

You and every living creature, the seas, the rivers, the mountains, the very earth itself are all a temple of the Holy

---

6   Albert Schweitzer, *Out of My Life and Thought* (Baltimore: Johns Hopkins University Press, 2009), p. 147.

Spirit, because everything *is* that Creation and the name of his kingdom where he lives is called *life*. God cannot be separated from his creation. (Romans 8:31)[7]

Eventually, most men and women who know they are dying arrive at acceptance of their condition. This acceptance is when the spirit of the person takes over mind, body, and spirit. Guided now by the Holy Spirit, the person says, *I am ready. I don't want to struggle anymore.* Then, the person can relax in mind and body. Denial, isolation, anger, and resentment are gone. The fight against death is over. God has taken charge of the situation. The Holy Spirit reigns in the dying person. Such acceptance takes the form of finally accepting the will of God.

This is a profound final measure of faith in God's love and mercy. We have put ourselves into his mercy and compassion, as we should do all of our life. Our destiny belongs as it always did to him alone. The heart is at peace and together with the spirit it will say, *My heart is ready, O God, my heart is ready.* (Psalm 56:8)

---

7   St. Teresa of Avila, *Interior Castle, Seventh Mansions*, Chapter 2.

10 July—On never being alone in life or death

E OFTEN THINK we are forgotten. This is especially true if we live alone and even more so if we get ill. Having grown children or grandchildren or family living close by does not necessarily guarantee that we will never feel neglected. Whether this is true or not, we should be thankful. This thanksgiving is for our blessings including, especially in this case, the love we have enjoyed from others. It does not matter if it is now or in the past.

Sadly, our feelings of being alone often lead us to feel self-pity and despair or even anger. We forget that if we are to accept God's blessing we must also accept the suffering that befalls us. (Job 2:10) Indeed, in our suffering we should imitate the example set by Jesus himself and bear our cross with patience. In any case, judgment belongs to God alone and this applies to how we feel about members of our family and our friends. Only God can read what is in their hearts.

When we think we are alone and neglected we are in error, because a Christian can never be truly alone and is never neglected. It is impossible, since God never deserts us and Christ is always with us to give us consolation and comfort. In addition to these heavenly blessings, we also have the presence of our Guardian Angel, who has been at our side since the moment we were born.

Guardian angels and, indeed, the whole host of heavenly angels have an ancient history in the lives of men and women. They are there to help and comfort us. The incidences of such heavenly actions and appearances by Guardian Angels are not just those recorded in Holy Scripture, but have happened and continue to happen in the lives of ordinary men and women even if they go unrecorded in books and official records of the church. (Matthew 18:10; Daniel 10:4; Acts 12:6–12; Hebrews 1:13–14; Psalms 16: 6–7 & 91:11)

This being the case, we should not forget to turn to our Guardian Angel when we pray or we are feeling down about our life. In this way we acknowledge this holy presence and welcome it into our life. Here is a short prayer you might say to your own Guardian Angel: *My Guardian Angel ever bright, heaven sent to watch over me. Whisper to me of God above and bring me Christ's delight.*

The next time you are lonely remember that Jesus is always with you. Seek his company. Talk to him as your friend. Listen to him as your teacher. Let him help you with the comfort of his consolations. Remember to call on your Guardian Angel for help in not falling into judgment of the affection and sense of duty of those around you. Always be thankful and model any suffering on that example of obedience to God that Jesus showed us.

11 July—Feast of Saint Benedict of Nursia

AINT BENEDICT'S RULE for living in a religious community has been used by monasteries for over 1,500 years. The reason it has lasted so long and continues to be relevant is that it is generous and wise about human nature. It is a rule of living that works for men and women who want to live together in the peace of charity, the virtues of forgiveness and humility, the teachings of the Church, and in obedience to the precepts of God's commandments.[8]

However, it is not only nuns and monks who benefit from this rule. It also helps those who live an ordinary life in the world. We find the things covered by Saint Benedict's rule are practical, inspirational, and profoundly spiritual.

First and foremost in this great rule is that we put nothing before the work of God. This means going frequently to God in prayer and contemplation. It means seeking nourishment by meditating on his holy Word. (Matthew 4:4) It means fulfilling vows of charity, poverty, and obedience in the *Household of God*.

Saint Benedict instructs us *to listen* with our heart, because it is from this kind of inner hearing that love springs. Such charity is necessary if we are live in peace with others.

He asks us to have stability and balance in the way we live. This stability of self and place helps us to remain focused on God instead of always seeking the novelty of the new and displacing ourselves physically, emotionally, and intellectually, all of which brings anxiety and stress. With stability of self and place, we can more easily remain in that peacefulness which brings a healthy balance to our life.

---

8   David Parry OSB, *Households of God; The Rule of St. Benedict*, Trans. Justin McCann; Adalbert de Vogue, *La Règle de saint Benoit, VII, Commentaire doctrinal et spiritual; Rule of Saint Benedict*, Trans. Abbot Parry OSB.

As to his advice on possessions, he tells us to be attached to nothing, to live simply, and to possess little. This helps us to live an uncluttered life and to avoid greed, pride, and many other vanities of this world. In short, *less is more.*

Regarding other people, we are not to judge. Judgment and justice are the privileges only of God and, therefore, must be left to him. The guiding rule is that we are to practice forgiveness and treat every man or woman as if each were Jesus Christ himself. Charity once again dictates the way we are to live.

While in a religious life, we may owe obedience to a superior or to a bishop, but obedience in the ultimate sense is always obedience to God. In this obedience, we must not waver.

Finally, Saint Benedict writes of how necessary prayer is for our life in Christ. Here is the *Work of God.*[9]

These guide lines of listening, stability, balance, possessions, obedience and prayer written so long ago by Saint Benedict are the values by which all Christians should live, because they reflect the teachings of Jesus and fulfil the commandments of God.

---

[9]   *The Rule of St. Benedict,* 26–40.

12 July — Saint Benedict on humility

 aint Benedict reminds us that whoever exalts himself shall be humbled and whoever humbles himself shall be exalted. (Luke 14:11) He shows us that, like Jacob, we ascend a ladder of humility to God through stages or steps. (Genesis 28:4) He explains that there are twelve such steps of humility. Here are the first five:

The first step, he writes, is that a person should always keep the fear of God before his eyes. (Psalm 38:2) Such fear is based on respect for God. This makes us humble.

The second step we take is to love the will of God more than our own will. This echoes Jesus when he declared that he had come not to do his own will, but that of the one who had sent him. (John 6:38) This stirs in us the virtue of humility as we reach out to God.

The third step reflects the faithful obedience of Jesus to the will of his father in heaven, because he was obedient even unto death. (Philippians 2:5–11) We can follow Jesus in this by being obedient to our lawful authorities, but we do this out of charity for the well-being of our community and not because of force or fear. This kind of obedience makes us humble before men and women. (1 Peter 2:4–5)

The fourth step of humility is to embrace our suffering with patience during difficult and even unjust situations. We must bear our cross and be steadfast. (Matthew 10:22, 16:24–26; 1 Peter 3:17) In all this, we are helped by the knowledge that we are not asked to bear more than is possible for us. (Romans 7:14–25; Psalm 65:10 & 21:20) This deepens our understanding of God's mercy and fills us with humility.

If we are to safeguard humility, Benedict recommends a fifth step, which is regular confession of any secret wrongdoing we have hidden in ourselves. This wrongdoing is what we have done or omitted to do, especially in not loving others, and when our thoughts have turned away from God. Here is the cleansing power of God's forgiveness.

Use these five steps given by Saint Benedict for love of Christ and to keep humble.

13 July — On further steps to humility

 AINT BENEDICT TELLS us further that in order to have humility we must be content with a lowly status in the eyes of the world. To be humble in this way, we need to accept our fragile nature and that of others. All of us must plead guilty for often being ignorant about how others feel. We hear what they think but fail to recognize how they feel. Thus, we need to confess to God: I was stupid and did not understand, no better than a beast in your sight. (Psalm 72:22–24)

By acknowledging to God our confusion about how others and we may actually feel, we are humbled. In this humbled state, we are now in a better position to understand God's commandments, because we are not awash with vanity and no longer believe that we are important in this world and, especially, that we can know someone's deepest feelings. We have emptied ourselves of the demon of pride as best we can.

The next step in humility is one we often forget or neglect. It is about how we have squandered the many unique and beautiful talents that God has given to each of us.

Everyone has a special gift, no matter his or her intelligence, education or worldly status. Many people simply refuse to believe that they have these talents or special gifts, but everyone no matter who they are, has such gifts from God. A neglect or refusal to believe that we have such gifts shows that we do not believe in the promises of God. (Psalm 88:15) Awareness of this fault brings humility, because in failing to accept our gifts and to use them, we are failing God. We have refused his grace. This should make us very humble indeed.

The eight and last step in humility written about by Benedict seems at first to only apply to nuns and monks, because it is about upholding the Rule of Saint Benedict in a monastic communal life. What Benedict tells us is to do nothing except what is commended by the common Rule of the monastery and the example of the elders.

This maintains peace in the Community, but such a Community is found also in our family, our neighbourhood, town, and country. Indeed, our community is the whole world.

So this rule of Saint Benedict's puts first the well being of everyone else. How this applies to us outside monasteries is clear, because putting everyone else's well being before our own is to love our neighbour as God commanded.

Now, the reality is that even for hermits everyone lives in a community of some kind. There are always *others* some-place, near or far. So in this way, just as in the monastery, we are part of a community. This community can be a monastery but it is more likely to be our town, neighbourhood, family, or household.

Peace is what we want and pray for in this common life in any community. Here is the very place where we can practice love. Here in a community is where we find the people who are the body of Christ that is his church. We must seek as well to keep peace in the church itself for that too is a community, the community of believers, the holy community of souls. In all this we follow the example of charity set by Jesus.

Therefore, this last step of Saint Benedict on the ladder of humility is that we should abide by those rules of our community that make for peace between people and reflect the commandment to love our neighbour as ourselves. It does not matter whether that community is in a monastery or somewhere in the world or, indeed, the world itself.

14 July—On finding humility in silence and solitude

 HE APOSTLE JAMES warns us *that the tongue is a fire, a world of iniquity, and no person can tame it, because the tongue is full of deadly poison.* (James 3:6–12) Therefore, we must never trust our tongue, because it holds the power of life and death. Every judge and every victim knows this. Every command of the powerful, every injustice in this world, and every fair or unfair sentencing have words behind it.

St. John of the Cross declared that silence was God's first language, because it is only when we are silent and our tongue still that we can listen to God.[10]

Silence for Saint Benedict's Rule is his ninth step on the way to humility. He reminds us that a talkative person who goes about aimlessly chattering and is always in a flood of words cannot avoid sinning. (Psalm 140:3–4; Proverbs 10:19) Indeed, how often our talking to another person turns from idle words into the shame of gossip.

The problem with talking too much is that it eventually leads into our not listening to others. Such not listening to others takes away our means of understanding them. This lack of understanding the other person and how they are feeling affects our charity. Much talking, as mentioned before, also easily falls into gossip. Gossip quickly becomes secrets, whispers, slanders, and rumours. Most of these become false and deceitful in the repeating of them. Words are added to words until truth is distorted. We are told many times in both the Old and New Testaments to avoid gossip. (Ephesians 4:29; Proverbs 15:2 & 16:28; Psalm 33:14; 100:5; Ecclesiasticus 19:15–16) It always leads to disobedience of the commandment to love your neighbour, because gossip almost always lacks charity about others.

---

10 St. John of the Cross, *The Spiritual Canticle,* 1578.

If we are to learn to guard our tongue, it is necessary to practice solitude. In solitude we can find silence. In silence we can learn much about the nature of the spirit. We learn not to be always seeking the diversion and novelty of companionship, but to appreciate our own company and that of God. Solitude gives us an opportunity to listen to our inner voice, to gain a deeper understanding of how we feel, and to savour our joys and sorrows. When we find ourselves in such solitude, we should let go of our worries. We can become calm. We are able to make peace with ourselves and with the world around us. We move closer to Christ, because justice is sown in peace to those who make peace. (James 3:13)

These are some of rewards for guarding our tongue and being very careful when we do speak. It is the best way to live in harmony with others.

15 July—On laughter and the spiritual life

 HE WORLD IS very cruel so it seems harsh not to take every opportunity to laugh, but Saint Benedict warns us to watch out that we do not indulge in *excessive* laughter.

He says this, because those who are given too easily to laughter often take their lives too lightly. In this way, they forget that the holy journey they are on is a serious matter.

Instead of just being superficial about ourselves, we should laugh when *appropriate*. Saint Benedict tells us that our laughter should be *sincere*. Our laughter shouldn't just be for the sake of politeness. If it is, then it is insincere and hypocritical. Instead, our laughter should be good natured and joyous, using encouraging words when speaking to others, words that build up and do not pull down. (Ephesians 4:29 & 32) The same goes for smiling, so smile often and mean it.

Above all, we should be considering of others and how they feel. By our laughter, we should not embarrass them or in any way mock them. To do this is to alienate their affection and condemn yourself before God through your humiliation of another person. The kind of laughter that is misplaced humour lacks real joy. It demonstrates no love for the other person. By such wayward actions as these you show yourself to be judging others, which is forbidden. (Luke 6:37–38; Matthew 7:1–2)

Laughter, of course, has its place in our lives. To smile often and to laugh are to reflect joy in living and it raises the morale of those who look on your face, but the cautionary note about laughing from Saint Benedict is helpful if our aim is to please both God and our neighbour.

16 July—Memorial of Our Lady of Mount Carmel

UR LADY OF Carmel is none other than Mary, the woman favoured by God. This woman gives us the example of spiritual perfection by her obedience to the will of God.

But where does the word *Carmel* come from? Mount Carmel is a rugged mountain area located in modern day Israel. Its name in Hebrew means *God's vineyard.* The collection of early hermits, who once lived there, were like a fruitful vine, seeking God in silence, recollection, and prayer. They produced the harvest, which we know today as the world wide religious order of the Carmelites, named after the holy mountain where they had lived for so long. They see Mary as the model of inspiration in following an interior life given to prayer and contemplation.

Through out its more than 800 year history, the Carmelites have been inspired as well by Elijah the prophet. On Mount Carmel, Elijah challenged his people to choose one God for Israel. He told them, *God lives in whose presence I stand.* The Carmelites try to follow this model of holy wisdom by recognizing God in everyone they meet and serve. (1 Kings 18:20–39) This reflects the teachings of Jesus himself and Saint Benedict echoes this in his Rule when he tells us that *all who arrive as guests are to be welcomed like Christ.*[11]

The Carmelite Saint, Teresa of Avila, regarded Christ not just as her Saviour but as her dearest friend. Based on this, she declared that prayer is a conversation with a beloved friend. If Christ, then, is our friend, shouldn't we speak often with him? Isn't this what dear friends do?

---

[11] *Rule of St. Benedict*, 3, para.1.

17 July — The dark night of the soul

 NYONE WHO SEEKS God suffers at some point from what Saint John of the Cross, a Carmelite monk, called *the dark night of the soul*. It is a time when we feel abandoned and lost. A time of feelings often called *dryness* when all seems meaningless and we feel that God has forgotten us. We search for reasons and find none. We pray but our words seem hollow. It is a period of spiritual desolation It is, indeed, a dark night for our soul.

You do not have to be a mystic like Saint John of the Cross for this spiritual desolation to happen to you. For Christians, such desolation, such dryness of the spiritual life can be a mystical stage on their journey with God. It is a time when we feel discouraged, forgotten, and abandoned. Like the psalmist we cry out, *O God, listen to my prayer, do not hide from my pleading!* (Psalm 54:2) Millions of God-fearing and prayerful men and women and many saints have felt this despair. It is often part of our seeking God.

Since God is everywhere and in all things, where there is darkness so there must eventually be light. The best response in our darkest moments of faith is to keep searching for God. Keep praying. Do not give up.

Instead, fill yourself with hope. Trust in God. Recall his promises. Ask for mercy. In this way you will not feel alone. After all, God never really deserts you. The consolations of divine love will return to you. These will show you the way out of your spiritual desolation. Like Saint John of the Cross and millions of other believers, you will eventually return to God's embrace. All your fear, sense of desolation, and darkness of the soul will be vanquished.

So when hope seems to have fled from our heart and we feel forgotten and find we seem lost in that dark night of the soul, then appeal to Christ. We think we are alone, but we are not — Christ is *always* with us.

So turn to him now. Listen again to his teachings. Learn how much he loves you.

Many of us may live alone or often feel forgotten and this too is a kind of dark night of our soul. But we have no need to be lonely or to hunger excessively after human companionship, because we have Christ with us. The dark night will pass and faithful Mary, the Star of the Sea, and Christ the beloved, who is the light of the world, will guide us safely home.[12]

---

[12] *Ave Maris Stella* and St. Thomas Aquinas.

18 July — On the benefits of doing nothing

 E OFTEN PRIDE ourselves on how clever we are. We like to think we can do multiple things at the same time. For example, stirring the soup while talking on the mobile at the same time as watching the television news. Doing three things all at the same time! How pleased we are with our ability to be so busy.

This *being busy* is a virtue according to worldly wisdom and considered to be something of which to be proud. Being able to multi-task is something many people brag about. It is a modern conceit.

So it follows that to be still and apparently to be doing nothing is considered lazy or eccentric by most people. To do nothing is quite out of fashion. Yet, it can promote the biochemistry and responses of our body that make for good health. Doing nothing can be an act of healing.

Long before science did research about our brain and meditation and mindfulness became fashionable and before we made multi-tasking popular, Jesus told us all we need to know about the benefits of just being still. He told us not to worry about things and to accept life as it unfolds without anxiety or trying to do something about it. He told us that the lilies in the fields do not labour and yet flourish and that our time on earth is short and withers and dies like grass. (Luke 12:27; Matthew 6:28–31; 1 Peter 1: 24) Jesus tells us that being busy for the sake of being busy does not progress our spiritual life. Most people are so occupied with daily living that they neglect their spiritual life, forgetting God. They are concerned only with the passing things of this world. They worry constantly about those things which do not affect the life of their soul here or in the future. Are you one of these people? Undoubtedly, the story about Mary and Martha teaches us all we need know about our priorities in life. (Luke 10:38–42)

However in apparently doing nothing, we can in fact be very busy in our interior life. We can make ourselves available for the Holy Spirit. In seeking this calmness in which we are apparently doing nothing, we avoid pride since our attention is on spiritual matters.

In short, we must not become so busy that we forget the presence of God in our life. It is with stillness that we are able to listen and know him. (Psalm 47:10) It is with waiting and preparation that we give Christ space to fulfil his majesty in our lives and to raise us above our human weaknesses. In this way, our salvation becomes a new reality. (Psalm 61:2) We bloom with the lilies in the field.

If this is the case, then we cannot make our lives hectic, anxious and over-filled with activities. We balance what we must do with our need for stillness, being calm, and at peace with the world and ourselves. We withdraw into our interior life to make space and time for the holy. Our faith comes through hearing the Word and it is best heard in the circumstances of stillness and apparently doing nothing. (Romans 10:17; Lamentations 3:*Tet* 26)

19 July — On the benefits of solitude

HE APOSTLE LUKE tells us that Jesus would withdraw to isolated places and pray. Also when the apostles were weary of the large crowds gathered around them, Jesus told them to go somewhere by themselves to a desolate place and rest a while. Jesus often withdrew to an isolated place where he prayed alone. (Luke 5:16) Here, Jesus teaches us the importance of solitude in our lives. This solitude helps us to step away from the busy world. In such solitude, like Jesus, we rest in the peaceful embrace of God.

But solitude with its surrounding stillness and lack of noise and distractions is rare today. Cities may have parks but deserts are in far lands. Praying in church, we find ourselves amidst chattering people and often there is music. It is difficult to concentrate, let alone feel any degree of solitude. At home few of us have a space to which we can withdraw from our family and others. Even in the countryside we usually hear traffic in the distance. In cities desolate places are almost impossible to discover. Most of us live in urban environments and this makes solitude truly hard to find. We can go on a retreat and that can be good for us in mind, body and spirit, but solitude and rest even on a retreat can be difficult to achieve.

The physical solitude we need is a place where there is silence or at least where it is relatively quiet. Here, we can empty our minds of worries and relax our bodies from their hectic round of activities. This is why Jesus told us that when we pray, we should go to our room and shut the door and pray to God in secret and alone. (Matthew 6:6)

Such solitude gives us inner space, a place where God may have his presence felt. This gives us the best situation in which to pray without distractions or interruptions. Solitude's accompanying silence brings us that necessary peacefulness in which we can find rest for mind and body. In such peacefulness, we can enter our interior self. Here is that place of more perfect solitude, that inner place of interior desert, where our heart can invite the Holy Spirit to become more active in our life. Then, our spirit soars and finds itself in rightful first place.

All this is yours in that solitude of inner space, which Jesus called *desolate*. It is not really desolate in the sense of ruin or unfriendliness but simply empty of the world's distractions. It could not, in fact, be a more beautiful place for all our senses and intelligence are gathered into the mystery of heaven. It is filled with treasures of the spirit, invisible at first, then gradually appearing to us. We will be prompted to pray, because everything without and within us is ready for this most secret and precious conversation with God. We will be raised above the spoiled and selfish values of the world. We will be made whole again and find completion through the state of love.

Could we ask for more benefits from that solitude which is our being alone with God?

20 July — On the benefits of simplicity

OLY SCRIPTURE SPEAKS of simplicity in our lives. We are told we brought nothing into the world and we can take nothing out of it, but as long as we have food and clothing we should be content with that. (1 Timothy 6:6–10)

Just to make certain that we understand that we are to keep our lives simple and not cluttered with worldly values, vices, and possessions, the Apostle goes on to warn us that people who long to be rich are prey to trial. They get trapped into all sorts of foolish and harmful ambitions that plunge them into ruin. He concludes that the love of money is the root of all evils and there are some, who in pursuing it, have wandered away from the faith and so given their soul any number of fatal wounds. They have become ill in mind, body, and spirit.

Wisdom then is not to be found in a life lived for possessions, social prestige, worldly power, and being busy with nothing more than passing distractions or entertainment.

The first and most important benefit of living a more simple life is that we keep focused on God. If we keep daily life as simple as possible, seeking the presence of God will arise, because our mind is not cluttered with ambitions and our body not tired from working for material goods. We have room for the spirit to flourish.

We know that no one can add a single hour to his or her life span by worry. (Matthew 6:27) Believe it or not *less is often more* when it comes to contentment. A great many people believe *more is better* but this is an illusion. Ask most of the wealthy — they will tell you that treasure does not bring contentment. Be assured that when we set aside the accumulation of what the world deems wealth, many people will criticize us or deem us lazy or tells us that we are not ambitious enough. However, when we find joy in simplicity and seek God, he will add to our blessings in many ways.

(Matthew 6:32–34) Thus, the benefits of simplicity are manifold. (Deuteronomy 28:1–8)

Our boast should be that we live in the world simply and that we able to live this way by the grace of God and not because we are wise in the ways of the world. (2 Corinthians 1:12-14)

So why not start today to reduce the clutter of possession that surrounds you—those clothes, shoes, china, pots and pans, all the other stuff you have not used in years, because we cannot live simply if we have more than we truly need. As to excessive savings at the bank, share what extra money you may have with the poor and needy, because you know that *it is easier for a camel to go through the eye of a needle than for someone who is rich to enter the kingdom of God.* (Mark 10:25, Luke 18:25,

If we make love our guide and the teachings of Jesus the manifesto by which we live, then all the benefits of simplicity will be a harvest of blessings for us.

21 July — On the benefits of solidarity

OLIDARITY HOLDS MUCH meaning in the Christian life, because it is the expression of a union by individuals brought together by their common interest. For Christians, such solidarity comes from sharing religious beliefs. It means we have unity, harmony, stability, cohesion, team spirit, a singleness of purpose, and like-mindedness in a community of shared interests. Does this sound like the Church of which you are part? If not, then make it so. Isn't this the basis of the relationship you desire with other Christians? If not, then make it so.

Such solidarity means Christians recognize that we are *one* in Christ. We practice this truth by the way in which we live our daily life. Since we are all equal in the sight of God and there is neither Jew nor Greek, neither slave nor free, and no male or female in God, why not make this *one in Christ* a living truth? (Galatians 3:25–29) After all, we are all one, because we were all baptized into the one body and drink of the one spirit. (1 Corinthians 12:13) Here is the foundation of our solidarity.

This sense of oneness should not be just about our fellow humans, but be extended to all God's creation– his animals, plants, the bees and insects, the waters of rivers and seas, the leaf that falls, the leaf that holds tight. Indeed, all Creation shares this earth with us. We are related and connected to each and everything around us. But our oneness with everything else is a reality. To believe we are superior or not related to other forms of life or that we are not one together in creation with all other life is to be arrogant and dismissive of what God has created. For example, the next time you throw away a plastic cup in the sea and a fish swallows it and dies, then you are throwing God's creation away as well. (Genesis 1–31)

The feeling of being one with everything in creation is an awareness raised up in us by the Holy Spirit, because in feeling this way we are showing a reverence for life, that *the will to live* which God has given to each and every living being.[13]

This will to live is both individual and collective—that is we are both individual beings while at the same time we are joined with all other life in forming the whole of God's creation. The tree in our garden bends to the same wind that blows us about. The rain is as wet on the nose of a mouse as on our nose. We cannot be separate from the tree, the wind or the mouse anymore than we can be separate from the people who may live down the street from us. The world is *one*, united in being of God. Does not Scripture exclaim: *all the trees in the wood shout for joy!* (Psalm 95:12; 1 Chronicles 16:33; Isaiah 55:12)

When we feel this awareness of being one with all Creation, whether in the smallest or grandest ways, it brings joy to the heart and wonder to the mind, because we understand that everything is *one in God*. There is no separation. When we realize that this oneness of being is our shared common ground of life, we know that everything that lives sings out in its own way: *Glory to God in the highest! Alleluia!* (Psalm 148; Luke 2:14)

When this happens, we see beyond our ordinary of daily living. We begin to understand that such a holy vision goes far beyond the landscape around us, that this vision is unlimited, universal and timeless. We begin to share as part of Creation as God knows it. Did not God find what he created *good*? (Genesis 1:31) So we bow down in thanksgiving before God, who is glorified forever in his dominion. (1 Peter 4:10–11)

---

[13] Albert Schweitzer, *The Ethics of Reverence for Life* in *Civilization and Ethics* (Macmillan New York, 1929).

22 July—Feast of Saint Mary Magdalene

 LL SCRIPTURE IS breathed out by God through the men and women he has chosen as his holy instruments. Therefore, every word, every thought, each teaching and prophecy in Scripture can be profitable for our learning, correction, training in righteousness, and inspiration. (2 Timothy 3:16-17) Yet, even with the most holy intentions we can still be confused about what Scripture is actually telling us. In this way we create myths and false stories about people in Scripture from time to time.

Such was the case with Mary Magdalene, the person named in the gospels to be the first to know Jesus was resurrected from death. (Matthew 28:1 & 9; Mark 16:9; John 20:11–18) But this holy and beloved woman was been presented to Christians for many generations as an example of the sinner who finds redemption with a decided emphasis on the sinner part of her life. In some cultures her very name became a synonym for an unworthy immoral woman. She also became at the same time the symbol of repentance and, most of all, the prize example of devotion to Jesus. It is this latter person, a most faithful woman, whom we remember today.

The history of Mary Magdalene, so mixed up with myth and invention, tells us a lot about how different biblical interpretations can be, about the gullibility of people, and, most importantly, about how women have been viewed over the centuries. We begin to grasp how power and sanctity are understood or misunderstood, depending on cultural behaviour more than on Scripture. We learn how the past is remembered or forgotten or made into something it never was. In short, how humans, not God, see such things.

Today we understand that Mary Magdalene was a woman devoted to Jesus. We learn God gave her a holy place in the life of Jesus. For example, she was present during Jesus' Ministry, during and after his Crucifixion, and she was there at his resurrection. (Luke 8:1–3, 24; Mark 15:40 & 47, also 16:1; Matthew 27: 56 & 61, 28:1; John 19:25, 20:1–2) Indeed, she is named by the Church as one of Christ's disciples.[14]

Resolve on this day of remembrance to take this esteemed woman of God as an example of our need of devotion. Make devotion to Christ as to your beloved, because that is what he is in your life. In this way, you will surely be as pleasing to God as was Mary of Magdalene.

---

[14] See Pope Francis, *Decree of Congregation for Divine Worship* (2016) and Pope St. Gregory the Great, *Homilies on the Gospel*, 25, 1–2, 2–4 & 5.

23 July—On the spiritual basis for a Christian life

OR SAINT BENEDICT as for Saint Teresa of Avila, God is *not* somewhere else, but present at this very moment, right now, right here. Benedict and Teresa understood that once a person has entered into a relationship with God, he or she couldn't go on living with a lukewarm religious life. A person in such an unfolding spiritual journey becomes aware of the need to anchor such a life in solid spiritual guides.

Such spiritual guides are based on Scripture and have been used in daily life throughout Christian history from the Church Fathers to Mother Teresa of Calcutta. Their rich diversity of writings, sermons, bible commentaries, and holy life stories give us support in our spiritual journey. Such a treasure is an inheritance that belongs to the whole world.

Fortunately, spiritual guides are still available today to help us. Some are bishops, priests, deacons, religious, saints, or other Christians. From time to time, their objective and informed guidance is helpful on our pilgrimage to God, because they help us to bring a better clarity of vision to our journey. Their help steadies us when we may be straying from the path of God's calling.

This spiritual guidance has the effect of bringing a life focused on what God wants for the person. It is a life guided to a balance between prayer, work, and living in peace and love with others. In this way, we are able to see God is in *all* his works, including the little things of our living. As Brother Lawrence put it: *God is present even as we cook an omelette.*[15]

Such a vision of God about which Br. Lawrence speaks takes away muddled thinking, clarifies intentions, focuses

---

[15] Letters of Br. Lawrence of the Resurrection, *Practice of the Presence of God*.

minds on what we are doing, and helps us to hold to high moral standards. We are focused on what we are doing and never forget God. In this way, as Brother Lawrence pointed out, we keep God present in our life as we go about the very ordinary events of living—even when scrambling eggs. As Jesus told us, *Ask, and it will be given to you; seek and you will find; knock and it will be opened to you.* (Matthew 7:7–8)

24 July — Lessons from women in Scripture

HE BIBLE TELLS us that in God there is neither male nor female, yet we are given many examples where woman have played roles that at first may seem defined by their gender. On closer examination we find that their gender is quite incidental to their holiness. For example, Queen Esther in *The Book of Esther*.

As we learn of their stories in Scripture, all these women rise above any gender stereotype to become instruments of God's will. In the *Old Testament* especially, many of the women mentioned dared to fear nothing, risking all and becoming holy heroines. They raised themselves above self-interest, above the defined place and role of women in their society, and above consideration of what other people, even kings, might say about them. They do this in order to save their people or courageously act on behalf of what is just and righteous, prompted by God. Like the Virgin Mary herself, they become willing instruments for God intentions.

Many women are mentioned in the bible by name, but there are many more who are not identified. Each woman, named or not, has her place in the life, death and resurrection of Jesus Christ and each is an essential part of the history of God. The following are named in the bible: Mary, the mother of Jesus; Mary Magdalene; Mary Salome, wife of Zebedee; Mary and Martha of Bethany, the sisters of Lazarus; Mary of Clopas; His wives (2 Samuel 2:2, 3:2–5); Joanna; Susanna; Priscilla, Tabitha, Lydia, Phoebe, Junia, Tryphena of Rome and Tryphosa, Julia, Nympha, and Apphia. Many women, unnamed but whose presence is noted, received the power of the Holy Spirit at the Pentecost. The histories of the Jewish people and of Jesus could not be told without including women. From the very beginning, women have always been an essential part of our faith.

If women are prophets of God (Luke 2:36) and if such equality is found in Jesus Christ and if God claims no difference because of a person's gender, and if heaven itself does not recognize male from female, then we need to ask ourselves why any of us should treat a woman differently than Jesus would have done and why would we want to treat women differently than how God treats them.

Resolve to imitate Jesus in the love of everyone regardless of gender, race, religion, nationality or situation in this world.

25 July—Feast of Saint James, Apostle

HE APOSTLE JAMES was one of those disciples to whom our Lord showed a special favour in choosing him as one of the three to be witnesses of the glory of his *Transfiguration*. James was also allowed to be present when Jesus raised to life the daughter of Jairus. Jesus also took James with him when he went to pray and suffered agony in the garden.

How great must have been the faith and the love by James for Jesus for all this to happen to the disciple. How happy must be men and women, who like the Apostle James, keep close to Jesus in his holy sorrows and sufferings no less than in his holy joys and glory.

Now this means we are a spiritual dwelling place for God. We have become the palace of God. (Ephesians 2:19–22) It is as if this palace were made of a single precious jewel –a jewel that is unique, enchanting, beautiful in its perfection, and built entirely from divine love.[16] But if we are this close to Jesus and so intimate with God that his dwelling place is this splendid palace within us, then we too suffer with Jesus when he goes to his Cross and we too are with him in the joy of his resurrection. We are held fast by faith in the promises of God.

Yet, like Saint James, we also carry within us ambition and self-seeking. Even after years with Christ, the Apostle James still wanted to be the one chosen to sit at Jesus's right hand, the place of the most favoured. (Mark 10:35–45) James showed that ambition and pride still rose up in him even as he shared food with Jesus, even as he listened to his teaching, and even though he was an Apostle of the Messiah.

This example of self-concern should teach us not to assume ambition and the desires to be honoured and praised have somehow left us just because we have been following the

---

[16] St. Teresa of Avila, *The Interior Castle*.

way of Christ. It does not matter how virtuous and obedient we have been in our prayers, contemplation, loving, and in ordinary living, we remain sinners for we are still human. Our plea *God have mercy on me a sinner!* must be always on our lips or in our thoughts, because ambition and a desire to be praised are expressions of our pride and self-love and our declaration to heaven that *the spirit is willing but the flesh is weak.* (Matthew 26:41) This pride, self-love and weakness of the flesh which is in the nature of every human being waits to test us as they did with Saint James.

Today we celebrate Saint James's virtues but we also need to remember the lessons of his spiritual errors.

26 July—On making pilgrimages to sacred places

HERE ARE TWO kinds of pilgrimages. The first is an interior one in which we walk in our inner life along the path set out by Christ. We try to imitate him on this narrow way and forego the easier worldly ways we might take. This interior pilgrimage is the most difficult of all pilgrimages, because it asks us to leave self-concerns and vanities behind us and concentrate on the teachings of Jesus.

The second kind of pilgrimage is when we leave our ordinary daily life with its responsibilities, pressures of work and relationships, anxieties, and daydreams for a short time and go somewhere spiritually special or deemed sacred. For example, the Shrine at Lourdes, the Holy Land, or even to a church nearby where we sit quietly, perhaps light a candle, and be with God.

At its most basic such a pilgrimage puts us into a place where prayer is the environment. Going there promotes a renewal of the sense of the community of the faithful, the body of Christ. It allows us to focus on God without the usual interruptions and temptations of daily life. Holy sites, monasteries, the silence of churches, and retreat places all can have this effect. But do not be surprised if you meet people who are visiting as tourists, because not everyone visiting holy sites is on a spiritual pilgrimage in these days of global tourism. Be warned that you still can never read what is in another person's heart!

Whether or not you go to a sacred place by yourself or with a local group of other Christians, you will be probably more affected by the *process* of your pilgrimage than by your actual achievement in arriving, especially if you walk as many do in getting to Saint Jacques de Compostela. On your way or once there, ignore all the signs of human carelessness like discarded trash and plastic. Concentrate on the signs of God that you feel and see. Look for the Christ in others. This is what is important on our pilgrimages.

27 July—The pilgrimage route of St. James of Compostela in Spain

 ROM ALL OVER the world people now travel on this pilgrim route, which honours the Apostle, Saint James. Some go for religious or spiritual reasons. Many go as a tourist challenge. Regardless of the reason for their going, many are changed. As we know the Holy Spirit, like the wind, goes where it wants.

This pilgrimage developed in medieval times after the claimed discovery of the Apostle's burial site in what later became Santiago de Compostela in Spain. The story is that St. James' remains were brought from Jerusalem and were buried there. Later, a large church was built there to commemorate him. Once a pilgrimage made mainly by Christians, it is now one of the most popular holiday hiking challenges. It takes about four to five weeks to do the 778km (483 miles) trek through northern Spain from the Pyrenees to Santiago de Compostela and onto the North Atlantic coast. Many of the pilgrims you will meet may not be Christians. Some may be of other faiths. Indeed, many may be agnostics or even atheists. This should make no difference to you for each is a child of God and his creation. In your practice of love, there are no strangers.

Like most pilgrimages, the doing of it is what is important—that is *the process of the pilgrimage itself* is much more important than the goal of arrival. Whether Christian or not, pilgrimages to sacred places and shrines are likely to have a spiritual effect on us, because God is at work in every man and woman.

28 July—On visiting the Sanctuary of Our Lady of Lourdes

OURDES IN FRANCE is one of the most popular places of Christian pilgrimage in the world. It is visited by millions of people every year so it is almost always crowded.

The history of this great Christian shrine is a simple one: A fourteen year old peasant girl, Marie-Bernarde Soubirous (1844–79) received 18 appearances of the Blessed Virgin Mary at the Massabielle Rock in Lourdes over a period of months. During this time, a spring appeared in the grotto of the rock, the waters of which are believed to be miraculous. Almost from the beginning people visited the grotto to seek cures for their illnesses and fulfilment of their prayers. Marie-Bernarde later became a nun and is known today as Saint Bernadette. The grotto today is filled with candles, prayers, and silence, because pilgrims there are focused on *spiritual intentions*. Many seek healing and recovery, remembering that Jesus Christ told us, *If you ask me anything in my name, I will do it.* (John 14:13-14)

There have been miracles at Lourdes attested to by the Church and independent medical authorities. We have no reason to think God will not favour us but every reason to hope that his grace and mercy will descend and heal us. We only need faith and even the mountains will move. (Mark 11:22–23) Sometimes these miracles happen at Lourdes, but in any case men and women find hope there.

Hope is a cardinal virtue that springs from faith in God and his Christ and in the power of the Holy Spirit. Hope is what Lourdes and all other such sacred places offer us. It is the gift made to every pilgrim at Lourdes when he or she reaches out to God in prayer. Not everyone is favoured by a miracle of physical healing, but everyone is favoured by the miracle of hope. Hope renews all the promises of God in our heart. Hope lifts our vision to one of a better future. Hope is the healing charity of God himself.

29 July—On visiting the Basilica of Our Lady of Guadalupe in Mexico

UR LADY OF Guadalupe is the Virgin Mary who appeared to Saint Juan Diego Cuauhtlatoatzin of Mexico in 1531. Juan Diego, an Aztec descendent converted to Christianity, was walking from his village to Mexico City when the Virgin Mary appeared to him. She told him to build a church there. Not knowing what to do, he went to his Bishop, who did not believe his story and asked the poor peasant to bring him a miraculous sign to prove he was telling the truth.

The Virgin appeared to Juan Diego again and told him to gather the roses, which he found blooming at his feet even though it was winter and to take them to the bishop. Juan gathered the flowers up in his cloak and carried the bundle to the bishop. When he opened his cloak before the bishop, roses as fresh as when he picked them tumbled out to reveal an image of the Virgin Mary on his cloak. The bishop was astounded just as are millions of people, who have made the pilgrimage to the *Shrine of Our Lady of Guadalupe in Mexico* and beheld this miraculous image of Mary still on Juan Diego's cloak.

The church Mary requested was built and dedicated to *Our Lady of Guadalupe,* attracting Christians from all over the world. In the last hours of their pilgrimage many Mexican Christians make their way to the church on their knees in devotion to Mary. The original miraculous cloak containing the image of the Virgin continues to hang above the altar and by its presence invites all who see it to praise the wonderful and mysterious glory of God.

While it is true that our devotion and prayers are often enhanced by using images of Jesus Christ, his mother and those of saints to focus our attention and help us in our meditations, prayers and contemplations, we are warned by Saint John of the Cross about them. He said to treat such things as *spiritual inspiration*, which draw us closer to God and help make our real veneration for what such images, icons or statues *represent* of God and Christ and their holy servants. He reminds us that we are never to forget that these objects, no matter how holy in origin, are meant to bring us closer to God and to help us in our prayer and contemplation of him and his wonders.[17]

So we need to remember that the rosary beads you may hold, the images of Christ or Mary in paintings, statues and icons, the various pictures of your favourite saint that you may have by your bedside or which you favour when in church, and the little prayer cards tucked in your bible or Mass missal, all these are there to help you focus on God. They call us to the ways of virtue.

But remember that these are only aids to help you in your spiritual life, because there is only one God for you to worship and that God is ineffable and unknowable. You will find him perfected in his Word.

---

[17] St John of the Cross, Book 3: 35 & 36.

30 July—On praying to your favourite saint and the use of holy images

 E CAN HARDLY do better than to follow the advice of St. John of the Cross in the matter of prayers to saints and the use of various religious images.

First, Saint John points out that there can be a considerable vanity of pleasure in relation to statues, paintings, and other holy images. The aim of such images is to awaken us from our lukewarm feelings of devotion. However, he says many of us seem to rejoice more in the image than in what it represents.[18]

Saint John tells us that truly devout people direct their devotion mainly to the *invisible* object represented by the image and that they have little need for many images to spiritually stir them up. He claims they use those images that seem to project holy traits more than human ones.[19] Therefore, we should occasionally re-examine the images we use in our devotions when those images are other than of Jesus and Mary.

So it is proper to ask if the images or favoured saint we use awakens our dormant or lukewarm devotion. Our devotion should be rekindled and set aflame with love for God by our being reminded of the holy. Saint John of the Cross tells us, *Where there is devotion and faith any image will be sufficient, but if they are lacking none will suffice.*[20]

---

[18] *Ibid.*, Book 3, Chap 35: 2.

[19] *Ibid.*, Book 3, Chap 35: 5.

[20] *Ibid.*, Book 3, Chap 36: 3.

31 July—Memorial of Saint Ignatius of Loyola

OUNDER OF THE Society of Jesus, Saint Ignatius lived in the 16th century and was a priest, hermit and mystic. He developed a retreat programme lasting four weeks called *The Spiritual Exercises.* These form a process of spiritual discernment and renewal still offered on retreats around the world. This kind of retreat is still very fruitful for Christians.

Saint Ignatius believed the spiritual life to be centered on the basic tenants of the Christian faith, that is the Trinity, Jesus Christ, and the Eucharist for the greater glory of God. Those last words, *for the greater glory of God,* are the motto of the Jesuits.

To all who came to him in repentance, Saint Ignatius of Loyola recommended this prayer:

> Receive, O Lord, all my liberty. Take my memory, my understanding, and my entire will. What so ever I have or hold has been given to me by you. I give it all back to you and surrender it to be governed by your will. Give me only your love and your grace and I am rich enough and ask for nothing more.[21]

Are we willing to surrender to God like Saint Ignatius? This is the question our heart must ask. This is the question our faith poses. Until we, like Jesus himself, are willingly with gladness to submit to the will of God, we are not obedient, because in spite of all our devotions and the church services we may attend, we still believe we have control over our life.

But if we truly love God we will be happy in submission to God's will. Our heart is ready for such obedience when it is empty of all self-love. Our soul is ready when it desires God's will above all else. When this happens, we can freely choose submission to God. Then, we will find true freedom.

---

[21] Saint Ignatius of Loyola, Spiritual Exercises, No. 234.

We are released from the chains of a false belief in our control over our life. In such submission to God we are bound no longer by discontent and uneasiness about life. At long last we will have embrace the fullness of charity.

AUGUST

Theme: The promises of God and the benefits of virtue

Jesus declared to the world, Whoever believes in me, believes not in me but in the one who sent me and whoever sees me, sees the one who sent me. I have come into the world as light to prevent anyone who believes in me from staying in the dark anymore.

John 12:44–46

1 August — On being denied universal good

 OD IS THE source of universal good, the being of infinite good and the unending source of good in his creatures and creations. (Luke 18:19; Mark 10:19) Since any good comes from God alone, people who lose God's favour have lost everlasting good. There has come a gulf between God and themselves that can never be bridged. Even to imagine this is terrible. Yet millions pass their days taking God's goodness for granted and testing his patience by their trespassing of his commandments. Without repentance and reconciliation, their end will be despair, sadness, rage, and hatred. Any good has deserted them. We are left in darkness.

If we find ourselves in such a state of trespass and neglect of God's Word, then we must fear his displeasure and repent at once. We need to promise never to turn away from him again in this life. We need to be obedient to his command to love. In this way, we can hope to remain in God's goodness and in the light of his Christ.

2 *August* — *On where to find the strength to resist worldly values*

 HO CAN OVERCOME the seductions of this world? Christians know the answer, because Saint John told us: *Who can overcome the world but the one who believes that Jesus is the Son of God.* (1 John 5:5–6) So there we are — we have been told!

If we believe this to be true, then it follows that we must believe all that Jesus taught. The path he showed allows us to overcome the values of this world with that discipline and hope that is the strength of all his disciples. We have been told that Jesus himself is that holy path. *I am the way, the truth, and the life*, he told us. Moreover, Jesus added that no one could come to God except through him. (John 14:6)

Have we forgotten these basics of our faith? Are any of us still looking for solutions and answers when it has been made clear what we should do? If this should be the case, then it high time to renew our Christian discipleship.

What then is *the way* if not simply to follow the examples of love and obedience to God that Jesus himself showed us in his earthly life? What then is *the truth* we seek if not in that ultimate sacrifice that forgave all men and women through the salvation offered by Jesus? What then is *the life* but living in and with Jesus himself? In following this holy way, we are made complete with a rightness of mind, body and spirit, all of which fosters the contentment that comes from the constant presence of God in our life.

Resolve to study once again the doctrines of your faith so that Christ's message lives in your heart. (Colossians 3:16–17) In this way you will persist on the path that leads to peace. When you struggle, as surely all of us do from time to time, call on God who will increase the strength of your mind, body and spirit. (Psalm 137) Then you will find the courage we all need to overcome the temptations, false promises, and seductions of this world.

3 August — On the happiness of earthly life

VEN THOUGH THE Word of God and many holy men and women tell us that the world's praise, achievements, and admiration are vanities, we persist in running after them. Somehow we still believe that these are sources of happiness in spite of all warnings and wise words to the contrary. (Ecclesiastes 1:2)

It is true, however, that these feelings most often arise from our triumphs in this world, which are achieved through worldly values. This fools us into believing in them. At such times we feel all is right with our world and that, somehow, what we do and are in this world holds the meaning of our life. This is an assumption that almost all of us make, because it is based on how we *feel,* since we like achieving our goals and the praise and admiration that comes from winning.

But how we are feeling is the most misleading of all our senses, especially when it comes to our happiness. It is a superficial emotional moment that may please our mind and body at the time, but does little for our spirit. When this passing moment of happiness goes, as quickly as it always does, we are left searching for the next instalment of happiness in our lives. As is often said, *Happy one moment, unhappy the next.*

But if we are continually seeking to feel happy in this life by worldly values, it must mean we are seeking what will be pleasing to us rather than to others. How is this charity? How is it possible then for us to receive each man and woman as Christ himself when we are so overwhelmed with such self-love. (Matthew 25:35)[1]

None of us can achieve love for our neighbour if our goal is in worldly happiness. The joy of knowing you are pleasing to God is the happiness that last. (Psalm 43) All else is vanity. (Ecclesiastes 1–14)

---

[1] See *Rule of St.Benedict*, Chapter 53.

4 August — On the happiness of heaven

 F WE CAN know God's mercy and abounding love in this life, what then must be his magnificence to us in his heavenly kingdom? It is happiness beyond anything on earth, because God has prepared for us *what no eye has seen or ear has heard, what the mind of man cannot visualise; all that God has prepared for those who love him.* (1 Corinthians 2: 9) This happiness is *Paradise*.

God has provided us with the necessary means to obtain this heavenly happiness. Resolve now to be diligent in using all these means for your salvation, but bear in mind that God, who made us without our consent, will not save anyone without their agreement.[2]

---

[2]   See St. Augustine, *Sermon* 169,13.

5 August—The good things of Our Lord in the Land of the Living

 ONSIDER THE THINGS that most allure people and draw their affection. We all know these things to be honours, riches, and pleasures. The mistake many men and women make is that they seek these things where they are *not* to be found. False appearances fool them. Such allures are not to be found in the broad road of the world, which is full of traps baited with desires, false turnings, and misleading directions. True honours, true riches, and true pleasures are found together with all other good things in the *Land of the Living*. (Psalm 26:17; Psalm 114:9) This expression *Land of the Living* means to be fully awake and alive in God as the temple and palace of his kingdom. (Luke 17:20–21)

In this land, all the inhabitants have the highest dignity in a fellowship with God and a partnership with Christ. Here all men and women are noble, wise, and holy. All are kings and queens and their crowns shine like sunlight for they are the heirs of immortal glory. This *Land of the Living* is nothing less than heaven, that once lost Eden now returned in the fullness of God through Jesus the Messiah. Everyone there feasts on the riches of his house, they drink from the stream of his delight. (Psalm 35: 9) The great river of the water of life, which runs out from the throne of God, washes all the streets of the heavenly Jerusalem with light and nourishes the great tree of life growing upon its banks. (Revelation 22:1)

6 August—Feast of The Transfiguration of Our Lord

 ESUS TOOK PETER, James, and John up into a high mountain and was transfigured before them. They beheld his face shining like the sun and his garments turn as white as snow. Then Moses and Elias appeared and spoke with Jesus. (Luke 9:31) Peter with the glory of this vision, cried out, *Master, it is wonderful for us to be here; so let us make three shelters, one for you, one for Moses and one for Elijah.* As Peter was still speaking, a bright cloud overshadowed the three Apostles and a voice spoke out of the cloud, saying, *This is my Son, the Chosen One. Listen to him.* (Luke 35; Matthew 17:5)

This mystery of the transfiguration of Our Lord confirms our faith and adds to it the testimonies of the prophets, who bear witness to the gospel, such as shown by the appearance of Moses and Elias with Jesus. God himself testifies in all the three manifestations of himself by the voice of the Father, by the glory of Jesus the Messiah, and by the Holy Spirit in the bright cloud that appears.

7 August — The heavenly Jerusalem

 ERUSALEM IS INTERPRETED in Scripture as the vision of peace. For this reason, it is often called the *City of God*, because it is the seat of eternal peace. Saint John tells us that in this New Jerusalem *is the tabernacle of God. There, God dwells with men and women and wipes away all tears from their eyes. There, death is no more nor mourning nor sorrow, because all these things have passed away.* (Revelation 21:3–4)

This means that in this New Jerusalem there are no heat waves, no wintry colds, no harsh rains, no storms, no diseases, no pains, no conflicts or adversities of any kind near this blessed abode. What does reign there is a wonderfully bright day, a serene calm, and a solid peace. A peace never to be disturbed and always secure. A peace both within and without each person. Peace abounds.[3]

In this New Jerusalem, you would meet a multitude of people living eternally in fraternal charity, friendship, and union. Indeed, the perfect realisation of the psalmist's words in declaring, *How good and how pleasant it is when brothers live in unity!* (Psalm 132:1)

If we desire to be in this New Jerusalem, the *City of God*, we must give up the ways of Babylon, the way of sin, and as much as possible become true servants of God.

---

[3]   See Thomas à Kempis, *The Imitation of Christ*.

8 August—On the glory of the heavenly Jerusalem

 OW WONDERFUL MUST be those mansions in the heavenly Jerusalem that God prepares for his servants. We cannot begin to imagine such beauty and surely we cry out with the royal prophet, *How lovely is your dwelling place, Lord, God of hosts. My soul is longing and yearning, is yearning for the courts of the Lord.* (Psalm 84)

When we think about the heavenly Jerusalem, this City of God, we also see the glories of our earthly life. Just as God has built us many mansions in heaven, so he has given us great gifts while we remain in this world that is the waiting room of heaven.

Just consider how noble a place this waiting room on the earth really is. God has been generous beyond measure in his gifts for our life here—the sheer beauty of the sun, moon, and stars; the bounty of an infinite variety of minerals, plants, flowers, and trees; the usefulness and companionship of living creatures; the fruitfulness of a rich earth; and the nourishment of air and water. Every single thing on this earth is wonderfully made and beautiful in its own nature from the spider and its cobwebs to the arch of a human foot. Everything was created perfect in its own form. This is why an elephant is an elephant, a rose a rose, and a human a human. Each creature and creation is unique, yet sharing *the will to live*, which is the presence of God in all life.[4] It is this presence of *God as being itself* in everything on earth that makes us all one. (Acts 17:26–28)[5]

So acclaim with great joy: *Our Lord is magnificent!* (Isaiah 33 & 35:3–4)

---

[4] See Albert Schweitzer, *The Quest of the Historical Jesus; My Life & Thought.*

[5] See writings of Blessed John Duns Scotus 1266–1308 and Saint Thomas Aquinas 1225–1274.

9 August—Optional Memorial of Saint Teresa Benedicta of the Cross (Edith Stein)

t. TERESA BENEDICTA, a Carmel nun, was a martyr of the Holocaust. Her murder reminds us of the cruelty of people and we pray that the world will see the end of such inhumanity. Born of Jewish parents, Edith Stein converted to Catholicism and entered the Discalced Carmelites. Later she was sent to live in a Dutch convent for safety, but in retaliation for fascism being denounced by the Dutch bishops, the Nazis arrested all Dutch Jews who had become Christians. Sister Benedicta along with other Catholics of Jewish extraction, was arrested, transported by cattle train to the death camp of Auschwitz, and died in the gas chambers there. Today she is one of the six patron saints of Europe.

Many of us think that not to live out in the world, as in an enclosed religious life, keeps us safe and permits us to concentrate on the things of God, but this is not so. In a life of prayer and contemplation, one is drawn to others that is into the world of the living even though secluded from it. Long before she died, Saint Benedicta found this out and it provided her with a deeper understanding of her life in Christ. She wrote, *I even believe that the deeper someone is drawn to God, the more he has to "get beyond himself" in this sense, that is, go into the world and carry divine life into it.*

10 August—Feast of Saint Laurence

 HAT MADE THIS Deacon, St. Laurence, so great a saint was his charity in his love for God and for his neighbour. He understood that just as Jesus died for us, so we should be prepared to die for the sake of others. When such a choice faced him, St. Lawrence acted accordingly imitating Jesus in his death. Many Christians today still die rather than deny Christ.

Loving life in this world means living according to the standards of God and not those of the world. Further, that the servant of the Christ must follow him and where Christ is found, there also his servant must be. We can all be martyrs of Christ by at least dying to ourselves for the love of him. (John 12: 24) If Christ was humble and obedient, why then should any of us be proud? (Philippians 2:6–8)[6]

Honour the martyr Saint Laurence by imitating his constancy in the cause of God and by his love for God and his neighbour. This means we must cast out all self-love. This is the best way to celebrate his feast.

---

[6]   St. Augustine, *Sermon* 304,1–4.

11 August—The glorified in heaven

T OUR RESURRECTION, our bodies will be wonderfully changed. *This perishable nature of ours must put on imperishability and this mortal nature must put on immortality. What was sown is contemptible but what is raised is glorious, what is sown is weak but what is raised is powerful and what is sown as the natural body is raised up as a spiritual body.* (1 Corinthians 15) In short, both the body and the soul will be immortal.

We are told the very least of God's servants in that eternal kingdom shall be far more beautiful than anything that can be seen here on earth or even represented by man's imagination. The upright, said our Lord, will shine like the sun in the kingdom of their father. (Matthew 13:43)

Just the thought of such a beautiful change in us should be enough to spur us on to imitate Christ and please God. Hopefully, our devotion to such a life will earn us a place in paradise. Everything there will be beautiful, including us if we get such judgment.

12 August — On a happy eternity

 HILE THE REWARDS of heaven are eternal, the honours, riches, and pleasures of this world are short and momentary. They are just like a little puff of steam, which appears for a time then vanishes, never to be seen again. (James 4:14) It is in their worldly nature not to stay with us for very long, no matter how much we may want them to do so and no matter what powers or riches we hold in this world.

The thought of this inspired St. Teresa with a contempt of all those things that pass away with time and filled her with a desire to give her life to Christ, because the things of heaven are eternal. She often repeated again and again the following word when contemplating heaven: *Forever. Forever. Forever.*

Conclude to take to your heart the delight of paradise, that *forever* which fully satisfies the yearning thirst of our spirit. Sing out your praise in hope for that promised land of forever —*how blessed then must they be that dwell in your house, O Lord. Forever and forever I shall praise you. How lovely is your dwelling place, Lord Almighty! My soul yearns, even faints, for the courts of the Lord.* (Psalm 83)

13 August — On conforming to the will of God

 HO WOULD NOT wish that his or her own will was always in perfect union with the will of God? Such a union would be a perfection of love. This kind of love resembles the love of the angels and, like them, we become heralds of praise, glorifying God with all the heavenly choirs.

However, most of us in our frail humanity cannot achieve such a high standard. But *trying* for such love is what is important, because the most acceptable offering we can make to God is our willingness to please him. No matter what else we give him as long as we keep any part of our own will from him, we have withheld our love. He claims our whole being without reserve and asks that we give him all of our heart. (Proverbs 23:26)

When we give God our heart, it is in Christ as well. This means we are given back a new heart in return, a heart in union with God through Christ. We possess a new heart and with it a new life, a life in which we give our will over to God. We become the *New Adam*, the *New Eve*.

At best, most Christians manage to give God a divided heart, a heart always going back and forth from the values and vices of this world to the practice and virtues of a new life in Christ. This divided heart makes us unhappy and discontent. No sooner do we feel settled in obedience to God, than the world beckons us into sin. Our path of life is filled with many traps of temptation.

When we find we are drawn away from the things of God into the things of this world, remember anyone who is in Christ is a *new* person. Old things have passed away and a new life has been given to us. (2 Corinthians 5:17) We do not, therefore, conform to this world and its values, but we are changed by our new life so that we may prove that the will of God is good and perfect. (Romans 12:2)

So we must believe in our new life and not just pay lip service to it. We must let our whole heart be ready for God. (Psalm 57:8)

14 August—Memorial of Saint Maximilian Kolbe

HEN A PRISONER escaped at the Auschwitz concentration camp, ten others were sentenced to death. Seeing that one of those sentenced to die was a father, Maximilian volunteered to take his place. His request was granted and he was sentenced to death by starvation. In that prison of cruelty, he sowed love and showed us that our actions are what count in a life in Christ. He is said to have spoken these words when the Nazi persecution was raging: *Hatred is not a creative force: only love is creative.*[7]

As their slow starvation began in the darkness of their prison cells, there was no crying out or screaming. The prisoners with Saint Maximilian sang with hearts full of courage in God, echoing those three young men thrown into the fiery furnace of King Nebuchadnezzer, who singing in one voice, glorifying and blessing God. (Daniel 3:51–90, Psalm 148) In our own moments of trouble and despair do we cry out in despair or do we sing praises to God. The crying out will bring us nothing but more despair while the second one of praise will bring us hope and courage, strengthening our faith.

Saint Maximilian's death was not a spur of the moment act of heroism. His whole life had been a preparation for this moment. When that moment arrived, he was able to answer with an act of love, imitating Jesus.

The lesson we learn from his example is that the practice of love in imitation of Jesus prepares us for the challenges of this life and the gaining of favour with God for the next. This practice of love must be for us, as it was for Saint Maximilian, not an occasional thing but a way of life.

---

[7] See Pope Benedict XVI, *Discourse* (13 August 2008).

15 August—Solemnity of the Assumption of the Blessed Virgin Mary

 E MAY WONDER at how few times Mary is mentioned in Scripture, either directly or indirectly. The reason is a simple one, because each time Mary is mentioned her actions and reactions set before us outstanding examples of true faith in God. It is by her willing obedience to God that Jesus was born. It is by her good parenting with Joseph that he was raised to manhood and able to set out upon his holy mission to the world. At the marriage at Cana, it is by her declaration that everyone should do as Jesus says that we understand we are to be obedient to him. It is by her forbearance at his crucifixion that we understand that we are *never* to forsake Jesus, no matter how terrible our situation or how broken our heart.

Rejoice on this day then in the remembrance of Mary. Pray often these words that echo that declaration of this most favoured of women who changed the world by her obedience to God: *My soul proclaims the greatness of the Lord and my spirit rejoices in God my Saviour.* (Luke 1:46–55)

16 August—Lessons from the story of Martha and Mary

 N THE STORY of the visit by Jesus to Martha and Mary, we are shown two ways of devotion to God and which one Jesus values the most. Jesus came to a village where a woman named Martha welcomed him into her house. She had a sister called Mary, who sat down at the Lord's feet and listened to him speaking. Now Martha, who was busy with all the serving, came to him and said, *Lord, do you not care that my sister is leaving me to do the serving all by myself? Please tell her to help me.* But Jesus told her, *Martha, Martha, you worry and fret about so many things, and yet few are needed, indeed only one. It is Mary who has chosen the better part, and it is not to be taken from her.* (Luke 10:38–42)

How very differently these two holy sisters were at that moment—the one being busy serving and full of care in providing hospitality for our Lord while the other sat at his feet, still and silent, listening to him. Both were dedicated in different ways to his love and service. In this they represent to us two different kinds of lives of the servants of God: the active life and the contemplative life.

We might say these are two different kinds of functions in the Christian life. One function is the active life consisting of an action with good intentions for the service of Jesus Christ. This is what Martha was doing. The other function, the contemplative life, is one of spiritual devotion. This is what Mary was doing.

Both of these functions are good and highly commendable in the life of a Christian, because both of them are done for the love of God. Yet, the sister Mary in her attentive contemplation of listening to the *Word of God* is to be preferred and we are told this by Jesus himself. (Luke 10:42)

Are we like Martha, worrying about so many things, finding stress over worldly ideals of hospitality that we leave no time for listening or studying the *Word of God*? Are we rushing about in service to God so much that our spirit never has a moment's rest in his *Word*? Are we always a Martha and never a Mary?

17 August—Further lessons from Martha and Mary

 OW HAPPY WERE these sisters when given the opportunity to receive Jesus into their house, to entertain him there, to hear his word, and to converse familiarly with him. Just imagine if we had lived at that time and had been so favoured. But think for a moment and you will see that Jesus Christ offers you such a favour today, because he is here among us, abiding in the Blessed Sacrament, embracing us within himself, filling our lives with meaning, and helping us to find hope, faith, and charity. Sometimes we are a Martha. Sometimes we are a Mary. Both are disciples of Christ.

18 August—More lessons from Martha and Mary

 HE JESUS' MEETING with Martha and Mary echoes the holy devotion of his mother herself. Let us read again about this event, bearing in mind the significance of it in terms of the Virgin Mary. We see that Martha was busy serving the needs of Jesus just as his own mother did in raising him along with the help of Joseph, both making certain that Jesus was well fed, clothed, warm, and kept in good health. Yet, where did his beloved mother's service begin and end?

It begun with God, because when the Angel spoke, Mary heard with her heart as well as her ears. She trusted in the will of God and submitted freely to his plan for her life. So Mary first began her service to Jesus by listening to God just as Mary the sister in the Gospel did when Our Lord visited her and her sister, Martha.

We also know by the events at the wedding in Cana that his mother did not stop listening to Jesus after her original obedience to God. (John 2:1–11) When the wine ran out at the wedding Mary told Jesus, but he replied, *Woman, what do you want from me? My hour has not yet come.* Mary simply turned and said to the servants, *Do whatever he tells you.*

We do not know what Mary thought of his mysterious but prophetic words, but what she says in few simple words affirms that the *Word of God* is both her earthly son and her heavenly Lord. Her expectation that he will be able to do something about the wine is an act of faith in him as holy, since she could have no other reason to expect a carpenter's son to be able to perform miracles. Her expectation is for something beyond natural human ability. She is not disappointed because Jesus turns the water into wine.

This marks his first miracle and the beginning of his ministry. It also shows us Mary's faith in Jesus arises because her faithfulness never wavers, since God is always present in her heart. Like Mary, the sister of Martha, the mother of Jesus has chosen the better part and it is not to be taken from her. (Luke 10:42)

In these lessons taught by the Lord's visit to the two sisters and through the events from the Angel speaking to Mary to the wedding at Cana, we know to keep our heart always on God even in the midst of the duties of an active life. We need to be both active and contemplative. In this way we shall never forget that the *Word of God* is eternal and that his truth lasts from generation to generation. (Psalm 118:89–91)

19 August — On self-denial

 HE ENEMY OF love of God is the vice of self-love. The world tells us that it is permissible to try to get all that we may think will make us happy. *Grab! Grab! Grab! More! More! More!* are the world's slogans and instruction. It all amounts to greed, the result of self-love. This includes material things, power, wealth, social position, and fame. Yet, we know from our experience as well as that of observing others that real happiness does not follow automatically from even the most rewarded self-love and that such happiness if it comes is short-lived and fleeting.

Further more, self-love demands the constant replenishment of what may please us at any given moment. Such unrelenting demand for the constant satisfying of this fleeting happiness of self-love brings stress and no peace. How quickly we feel disappointment. How rapidly we can descend to depression and sadness in the midst of plenty. Self-love has an unquenchable thirst and hunger, always demanding more from us.

Self-love, therefore, leads not to any lasting happiness but to an insatiable yearning to always satisfy our craving for *more.* Such is the nature of greed. If we have plenty and many comforts and yet wonder at the lack of meaning in our life and why we want yet more when we have so much, then perhaps our self-love is the reason?

If we do not think this applies to us, then count how many pairs of shoes we own or the number of shirts and dresses in our wardrobes and cupboards. We are told to glorify the body, not to adorn it. (1 Corinthians 6:19–20; 1 Peter 3:3–4)

Yet, we actually need few clothes, and even fewer mechanical or electronic devices. (Luke 3:11) If we are constantly seeking such things we will be anxious about life. This includes what we eat or drink and about our body, always seeking the latest improvements, changes, products or diets.

Fashion will hold us in her shallow but powerful embrace and prove an unfaithful lover, promising much but delivering little. Surely our life is more than food and fads? Surely our body is more than its clothing or some fashion idea of the ideal silhouette? (Matthew 6:25–34)

By denying ourselves of what we do *not* truly need, we forget greed and realise that often *less is more*. We are restored as a glory of God in need of no extra adornment and wonderfully our true self. Then, the garden of our spirit flourishes. (Romans 8:5, 12:1–2)

20 August—Optional Memorial of Saint Bernard of Clairvaux

HE FIRST CISTERCIAN to become a saint, Bernard was a theologian, a contemplative, and a mystic.[8] It was a life characterized by a deep devotion to the Virgin Mary. He urged us to call upon Mary, saying that *in dangers, in doubts, in difficulties, think of Mary, call upon Mary. Let not her name depart from your lips, never suffer it to leave your heart. And that you may more surely obtain the assistance of her prayer, neglect not to walk in her footsteps. With her for guide, you shall never go astray; while invoking her, you shall never lose heart; so long as she is in your mind, you are safe from deception; while she holds your hand, you cannot fall; under her protection you have nothing to fear; if she walks before you, you shall not grow weary; if she shows you favour, you shall reach the goal.*

The Rosary is entwined with thoughts about Mary as it leads us through these joyous and sorrowful mysteries of God. Cardinal John Henry Newman (1801–1890), an important figure in the religious history of England, believed that the power of the rosary rests in the fact that it translates the Creed into prayer and allows us to meditate on the great truths of the life and death of Jesus.[9]

In this way, Our Lord is brought closer to our hearts. *There is no prayer*, claimed St. Francis de Sales, *as powerful as the Rosary when you meditate on its mysteries.*[10]

---

[8] See Pope Benedict XVI, *Discourse at General Audience* (2009).

[9] *To Boys about the Rosary* in John Henry Newman, *Sayings of Cardinal Newman*.

[10] Edward J. Carney, OSFS, *The Mariology of St. Francis de Sales*.

21 August — On the virtue in renouncing our self-will

 F THE VIRTUE of self-denial rests in its ability to suppress and root out our self-love, then it is clearly one of the most necessary of all Christian virtues. It must go, therefore, hand-in-hand with conformity to the will of God, which can never take root in our souls as long as we are attached to our own will and fond of gratifying our own inclinations. It is for this reason that the very first condition Jesus requires of his disciples is that they deny themselves. (Matthew 16:24) This self-denial by renouncing our self-will is the great lesson he taught, because through it we willingly put ourselves into the hands of God.

Traditionally, this virtue of self-denial is often called *mortification* from a word signifying *slaying* or *putting to death*. This is exactly what we are doing if we obey the teaching of Jesus; since we are putting to death, as it were, our own corrupt inclinations and passions and crucifying the former self, which belonged to sin. (Romans 6:6) Scripture confirms that all who belong to Jesus Christ have crucified the self with all its passions and desires. (Galatians 5:24)

Thus, we have died to ourselves that we may become the new man and the new woman, living in such a manner in Christ as to be able to say with Saint Paul: *I have been crucified with Christ and yet I am alive; and yet it is no longer I, but Christ living in me.* (Galatians 2:20)

The message is clear that if by the Spirit you put to death the habits originating in the body, you will have life. (Romans 8:13) Moreover, all who are in the flesh, that is alive, and does not do this not cannot please God. (Romans 5:8–11) Without such restraint of passions and the wayward inclinations of self-love, there can be no soundness in our mind, body or spirit. We may even hurt other people and make them unhappy by giving into such self-love. Indeed, our whole being will be sick and our heart diseased. (Isaiah 1: 5)

22 August — *On keeping the flesh from sin*

HILE OUR BODY is a glory of God and an infinite mystery of amazing creation, it is also the source of many legitimate pleasures. Here is where the trouble starts, because our flesh is also full of passions and lusts. This is why the flesh is reckoned to be one of the great enemies of the soul.

Our flesh is constantly inviting us to enjoy desires that are contrary to the commandments of God. However, if we ourselves did not pave the way for these illegitimate desires to enter our life, the vices of the flesh could not happen. We alone open the gates to let them into the garden of our soul.

To prevent this means we must first put a stop to our unwarranted self-love. We must search the darkest corners of ourselves to discover the whole truth about this self-love before we can do anything about it. We will probably find this seeking an unpleasant and distasteful revelation, because we hide secrets, things that we don't want others to know about us, things that we often think rather nasty and not at all pleasant to God or anybody else. This is especially true of those things that take us away from God and make us a servant to the world's values and vices such as lust, hate, greed, and selfishness about our time and space, and our loving, because we are consumed by what we like, need and feel. We never share ourselves or what we may possess with others. Indeed, the vice of such self-love denies any love of our neighbour.

Consider then that the basic business of getting rid of self-love is to reform the *whole* person — the mind, the body and the spirit. It is to put to death all that prevents us from loving others. In fact, everything that might disqualify us from union with God. As Saint Teresa of Avila put it, we must clean up the palace of our soul so it is fit for the king of kings. In order to do this, you must be aware of all the irregularities to which our inward powers and faculties are liable. Is it pride, self-conceit, self-sufficiency, or presumption? Is it false pride? Is it a variety of empty curiosities about this and that in the world, all of which take us away from focusing on God and those spiritual practices that keep us close to him?

We cannot keep control of our passions and desires unless we know what they are *before* we are tempted by them. Remember our self-will can be mistress of our interior life. (Ecclesiasticus 18:30)

23 August — Optional Memorial of Saint Rose of Lima

ATRON SAINT OF Latin America and the Philippines, Saint Rose lived her life in penance and solitude at home after taking her vows as a Third Order Dominican. Her deepest desire was to imitate the life of Christ and so she lived in daily contemplation of God, in continual prayer, and in very strict denials of mind and body. So great was her devotion and love of God that her many severe penances and poverty withstood the ridicule of others, who thought she was misguided and confused—but when she died the people of her city turned out to mourn her.

Are we willing, like Saint Rose, to discipline ourselves when in the midst of plenty? Do we understand the real life-changing experiences of living in imitation of Jesus even in a modest way? Saint Rose believed in this imitation of Our Lord and said that *apart from the cross there is no other ladder by which we may get to heaven.* (Matthew 19:16–30; Mark 10:17–31; Luke 18:18–30)

24 August—Feast of Saint Bartholomew, Apostle

 ONSIDER HOW JESUS went to an isolated place to pray before making decisions or when needing to settle his thoughts about anything. This retirement from the world and all its concerns leaves the worries, cares and noisy interruptions of the world behind. This allows us to reflect in solitude and pray with an interior quietness. Such seeking of God's help in any matter facing us is to place us entirely into his will. In asking him for guidance and blessing, you imitate his Messiah. (Luke 6:12)

Endeavour, then, to keep close to Christ and pray in all cases to let your refuge be in God. The Lord will support and help you for he will never forsake those who seek him. (Psalm 45)

25 August — On humility

 UMILITY IS THE favourite virtue of heaven, because all other virtues are nothing without it. Humility makes us aware of our own lack of merit and teaches us to divest ourselves of all conceit about our own performances or abilities. Thus, humility puts us in the lowest place and makes us sincerely prefer all others before ourselves. It aspires to no esteem, praise, honour, or glory as due to any excellence of our own. We must ascribe any good to God alone. (Mark 10:18)

Humility is not only a virtue absolutely necessary for arriving at Christian perfection, but without it there is no going to heaven for *God opposes the proud but he accords his favour to the humble.* (James 4:6) Jesus bluntly tells us that unless we become as little children, that is innocent and without vice, then we will not enter Heaven. (Matthew 18:3) Do not be deceived, because there is no room in heaven for pride. God only dwells with those of a contrite and humble spirit. (Isaiah 56:2 & 57:15)

So we must not become one of those proud and arrogant people that God finds an abomination. (Proverbs 16:5)

26 August—The School of Humility

 HE SCHOOL IN which we learn true humility is the one where knowledge of ourselves and of God takes place. These two aspects of Christian knowledge usually go hand-in-hand, mutually promoting and assisting one another. The more we know of God, the more we are aware of our dependence on him. At the same time, the more we know about ourselves and our failings, the more clearly we perceive that God alone is good. (Mark 10:18)

If we want the virtue of humility, we need, then, to start by taking an honest view of ourselves. The harder we look inwardly at ourselves, the more darkness we will discover. That darkness is a cave of discontent, decorated with all the vanities and vices of which we are guilty, but which we hide so that we do not need to acknowledge them to others or ourselves. This means we are not being fully the person God created. God waits to help us to accept who and what we are so we should have no fear of this darkness. (Isaiah 41:10)

Enrol now in this school of humility by learning to know God and yourself. Bring all your foolishness of this world into the light of Christ. Let him, who died for love of you, destroy all the pride that stands in your way to becoming humble and poor in spirit. (Luke 6:20; Matthew 5:3; Psalm 32:18)

27 August — The Master who teaches us humility.

N ORDER TO teach us humility God has sent down a Master from heaven, Jesus the Christ. His teaching of humility is *by example*. This tells us at once the importance of humility. In becoming an outcast of his people Jesus showed us the way of humility without which we cannot live a life of love. (Psalm 22/6)

If we are unwilling to be humble, then we have refused the sweet invitation of Our Lord. The Lord who called us to come with him, to take his yoke upon ourselves and, bearing the Cross, to learn from him because he is meek and humble of heart. If we accepted his invitation, he promised we would be given refreshment and rest for our souls. (Matthew 11:28–30)

All this happens in the school of Jesus Christ. Isn't our heart crying out to accept his invitation? Isn't this the harvest of peace we want in life?

28 August—Optional Memorial of Saint Augustine of Hippo

ERE IS A great sinner who became a great saint. Eventually after many struggles and refusals, he finally stopped running away from the call of God. Like many men and women he resisted repeatedly until he could no longer refuse the call of God.

In this passage from his famous autobiography, *Confessions*, he tells us of the fire in his soul, which God lit with the flame of love:

> Too late have I loved you, O Beauty of ancient days, yet ever new! Too late I loved you! And behold, you were within, and I abroad, and there I searched for you; I was deformed, plunging amid those fair forms, which you had made. You were with me, but I was not with you. Things held me far from you—things that, if they were not in you, were not at all. You called, and shouted, and burst my deafness. You flashed and shone, and scattered my blindness. You breathed odours and I drew in breath—and I pant for you. I tasted, and I hunger and thirst. You touched me, and I burned for your peace.[11]

Is such a flame in your soul burning right now? Perhaps it is a quiet thing and not as overwhelming as St. Augustine experienced it, but it is still there inside you, that insistent voice inviting you to a better life, a life in the fullness of joy and peace. God calls us to live that life of joy. Like St. Augustine, we need to accept the call from God to embrace his eternal love and fall with rapture into the arms of the Christ, trusting ourselves completely to the mercy and will of God and praying we will be among the chosen.

---

[11] St. Augustine, *Confessions,* 10:27. See Job 7:1–21.

29 August — On the practice of humility

 s IN MOST things from riding a horse to playing the piano, practice may not make us perfect but it improves the quality of our efforts. So, if we wish to acquire the virtue of humility, then we should neglect no opportunity to practise it.

Since the humiliations we may suffer come from the hand of God or the unkindness of others, we must embrace them in such way that we become humble to both God and man. This is not something easy for anyone to do. The practice of humility calls for patience and perseverance. It is hard work so we are bound to struggle.

To succeed in being humble we need to have more than just a great desire for humility. We also need great patience, because when we feel humiliated we tend to fight back for none of us likes criticism or unkindness. We forget to turn the other cheek. (Matthew 5:38–40) We need to bow our heads and leave cruelty to the justice of God.

To do this, we must have spiritual discretion as well as personal patience for in the sufferings that come to us through the hands of wicked people we must always distinguish that which is the will of God from that which is the malice of men and women. While embracing that which comes from God, we must detest the other.

If the humiliations we endure from other people are accompanied with the evil of sin, either of our own or of others, we must humble ourselves under them so as to embrace the humiliation, whilst abhorring the sin. Again, the way to do this is to remember the humility of Jesus and that only God is good. (Mark 10:18)

30 August—The foundation for all virtues

 F WE ARE to enjoy the fruits of humility we must not just avoid undo satisfaction in the praise and esteem of others, but we need to deliberately take the lowest place in accord with the gospel lesson. (Luke 14:10)

We can practice humility by these three steps: First, learn to suffer with silence and patience being despised, reproached, or affronted by others. These insults probably will cause anger, resentment and sense of injustice to naturally arise in us, but we must learn to deny these feelings. Second, learn to receive this kind of unjust treatment with a willingness and readiness of mind. Indeed, be happy that someone has given you the opportunity to please God by your virtue—but beware of having false pride about it and feeling righteous because we must not deem ourselves to be spiritual rich. This is a judgment that belongs to God alone. Third, learn to embrace all these kinds of humiliations with joy for it brings us closer to being dead to this world and alive in God and sin is no longer our master (Romans 6:11–14)

Faith itself absolutely depends upon humility, even when that humility obliges the soul to adore what she cannot understand, to submit to the most humbling truths, and to *every presumptuous notion that is set up against the knowledge of God and we bring every thought into captivity and obedience to Christ.* (2 Corinthians 10:5)

31 August—On the degrees of humility

RUE HUMILITY DOES not consist in speaking ill of ourselves, nor in wearing plain clothes without jewellery or other adornments, nor in doing menial tasks, nor in looking down on the ground all the time in some guardianship of the eyes when our mind is on illicit thoughts and ideas, nor in making long prayers in public, nor in quoting the bible whenever we want to support an opinion, nor by appearing pious about our church-going, nor in any of those ways by which we may appear different or superior to other people by the beauty of our body, our brilliant intellect, or our devout spiritual life. Sadly, all these things may be done out of pride, either to acquire the esteem of others by our outward show of humility or to applaud ourselves with the spiritual conceit of our being so humble.

True humility, therefore, consists in the inward sentiments of our heart. *Humility,* says St. Bernard, *is a virtue by which a man, out of a most true knowledge of himself, becomes mean and contemptible in his own eye; so that for a man to be truly humble is to have a low opinion of himself.*[12] So if we do not have a low opinion of ourselves then we are not truly humble. In short, we have forgotten that Jesus came to save the sinner, not the righteous. (Mark 2:17; Luke 5:32)

The second degree of true humility makes us think of ourselves as unworthy of God and makes us willing that other men and women may have this low opinion of us in which we are pleased at such humble status and not upset or worried by it in the least. Since most of the time most of us want other people to agree with our opinions, why not want them to agree with how we want to consider ourselves? How harsh this sounds. How unlike what the world would value. Yet, it remains a requirement if we are to achieve the

---

[12] St. Bernard of Clairvaux, *The Twelve Degrees of Humility & Pride.*

virtue of humility. We must accept that we are sinners and in need of reconciliation with God.

The third and most sublime degree of humility is that of the saints and holy men and women. In spite of the greatest favours from God and all the gifts of divine grace, they are set so firm in God's truth as to ascribe nothing at all to themselves and everything to God. St. Thomas of Villanova said that *humility is the mother of many virtues because from it obedience, fear, reverence, patience, modesty, meekness and peace are born. He who is humble easily obeys everyone, fears to offend anyone, is at peace with everyone, and is kind with all.*[13]

---

[13] St. Thomas of Villanova, *Attributed saying.*

SEPTEMBER

Theme: The aims of a Christian life

My vows to the Lord I will fulfil
Before all his people,
In the courts of the house of the Lord,
In your midst, O Jerusalem.

Psalm 115:18–19

1 September—On the Eight Beatitudes

ESUS THE CHRIST came to us in order to reclaim us from all our errors, to dispel our darkness, to reconcile us to God, and to conduct us into the way of everlasting happiness. By his *Sermon on the Mount*, he laid down the principal maxims of true wisdom and all the fundamentals of Christian morality comprised in what we commonly call *the eight beatitudes*. The ancient philosophers with all their pretensions to wisdom were in the dark with regard to man's last end. They never once imagined that to be poor in spirit, to be meek, to mourn, and to suffer persecution could be ways to happiness. This was a new doctrine taught by the Messiah. The learning of it makes us wise and brings us to eternal union with God.

Yet, when we look around today we still find people claiming to know the secrets of true happiness, filling books with advice, broadcasting their solutions to our problems, speaking about science as they understand it, giving self-help instructions that they think will bring happiness or good health or better relationships, and so on. These men and women will tell you, like the ancient philosophers and those who thought they knew the truth about life, that the solutions of yesterday are wrong and that the real wisdom is what they say today. Millions of people believe this new wisdom, just as many believed the ancient philosophers and others who lead them astray.

These poor deluded citizens of a modern Babylon take no notice of those lessons that the Christ was sent from heaven to teach. They believe in every passing political, social or celebrity leader with a platform. They believe what they hear whether it is false or not. Among these foolish believers are many baptized Christians, who have forgotten or ignored or just do not understand the teachings of Jesus about what wisdom really is.

Conclude to be thankful for the virtues recommended in the eight beatitudes. They lead to happiness in this life and to God in the next. Here is the wisdom that lasts forever and does not change with fashion or the conceits of men and women.

2 September — On poverty of spirit

 HE FIRST OF the eight beatitudes says, *How blessed are the poor in spirit: the kingdom of heaven is theirs.* (Matthew 5:3) This beatitude bringing entitlement to heaven belongs in the first place to those men and women poor in material wealth or social power by the world's standards, provided they embrace such poverty as a mark of being the favourites of God. Indeed, we are told the first followers of Jesus possessed little. (Luke 6:20) Knowing that Jesus died in poverty, how can we disdain the poor?

This beatitude also belongs also to those that are poor in their affection for things of this life, that is they have not set their hearts on worldly possessions and, even when they enjoy wealth and social position, are quite ready and willing to part with it whenever God wills it. We often forget that those who are not poor may also be devout and virtuous Christians. Many such people decide to be poor or live simply by choice when they feel that such is the will of God for them.

We all know how hard it is to give up our comforts so just think how much harder it is to give up the imagined security of wealth. Recall again that virtuous young man who asked Jesus to tell him what he must do to have eternal life. When told to give up his wealth and be poor he could not do it. (Mark 10:17–31, Matthew 19:16–30)

Another aspect of this beatitude belongs to the humble for they are truly poor in spirit. They are not puffed up with pride nor with any conceit about any ability or talent of their own unlike the man to whom it was said in scripture: You say to yourself: I am rich, I have made a fortune and have everything I want, never realising that you are wretchedly and pitiably poor, and blind and naked too. (Revelation 3:17) Pray then that this may not be said of you and that the Lord will help you to be humble.

Since Jesus requires his disciples to leave all to follow him, we need to study true wisdom by applying ourselves to learning this first lesson of poverty of spirit. If you are in poverty or poor by the world's standards be thankful, because it can draw you nearer to God. If you are basking in wealth, put no trust in it, treat it with the disdain, do not believe it makes you somehow better or safer than others, and use it for love of others. Be charitable. Give away not just what you can afford to give up, but be generous with all you possess from the food on your table to the money in your bank account. In every case, poor or rich, make God your first priority and seek to be a person of poverty in spirit.

3 September—On meekness

LESSED ARE THE *gentle: they shall have the earth as inheritance.* (Matthew 5:5, Psalm 37:11) The two beatitudes of poverty of spirit and meekness go hand-in-hand. Jesus joins them together and calls on us to take his yoke and to learn from him, because he is meek and humble of heart. (Matthew 11:29–30)

Meekness is a virtue that restrains all anger and passion, suppressing our first reactions to real or imaginary provocations or injuries. Meekness stills the soul on all these occasions and keeps all violent words from our lips. We do not fight back. Meekness allows no thoughts of anything other than those of overcoming evil with good. Such was the practice of Jesus of whom it is written: *He was insulted and did not retaliate with insults; when he was suffering he made no threats but put his trust in the upright judge.* (1 Peter 2:23)

It is this evenness of soul, this leaving cruelty to the justice of God, this joining courtesy to our words and this being cordial and friendly to the poor as much as to the powerful and the rich, which makes up the proper character of a true follower of Christ. Let us embrace such meekness *and we will be beloved above the glory of men.* (Ecclesiasticus 3:18–20)

But to learn to be meek and obtain victory over our anger and passion, we must first set a watch on ourselves. If we watch over ourselves, we are not taken by surprise by the sudden first emotions we may feel. On such occasions, we must pray for divine help and resolve to fight with the best weapon of God against these wicked passions and that best weapon is love.

4 September — On mourning

 s TO THE third beatitude, consider the words of Jesus: *Blessed are those who mourn: they shall be comforted.* (Matthew 5:4) Since the term beatitude means happy, fortunate, or blissful, we see how very different are the world's notions of happiness from the meaning of this beatitude of mourning.

Most people imagine that worldly pleasures are the chief ingredients of a happy life, especially that laughing must mean happiness while weeping or mourning means the opposite. Yet, Jesus tells us differently and so does Scripture: *This laughter, I reflected, is a madness, this pleasure no use at all.* And again, *The heart of the wise is in the house of mourning, and the heart of fools in the house of gaiety.* (Ecclesiastes 2:2 &7:3)

What kind of mourning, therefore, is recommended in this beatitude? Not the worldly sadness of which it is written that such sadness kills many and there is no profit in it and that sorrow in this world leads to death. (Ecclesiaticus 30:25; 2 Corinthians 7:10) Not any mourning, which is turbulent or accompanied with impatient wishes for death or anxious solicitudes or despondency where any feelings of hope are abandoned. These are not the kinds of mourning Jesus is talking about.

The mourning he is talking about in this beatitude is a more calm mourning with our eyes turned to heaven, a mourning that we have within us everyday, because when we mourn the personal loss of a loved one, we become aware of the death of Jesus. Such mourning for Jesus that arises in us is different from the loss of a loved one or a best friend or even a parent or child. We mourn on God's terms, not our own.

This kind of mourning leads us ultimately to mourn for our great distance from God. It demands that we look around at the world in its wars, famines, and cruelties. We weep in our hearts for the length of time we must stay here in this

Babylon. We pray we will not be victims of such cruelty. Even when we think of the death of Jesus, we mourn in a holy way which means our hearts, filled with sorrow for him, are blessed for we are drawn closer to God.

Thus, the beatitude of mourning is that which makes us more keenly aware of our salvation and more determined than ever to overcome our passions and spiritual weaknesses and to eagerly seek the remedies of the soul, which are found in the consolations of Christ.

5 September—On yearning for justice

LESSED ARE THOSE *who hunger and thirst for uprightness: they shall have their fill.* (Matthew 5:6) It will help to understand this beatitude, if we recall how the desire to be good is the beginning of all good, just as the desire for wisdom according to Scripture is the beginning of all wisdom. It follows, then, that the desire for love of God is the beginning of the love of God.

So it is of all virtues, because to desire them is to begin to acquire them. But such desire must not be a half measure, one day desiring it, the next undecided or not wanting it. (Proverbs 23:17–18) When such desire is strong and a person perseveres, it grows to a hunger and thirst after divine love. It becomes a yearning that will not go away.

Here is found true justice. This hunger and thirst sets the soul seeking diligently, praying heartily, knocking earnestly at the gate of divine mercy, and employing all possible means to procure the satisfying of this yearning for justice. A person, who yearns like this, overcomes all obstacles and never stops until such justice triumphs. Jesus tells us that such men and women are truly happy who hunger and thirst in this manner.

Now, the nature of this yearning for justice is not just for a justice about the cruelties in this world. For the cruelties of this world must be left to the justice of God, like all judgments. The justice we must seek is about God in ourselves, the justice of God in our neighbours, and the justice of God in himself. Here is the foundation of all justice.

The justice of God in ourselves arises when we seek to fulfil our duty as Christians and when love for God takes full possession of us. The justice of God in our neighbours arises when we desire that others may know and serve God. When we are in love with God's infinite goodness and his glory in all things and we desire the perfect accomplishment of his holy will in our life, then we share in that justice of God himself—just as Jesus did while on earth, saying, *My food is to do the will of the one who sent me.* (John 4:34)

Are you hungry and thirsting for such justice or do you fret and worry and become anxious to do something about the cruelties of this world? Worse still, do you forget about justice and cruelties and God and only seek the fleshpots of this world? Is the distraction of pleasure the way you avoid the realities of this world as well as the spiritual blessing of this beatitude? Are you always running away from the truth about the world and, especially, the truth about yourself?

They shall have their fill, promises the Lord to those having this virtue of justice. Consider what this means in our life: to be filled with divine grace, true devotion, heavenly charity, good works, and the fruits of the Holy Spirit. In short, happily filled with the eternal enjoyment of God himself, which alone can satisfy the heart, knowing that we are part of that immense universe of the one God. Isn't this the happiness that you desire for yourself?

Conclude then to direct yourself towards the Lord's goodness in the land of the living. (Psalm 26:13)

6 September—On being merciful

HE FIFTH BEATITUDE, *Blessed are the merciful, for they shall have mercy shown them,* helps us reflect on the fact that we are always living under of the mercy of God. (Matthew 5:7) From God comes all our good, the forgiveness of our transgressions, and the graces we have not deserved. All this is given to us through God, the All Merciful, the All Compassionate.

Finding mercy with God is everything. In receiving his mercy, we are obliged to show mercy to others. *Forgive, and you shall be forgiven. Give, and it shall be given to you,* writes the Evangelist. (Luke 6:37–38)

Just being polite to others will not do, because our good manners and our showing concern for others are often not from love but from the habit of social politeness. God shows us true mercy. In turn, we must show a sincere compassion for others and not perform only in the way approved by society. Otherwise we may fall into hypocrisy, pretending to be something when we are not. Sincerity is the test of real mercy.

The many ways of showing mercy are explained to us in the *Word of God.* These comprise those physical and spiritual acts of charity for people in need which we can do. In this way, we imitate Christ and extend the mercy of God.

In physical works of mercy, we help others with their worldly needs. For example, feeding the hungry, giving shelter to the homeless, clothing the poor, visiting the sick and those in prison, burying the dead, and giving alms. Spiritual works of mercy are those that are also acts of compassion. For example, helping our family, friends, and neighbours with their emotional and spiritual needs. This includes supporting them in their emotional disturbances, listening to them with attention, focusing on what they are really feeling, consoling them with kindness and, often, giving them welcomed hugs to reassure them, forgiving them for the wrongs they may have visited on us, since it is often the people closest to us who strike out, making us the scapegoat for their frustration and anger. Works of corporal and spiritual mercy such as these help us on the way to the eternal kingdom. (Matthew 25:34–40)

Now, consider who can withstand the judgment of God if he should set aside mercy for us when we have not in our turn shown mercy to others? What would we do without such divine mercy in our life? What would we do if no one listen to us, advised us, consoled us, forgave us or put up with patience at our moods and acts of self-love? What if we did not have the consolations of Christ to turn to in our troubles?

Think how happy those people must be who are merciful to one another, because by such love they ensure for themselves the mercy of God. On the other hand, how unhappy are they who refuse to show mercy to others, forgetting that there will be judgment without mercy to those who have not shown mercy themselves. (James 2:13)

7 September—On possessing a clean heart and a clear vision

HE WORDS OF the sixth beatitude hold out an amazing promise: *Blessed are the pure in heart, they shall see God.* (Matthew 5:8) But God is not seen by the eyes of the body, but only by the interior eye of the soul. Just as our physical eyes must be clean and clear to see something, so the interior eye of the soul must be clean and clear in order to see God. It must not be clouded with any disorderly affection or attachment to anything in this world.

This cleanness of the inner eye requires two things: simplicity in seeking God and purity of love for him. These two things wash all the soul with delight, refreshing and lifting us above the things of the earth, because simplicity aims at God alone and the virtue of purity embraces and supports all our seeking. *Seek God,* says the wise man, *in simplicity of heart.* (Wisdom 1:1) This means we are to be sincere, free from all double-dealing and thinking, and not have any of the treachery of self-seeking.

8 September—On being peacemakers

LESSED ARE THE *peacemakers, they shall be recognised as children of God* is the seventh beatitude. (Matthew 5:9) We know that God's own abode has eternal peace and the heavenly Jerusalem is the enjoyment of that everlasting peace. It follows, then, that they who truly love peace should contribute all they can to make peace among those who are at odds with one another. We cannot make a heaven on earth, but we can make peace in this world. It is difficult to believe any enduring peace is possible in this world, but each time we make peace it contributes to the sanctity of life.

To make peace we must start with ourselves. Then, we can be peacemakers in our families, among our neighbours, and in the wider community in which we live. We can refuse to endorse any political, social or religiously inspired action that is forbidden by the commandments of God as given to us in Scripture. (Proverbs 6:23)

Consider the reward promised to peacemakers: They shall be called the children of God. Isn't it amazing that we fragile creatures are invited to this embrace of God? *See,* says Saint John, *what great love the Father has lavished on us by letting us be called God's children—which is what we are!* (1 John 3:1)

9 September—On maintaining the peace of your soul

 N KEEPING CONTINUAL peace in ourselves, an inner contentment takes place. Such contentment brings a sense of stability, a quiet courage, and strength of character. These are the favours God always shows to the truly peaceful person.

The first and most necessary means of preserving this peace within ourselves is to banish all wilful sin, because there can be no true peace where such sin resides. Wilful sin is a sign of self-love and this wreaks havoc of our best intentions, prayers, and repentance. We never know where we stand either with ourselves or with God. We do not know the state of our spirit. It means we are anxious, stressed, never still, always worried about something. Our heart is divided and never at ease or ready for the sufferings of this world or the graces of God. We become miserable, because no one can be at war with God and have any peace. We must not be one of those people who appear to others as calm and peaceful while inside they are churning with passions at war with themselves, their faith or church, and their family, friends or neighbours.

What peace can there be for the slaves of such pride, ambition, greed, worldly solicitude, anger, and envy? What peace can there be when we are at odds with our loved ones or our neighbours? All these and other such passions disturb and distract the soul. They put us in a state of agitation and uncertainty. They make us suffer from lack of inner tranquillity and emotional balance.

True peace of the soul is not acquired without subduing passions and keeping them in order as maybe our rightful concerns, but leaving any judgment to God. The way to acquire such true peace is to become a servant of God, always praying that the will of God may be entirely fulfilled in us, because God wants us to be at peace so our life is a joy.

10 September—On suffering persecution for the sake of justice

 OW COMPLETELY DIFFERENT the eighth beatitude is from all the worldly thinking about our flesh and blood, about the meaning of our life on earth, and all we claim to be our *rights*. Jesus gives us a different view: *Blessed are those who are persecuted in the cause of uprightness: the kingdom of heaven is theirs,* Jesus tells us. And he repeats this doctrine in another way, saying, *Blessed are you when people abuse you and persecute you and speak all kinds of calumny against you falsely on my account. Rejoice and be glad, for your reward will be great in heaven; this is how they persecuted the prophets before you.* (Matthew 5:11)

We usual feel pity for all those who suffer in this way. Indeed, we think of them as miserable. We do not see them as *blessed*. We forget that with suffering comes consolation. (2 Corinthians 1) We hope that we will not be a victim of rejection and abuse. Yet, Jesus tells us that this situation is a holy blessing should we so suffer it. How strange this sounds to our worldly ears. Far from rejoicing when we are the one suffering injustice, we become dejected, angry, or sorrowful. But surely we must be wrong to think this way, since truth itself, the *Word of God*, cannot deceive us.

Jesus tells us to take a long view of the situation. Are we not being prepared for the reality of being his disciples? Are we not the successors of the prophets of old, who were so often disdained, not believed, and visited by many injustices? Have we forgotten to leave the cruelties of this world, including those suffered by us, to the justice of God?

In our anxiety and suffering the consolations of the Holy Spirit are with us. We have the presence of Jesus Christ by our side, giving us the courage and endurance we may need. (Psalm 93:19) In bearing of our cross, we learn humility, patience, and the acceptance of the will of God. All this time, we are moving closer to an imitation of Jesus Christ, his teaching, his suffering and the meaning of his death and resurrection. If we gladly take up our own cross, we share in his suffering. Then we shall be glorified with him. (Romans: 8:17 & 18)

Our present burdens are momentary and light, because the aim of our life is to reach the glory that is invisible but eternal even if we may now suffer those visible things that are hurtful but transitory. (2 Corinthians 4) Suffering injustice as a blessing rather than a curse brings us a yearning for God and his realm of peace. This yearning increases our love of God.

11 September—On the virtue of patience

ATIENCE IS A virtue by which we bear up with courage under a variety of suffering to which we are continually exposed in this life. These may be exterior or interior afflictions of many kinds—illness and pains in our body or disturbances of the mind, losses, disappointments, unhappy memories that make us sad, feelings of rejection, insults and rudeness from others, physical and emotional injuries of all kinds, social or political injustices, and unwarranted cruelties here, there, everywhere we look. Indeed, all manner of such crosses in ordinary living come to all of us. They are hard to bear and more or less happen to everyone from the king to the beggar and from our childhood to our death. No person escapes personal crosses in this life. How each deals with such suffering defines their faith in God or lack of it.

However severe a trial, the Christian never gives up and continues on the road of virtue and does not allow it to hinder them from the love of God. Such patience imitates Jesus and, because of this, looks forward to the promises of salvation. This brings the necessary courage to carrying whatever cross God wills for us without murmuring or complaining about it. It even has the admirable quality of often turning the evils of this life into virtues by making them all serviceable on our way to God.

For example, when someone falsely criticises us, as Christians we should not be angry or resentful, but look upon what has been said to us as an opportunity to respond by practicing the love of neighbour. Indeed, we have been told to turn the other cheek. (Matthew 5:39) This action makes an injustice into a virtue. To do this takes patience and great self-control but we are helped by grace from God. At the same time, being a Christian sweetens all that is bitter in our life by seasoning it with the acceptance of the will of God.

Consider how often in Scripture the virtue of patience is recommended to us: *Your perseverance will win you your lives.* (Luke 21:19) *Perseverance must complete its work so that you will become fully developed, complete, not deficient in any way.* (James 1:4) *Mastery of temper is high proof of intelligence, a quick temper makes folly worse than ever.* (Proverbs 14:29) *You will need perseverance, said the Apostle, if you are to do God's will and gain what he has promised.* (Hebrews 10:36)

Patience then is the virtue of the martyrs and of all the saints and within the capability of every faithful Christian. Remember there is no going to heaven except through many tribulations. (Acts 14:22)

12 September—How to acquire patience

 ATIENCE, LIKE ALL good things, is not to be acquired just by wanting it. Saint James tells us that if any one wants this true wisdom, they must ask God for it, because God gives abundantly to all who ask in faith and do not waver in their hearts. (James 1:5–7)

Therefore, the first step toward acquiring patience is to know its true value. This understanding comes by considering what patience produces both for this world and the next. Its fruits are a peace of mind, body, and spirit with control over unworthy passions. Therefore, whoever shows such patience will eat of the tree of life and that the name of God will be written on such a person. (Revelation 2:7 & 3:7,12–13 & 21) Once we understand the great rewards of patience and what it means in the Christian life, then we may ask for it in our prayers with a sincere heart.

13 September—On preparation for the Exaltation of the Holy Cross

 OMORROW IS THE *Feast of the Exaltation of the Cross*, when we renew our sharing with Jesus in this extraordinary moment in the history of the world and in the mystery of God himself when the Messiah was crucified on Mount Calvary. So let us prepare.

Consider that a Christian in order to celebrate *the Feast of the Exaltation of the Cross* must refuse the pride, ambition, avarice, and vanity of the world and any doubts about the will of God. Such a person declares their heart is ready for God and is restless until it rests in him. (Psalm 56: 8; Psalm 107:2)[1]

Approach tomorrow's celebration with joy, remembering that Jesus the Messiah crucified on the Cross is the wisdom of God for the faithful. (1 Corinthians 1:18) Be crucified to this world, then, and sing out your thanksgiving *for God has worked wonders: All the ends of the earth have seen the salvation of our God. Shout to the Lord all the earth, ring out your joy.* (Psalm 97:3–4)

---

[1] St. Augustine *Confessions*, Book 1.

14 September—Feast of the Exaltation of the Holy Cross

HE DIVINE OFFICE antiphon for this feast tells us clearly why we celebrate this day: *Behold the cross of the Lord; let his enemies flee before him; the lion of Judah, of the stock of David, is victorious, alleluia.* (Also 1 Peter 1:3–5; Galatians 6:14) In these few words, we declare the commemoration of God's greatest gift to us in the birth of Jesus, his death on the Cross, which brought us salvation, and his resurrection through which death itself was defeated. This gift opened the gates of Heaven for all men and women.

Let us consider the meaning of the first two of these pillars of our faith: Christ is our *salvation* and our *life*.

Our *salvation* is Jesus Christ, because his dying saved us from the original fall of Adam and Eve from grace. In our salvation we are redeemed at long last from this original disobedience of our first ancestors. This brought us out of the wilderness of our separation from God and returned us to an intimacy with him.

As to our *life*, millions of people, rich or poor, destitute or comfortable, young and old often wonder about the meaning of their own lives and to what purpose they live. Such curiosity is misplaced because it tries to answer a question that our faith in God through Jesus Christ has already answered. All we need to know has already been told to us in Scripture: the meaning of our life lies not in the pleasures, goods, and values of this world, but in life as a child of God and in praise and obedience to God.

Saint Paul speaks for all of us, when he says of this redemption: *I have been crucified with Christ and yet I am alive; yet it is no longer I, but Christ living in me.* (Galatians 2: 19, 20)

15 September—On the meaning of our resurrection

ET US CONSIDER the meaning of that third pillar of our faith, our *resurrection*, which we celebrate is the *Feast of the Exaltation of the Cross*. To be resurrected is to be raised up. As we all died in Adam, so we are made alive in Jesus Christ, that is we are raised up and handed to God. (1 Corinthians 15:20–22)

While it is true that our final resurrection is in the future, but before that happens we pass through two phases of our resurrection in Christ. The first part of our resurrection is when we submit to the will of God and acknowledge Christ as the Messiah come to save us. We make a total commitment to God. (1 Timothy 2:4; Hosea 2:22, John 8:32; 2 Timothy 2:12) At that moment we are resurrected in Christ, that is to say *we live in him*. This means we follow the path of life shown us by Jesus and the commandment to love others as we love ourselves. (Mark 12:31) By such faith in Christ, we are pleasing to God and saved from God's judgment of eternal death through the original sin of our first ancestors, Adam and Eve. (1 Corinthians 15:22)

As he was given his divine mission as the Messiah to provide us with salvation, so Jesus will return on the last day for the final judgment. (Matthew 11:23–27,16:27, 24:4–5 & 24: 30–31, 24:36, 24:37–39, 24:40–44, 25:1–12; 25:13,25:31–46, 24:40–44; Luke 12:37–38,12:40,17:28–30, & 21:34–36; John 14:1–4; Mark 8:38) On that day when Christ descends to the earth once again and stands on the Mount of Olives, will we will be resurrected with him or we will we have long since fallen from grace and be judged unworthy of heaven? (Zechariah 14:4) We have been given the choice. What do you think will be your final judgment?

16 September—On being made free by the Cross of Christ

HAT DOES IT mean when we are made free by the Cross of Christ? This part of our resurrection is the mystery of our dying with Jesus on the Cross by which means we are freed from the anguish of worldly desires and values. By faith in Jesus, we are given this new liberty. Our spirit lives in Christ. Our mind is set on the things of God. We follow the path of virtue in accord with his commandments. We are given this dignity through a life in Christ. We are free in body and mind from all that is bad for us and against the commands of God, because our spirit has become holy and leads us toward heaven.

What is this dignity but to be recognized as an individual person who is entitled to justice and the respect that accompanies a righteous life? *Never forget*, Pope Leo the Great said, *that you have been rescued from the power of darkness.*[2]

However, our own dignity cannot exist unless we recognize that everyone else has such dignity too. In this way, we show respect for them as a unique child of God. Such respect that gives dignity to others is an aspect of love and we are called to love everyone without making any judgment about them. Indeed, we are called to praise the whole of God's wondrous creation. The best way to do this is by seeing Christ in every man and woman and God in everything on earth.

> Come then and sing out:
> Praise the Lord!
> Praise the Lord from the heavens;
> praise him in the heights!
> Praise him, all his angels;
> praise him, all his hosts!
> Praise him, sun and moon,

---

[2] Pope Leo 1, *Sermon 1, Nativitate Domini.*

praise him, all you shining stars!
Praise him, you highest heavens,
and you waters above the heavens!
Let them praise the name of the Lord!
For he commanded and they were created.
And he established them forever and ever;
he gave a decree, and it shall not pass away.
Kings of the earth and all peoples,
princes and all rulers of the earth!
Young men and maidens together,
old men and children!
Let them praise the name of the Lord,
for his name alone is exalted;
his majesty is above earth and heaven.
Praise the Lord! (Psalm 148)

17 September — On the presence of God

 HERE IS NO place in which we could hide from God. (Jeremiah 23:24; Psalm 138) All Christians know this and yet we sin and try to hide it. Our misery is that in thinking so little of God, we quite forget about his continuous presence in our lives. As St John the Baptist told the Jews with regard to their Messiah: *I baptise with water, but standing among you—unknown to you—is the one who is coming after me; and I am not fit to undo the strap of his sandal.* (John 1: 26)

As God is everywhere present and is witness to all our thoughts, words, and actions, nothing can be concealed from him. He is the searcher of every heart, unveiling and exposing everything in the light of his power and love. No creature is invisible to God. (Revelation 2:23; Hebrews 4:12–13) Do you flatter yourself as the one exception and somehow believe God does not know you with such complete intimacy? (Ecclesiasticus 23:20) If so, you have forgotten that darkness and light are alike to the Lord, because God sees all. (Psalm 138:12)

However, God is not only present in every part of his Creation and sees all that passes, but he is also present within each of us. In him we live and move. (Acts 17: 28) Indeed, we are not only encompassed on all sides by him, as the birds are with the air in which they fly or as the fish are in the waters of the ocean, but we are penetrated by him, so that he fills every part of our being with his whole self. A greater mystery even than this is that while he is always in us, we are always in him. The creature does not exist outside of the Creator.

Resolve that God's presence is real for you as your creator, consolation, and companion.

18 September—On keeping in the presence of God

 LIVELY SENSE OF the presence of God is one of the best ways to bring the worst of sinners back to God. It spurs on the lukewarm and makes them fervent. It advances the just in all virtues. To walk in the conscious presence of God is to walk the way of perfection.

When God spoke to his servant Abraham and told him to *walk before me and be perfect,* he was telling him that in every thought shared with God and with every decision made with God, the prophet would be more perfect in this life. This means, of course, that Abraham must live in the continual presence of God. As it was for Abraham and all the prophets and saints, so it is with each of us. All men and women must walk in the sight of God and seek his presence. (Genesis 17:1, 48:15; Psalm 16: 8)

This practice of the presence of God is done partly by our understanding and partly by our will, because our prayers and contemplation of heavenly things brings a more profound awareness of his presence, a greater feeling of love for him, and a vision that makes him our companion in all we do every day. It does not matter whether what we are doing is a household task, our work, relationships with others, or attending church services. This continual presence of God makes us strong in wisdom and willingly obedient to his laws. By this means we are so filled with God's presence that we anticipate the joys of heaven.

In order practise this heavenly exercise of the presence of God, we must rid our souls of three mortal enemies. These are *a dissipation of mind, an anxious solicitude for the things of this world,* and *a disorderly affection for others.* Where these three or any one of them reign in us, God is usually forgotten.

A dissipation of mind makes a person run after a multitude of shallow amusements and in the process of such diversions he or she forgets both the true self and God. Seeking worldly things does not allow the good in us to take root and to grow into vines of virtue.

As to *wanting the things of this world,* such shows a lack of wisdom since our experience clearly shows us that such desires quickly pass and possessions eventually fall into ruin while God remains eternal.

Disorderly affections simply means giving your heart to other creatures in a manner that turns you away from God. We often give too much of our heart to another person in our lives, such as making a best friend, child, grandchild or a wife or husband the centre of our affections and care to the exclusion of paying attention to God. *Disorderly affections* take many forms but what it always means that our heart is drawn away from God and given to another. It means that we suffer from a divided heart.

Conclude to guard against these enemies by setting a watch both upon your roving imagination, which is so fond of running after butterflies and other distractions. Do not let your heart be caught up in the nets of wanton love or other idle affections. Do this by your awareness of always being in the presence of God, not just in church or at prayer but in the ordinary moments and events of your life. God is present when you wash the dishes as well as when you worship him in church.

19 September—On the advantages of keeping in the presence of God

 UST AS THE forgetting of God is the beginning of sin, so the remembrance of his presence is the source of all good. Realising that the eye of God is on them has obliged many wicked men and women to stop their bad behaviour and to be drawn into repentance. Think how many men and women, justly condemned to prison for their offenses, have found God present with them in their cell and through him have repented and have been reconciled to God as well as to themselves and to the world in general. The power of the presence of God in any life changes it for the good.

God's presence everywhere demands of us a modest way of behaving on all occasions. (Philippians 4:5) Such a holy presence challenges us. To meet this challenge, we must turn to his mercy and show him the depth of our love.

Never think yourself alone, because this is impossible if God is with you. He offers the sweetest repose, so rest at peace in his promises.

20 September—On the virtue of obedience

 EING OBEDIENT TO someone else interferes with our sense of control over our lives. But reflect for a moment on considering obedience as a spiritual virtue, because it can put into action whatever is commanded by your faith. This may mean we are obedient not just to God's will but also to the commands of those who have their authority from God through holy gifts, ordination or by other ways showing that God has chosen them. We obey such people for God's sake. (1 Peter 2:13)

This kind of obedience, like humility, is a greater action of holiness than all other sacrifices we can offer him, because as Samuel told Saul, *Truly, obedience is better than sacrifice, submissiveness than the fat of rams.* (1 Samuel 15:22)

Let the great example of obedience by Jesus inspire you with an ardent desire of living and dying in the gladness of obedience to God. (John 4:34, 5:30, 6:38,7:49,10:18)

21 September—Saint Matthew, Apostle—Feast

 ONSIDER THE WONDERS of divine grace in the conversion of the Apostle Matthew. He was suddenly changed from a publican and a sinner to a companion and disciple of Christ. He became a pillar in Christ's church and a preacher powerful in word and action, a worker of miracles, a converter of nations, an evangelist, and writer of the gospel. What an amazing change in one man who answered the call of God when it came.

Learn from this example never to despair of the conversion of any one, no matter how remote he or she may seem to be from following Christ at this present moment. It is possible for even the greatest sinner to be saved. Remember the arm of God is not shortened. (Numbers 11:23; Isaiah 59:1–2) His power, mercy, and goodness are as infinite today as ever. He still calls sinners to himself, because as Jesus told us, *I have come to call not the upright, but sinners to repentance.* (Luke 5:32; Mark 2:27–28, 9:7–8)

But the questions are these: Are we as ready as Saint Matthew to answer such a call or do we prefer to remain sitting in the customs house of the world, counting our illusionary profits? Are we so entangled in vain affections and our comforts that we delay our call to follow Christ? Look at yourself and ask yourself what is keeping you from Christ? Why have you not sought repentance and reconciliation?

Saint Matthew answered God with his whole heart. He did not hesitate, when Jesus said, *Follow me.* We too are called to be followers of Christ, yet how few, who call themselves Christians, truly follow either the doctrine or the example of Christ in the way they live.

Now Christ does not call most of us to quit our job or leave our family and responsibilities behind or to give up all worldly goods, but he does insists that we take the burden of these things off our hearts and that we leave all affections which keep us distant from God.

Jesus the Christ waits for us. *Look,* he says, *I am standing at the door, knocking. If one of you hears me calling and opens the door, I will come in to share a meal at that person's side. Anyone who proves victorious I will allow to share my throne.* (Revelation 3:20) We entertain Christ by opening the gate to the garden of our soul. We keep him with us by recollection and prayer. We feast with him by giving him our hearts. We drink from the cup of joy he offers us in return by giving himself to us. This happy feast while we live is a foretaste of the eternal banquet awaiting us in heaven.

So then, imitating Saint Matthew by a ready compliance to the divine call, we surely cannot have a more glorious aim in this life. When God calls you, do not hesitate, but answer at once and go to his embrace and service.

22 September—On the first commandment

 N THE PREFACE to the Ten Commandments, God tells us, *I am Yahweh your God, who brought you out of Egypt, where you lived as slaves. You shall have no other gods to rival me.* (Exodus 20:2–3) By this simple statement he states his authority and gives us the motive we need to obey his commandments. No one but the foolish and those given over to passions and worldly values would dare to refuse his commandments or question his authority or not give him obedience.

The love of God is that we keep his commandments and by following them we can have a blameless life. (Psalm 118 Aleph 1–8; 1 John 5:1–4) Jesus told us: *You must love the Lord your God with all your heart, with all your soul, and with all your mind. This is the greatest and first commandment. The second resembles it: You must love your neighbour as yourself. On these two commandments hang the whole Law, and the Prophets too.* (Matthew 22:34–40)

Yet, many people who call themselves Christians live and die in a notorious breach of these great commandments from God. They neglect and forget God and give preference to everything else. Their lives are lead by material values, consumption, household duties, obligations of work, and by a thousand and one details of a life devoted to *being busy*. Such people are worshiping false gods. They have no rest, no hope, and no peace.

Let us not be like such fools and always remember the two great commandments so our life is sweet, contented, and love dominates everything.

23 September—On the prohibition of idol worship

E MUST NEVER worship images of God or icons of holy saints, but only use them as aids to our devotion. It is what they represent that is helpful to us. In themselves they have no other power. Unless they lead us to God, they are just useless idols.

As to the kind of idolatry that consists in the setting up of stones and animals to be worshiped, there is less danger these days of Christians doing this, because this kind of pagan worship has been abolished where Christianity has been preached and taught.

The idols of our modern age are of another kind. They are not stone nor wood nor gold nor made of any animal or metal, but idols of illusion created by an endless curiosity that wants to know the reason and workings of everything. Such relentless curiosity underlies the belief that more information makes us wise. In fact too much information, explanations, and data leads many people into confusion and doubt. While being informed can be a good thing, it is unlikely to bring us closer to God.

Modern idols are made not by the hands, but by the minds of proud men and women. The world is full of such people. Illogical as it may be, many of such people often believe in spirits and the spiritual and even angels, but not in God. Just look around you at the books, retreats, talks, events, expositions, and courses, which the world recommends to us as giving answers as to how to live our life and be happy. If only they claim we would do as they say, then wisdom and contentment would be ours.

Beware of such alternative messages unrelated to Scripture and detached from the commandments of God. You may not at first recognize it, but such people are setting before you false idols.

If we believe this does not apply to our own life, then look at the kind of books we read and the conversations we have with other people. Do we discuss Scripture and God or do we talk about the latest news? Do we mention Jesus when we talk to others or do we only speak of this or that politician or celebrity or what show last night we saw on television?

24 September—On the making of many kinds of idols

 OU CAN MAKE an idol of anything. For example, take Nature. Our interest may manifest itself as environmental, biodiversity or ecological concerns or just artistic and poetic admiration. These are important things to care about and may seem innocent as far as our faith goes, but we must be careful it does not wind up as worship of Nature. The same can be true of the birds, moths, and butterflies or whatever we find fascinating in Nature. Do not make these wondrous creations of God into signs or symbolic icons of Creation, because in doing so we make idols of them.

Such a curiosity and concern for Nature may certainly make us marvel at the creations of God, but it may also draw us further away from being concerned with the fate of our brothers and sisters. It is possible to see the hand of God in a butterfly but the greatest miracle of all Creation was surely that *the Word was made flesh.* (John 1:14)

By all means let us identify with everything God has created and certainly believe that everything is connected to each other and all is *one.* Indeed, the tree *is* you and you *are* the tree, and the birds that sing join our voices and lift us together up to heaven. But always remember that God is the one who created everything. His Holy Spirit interconnects everything and makes everything the *one of creation.* God is the *being* in everything on earth. This *being* is the essence of life, connecting us with each living thing and connects equally them to us.

There are other dangerous kinds of idols formed by our misplaced affections of the heart. Many people calling themselves Christian set up these kinds of idols in the temple of their body or the garden of their soul, those places that rightfully belong to God. When we were baptized, we were consecrated to God and not dedicated to possessions, fame, money or anything valued by the passing fashions and fancies of this world. All who make idols of worldly things, such as power, honours, and the fulfilment of passions and pleasures, think more of themselves and the opinions of this world than they do of God. In the language of St. Paul, these people are idolaters, because they all worship and serve the creature rather than the creator. (Romans 1:25)

Making an idol of the self is the most common idol of all, because it is the worship of self-love above the love of others and the love of our own will above God's will for us. Most people are guilty of this disordered love of themselves. To love life certainly fulfils God's intention that we should live joyously, but to love ourselves excessively is quite another matter.

Finally, we know that all superstition is forbidden, including the observance of lucky and unlucky days, omens, dreams, and magic. For all these are relics of paganism and serve for nothing but to delude us, laying us open to even further vices.

Renounce then every branch of idol worship and superstition. Let your life be to the glory of God. Then you will be in no danger from false idols.

25 September—On honouring God's holy name

ONSIDER THESE WORDS of the divine commandment: *You shall not take the name of the Lord your God in vain.* (Exodus 20) This commandment is perfectly clear and obliges us to show all respect to the holy name of the Lord our God and not to profane it by any kind blasphemy, swearing or cursing.

But how common this guilt is among Christians. How often we hear someone proclaim, *Oh, my God!* using the name of our Lord as slang and not as a cry for divine mercy or hope or help. How dismal it is to bring the name of God to such low rank. The wise man tells us that a person who swears much shall be filled with iniquity. This is so because when we continually take the Lord's name in vain, we become gradually insensitive to hearing his name. Such numbness ceases to call forth in our mind and heart those things of God. Instead the holy name of God becomes just another word in our everyday chatter. When this happens we become more open to other vices.

Remember that the great business of a Christian is to glorify the name of God both by the lips and by the way we live.

26 September—On keeping Sunday a holy day

OW PROPER IT is that we should remember to keep the Sabbath holy. (Exodus 20:8–9) Jesus defined for us the true meaning of the law when he declared that the Sabbath was made for man, not man for the Sabbath. (Mark 2:27) He explained that as he is Master of the Sabbath, all things related to the salvation of men and women are under his authority. (Mark 2:28) This means the Sabbath is *The Lord's Day.* This new Sabbath demands participation by us, because this religious keeping is the Eucharist, the meal of his remembrance and the celebration at the very heart of his church, the people of God. It is then that the paschal mystery is celebrated.[3]

Scripture reminds us not to neglect meeting together to worship and prayer and by this means to encourage each other. (Hebrews 10:24–25) As Saint John Chrysostom so correctly pointed out:

> You cannot pray at home as at church, where there is a great multitude, where exclamations are cried out to God as from one great heart, and where there is something more: the union of minds, the accord of souls, the bond of charity, the prayers of the priests.[4]

Our worship on this day fulfils the commandment of the Old Covenant with God while bringing its spirit to a weekly celebration of the Redeemer of his people, Jesus the Christ.[5]

---

[3]   CCC 2177.

[4]   St. John Chrysostom, *De incomprehensibili* 3, 6: PG 48,725.

[5]   CCC 2176.

27 September—Memorial of Saint Vincent de Paul

 NOWN AS THE *Apostle of Charity*, St. Vincent de Paul created services for the poor that have shaped the role of the Catholic Church in the world and influenced many to serve God through helping the poor.

But what is charity for Christians? It is more than mere sentimentality about those who are struggling. It is more than simply giving some of our income to those who organize charitable causes. We must feel love in our hearts for others and be moved to do something about it. This is to imitate Jesus and to think like St. Vincent de Paul.

To understand the spiritual significance of our acts of charity, we need to understand what happens to us when we act in this way toward others. People, who volunteer to work with the poor and those in need, often claim they receive more than they give. Here is the key to the spiritual effect of charity. When we give love, God fills our own heart with his love in return. Through such charity, we learn to recognize that we are *not* different from our brothers and sisters in Christ and that we all share the same world of joy and sorrow. This unites us to Our Lord and, through God's grace, to all men and women everywhere.

As Jesus told us: *For I was hungry and you gave me food, I was thirsty and you gave me drink, I was a stranger and you made me welcome, lacking clothes and you clothed me, sick and you visited me, in prison and you came to see me. Then he explained: In truth I tell you, in so far as you did this to one of the least of these brothers of mine, you did it to me.* (Matthew 25:35–46)

Here is the love that God wants us to have for each other.

28 September—Feast of the Archangels Michael, Gabriel and Raphael

OLY SCRIPTURE WITNESSES to the existence of angels as a truth of our faith.[6] In this feast, we honour the angels, especially the Archangels, who have exerted such a powerful influence in the development of our history with God and Jesus the Christ.

While being in the service of God and acting as his messengers, angels have their own intelligence and will. Without this, there would not have been the fallen angels in rebellion against their duty to God.[7] It seems natural then that all angels belong to Christ, because he is at the centre of their world since all things in heaven and earth were created through him and for him. (Colossians 2:10–11; Hebrews 1:6) When the Christ returns in glory, he will bring *all* the angels with him. (Matthew 25:31)

Just think for a moment how the angels have been present in our lives. For example, they closed the gates of earthly Paradise at God's command; protected Lot; saved Hager and her child; helped Daniel facing the lions; stopped Abraham's hand from killing; assisted the prophets; and protected Jesus in his infancy, strengthening him in his desert trials and in his agony in the garden. (Luke 22:43) Finally it was the Archangel Gabriel who announced the coming of John the Baptist to Zechariah and then proclaimed to Mary the birth of our Saviour, filling the air with that praise we still sing out: *Glory to God in the highest!* (Job 38:7; Ex 23:20–22; Judges 13 & 6:11–12; Isaiah 6:6–7; 1 Kings 19:5; Hebrews 1:6)

For all these reasons and many others, we should celebrate this Feast Day with great joy. But we should remember the angels during the ordinary days of our life as well, because

---

6 CCC 326, 327,328; Fourth Lateran Council 1215.

7 CCC 329, 330.

417

they are present in the cause of our salvation, serving the completion of the divine plan for all creation.[8] Our guardian angel stands guard in the soul itself. (Matthew 18:10; Luke 16:22; Psalms 33:7–8 & 91:10–12; Job 33:23–24; Zechariah 1:11–17; Tobit 12:12–15) This is why we are never alone in this world, because our guardian angel is always with us.

Do not neglect to acknowledge your guardian angel and be sure to practice hospitality at all times, because, as Tobias discovered, some have entertained angels and not known it. (Tobit)

---

[8] CCC 322.

29 September—On the visitation of the Archangel Gabriel to Mary

N THE SIXTH month the angel Gabriel was sent by God to a town in Galilee called Nazareth, a city in Galilee, to a virgin betrothed to a man named Joseph of the House of David. and the virgin's name was Mary. (Luke 1:26–27) This announcement changed the history of the world.

No kingdom, no empire, no political, social, or scientific idea, no philosophy, war or peace has so changed our world as what happened when the Angel Gabriel visited this young Jewish woman. We must be thankful everyday to Mary that she trusted in God when Gabriel announced the creation of Jesus in her.

For over two thousand years we have enjoyed the priceless inheritance of this one moment in time, when the holy obedience of one woman brought us eternal salvation.

Scripture tells us that the Angel Gabriel visited earth four times to bring messages from God to certain chosen men and women. (Daniel 8:16 & 9:21; Luke 1:19; Tobit) Gabriel appeared twice to Daniel, reassuring him of God's love for his people in the dark days of Israel's captivity. (Daniel 8:15–16 & 9:21) Generations later, Gabriel appeared to Zechariah to tell him that God had not forgotten and that his wife, Elizabeth, would have a child, John the Baptist, who would prepare the way for Jesus the Messiah. Then a few months later Gabriel visited Mary to tell her she will give birth to Jesus, which announces that the Word is to be made flesh and to come among the people. (Luke 1:26–28)

Every message brought by Gabriel is one of hope. Remember this when you feel depressed or things are not going as you planned or when you hesitate a little on your path of life with Christ. Always have hope, because this is what God wants for you just as he did for Daniel and Zachariah. Always have faith as Mary did and God may favour you too with grace. Be patient. Be full of hope.

30 September — On our ultimate treasure

 LL THE MONEY in the world is not enough to purchase you the gifts of virtue, grace, and merit in God's eyes. Yet beyond this treasure of holy gifts lies an even greater one. This greater treasure is in our possession already, because we belong to God and God belongs to us and we have the chance for an eternal life with God through Jesus the Messiah.

Here then is our ultimate treasure, a gift beyond price, because if we have God as our true treasure nothing can make us miserable for long. (Genesis 15:1) Turn to God and in his comfort you will find your fears and worries vanish. But if we do not have God in our life, then be assured our happiness will be fleeting and we will not be content.

So put on the likeness of Jesus the Messiah, the man of perfect virtue, who is everlasting. (1 Corinthians 15:47–49) You were made for this joy, because the great gift of God is with you now.

OCTOBER

Theme: Angels, duties, and vanities

I rely on your constant love;
I will be glad, because you will rescue me.
I will sing to you, O Lord,
because you have been good to me.

Psalm 13:5–6

1 October—Memorial of Saint Thérèse of the Child Jesus

ARIE FRANÇOISE THÉRÈSE Martin was born in France in 1873. She became a nun at a Carmelite convent, fell ill, and died at the age of 24. She would have remained forgotten except God had other plans.

Her prioress had commanded Thérèse to write her memoirs and a year after Thérèse's death, this memoir was published in a small edition. Soon her words had swept the world, setting the hearts of millions on fire with love of God. Miracles started to happen. There were conversions, cures, and holy apparitions. Some hundred years after Thérèse's death, she was declared a *Doctor of the Church*, joining St Catherine of Siena and St Teresa of Ávila.

What makes St Thérèse so special? She was physically and emotionally weak. She had no confidence in herself. In spite of such fragility, she was not discouraged in seeking God, because she believed that God never calls us to do anything for which he does not give us the courage and strength to complete.

St Thérèse showed the entire world that our weaknesses are no excuse for a lukewarm faith when it comes to trying to be perfect in God. By her life, she endorsed what Apostle Paul told us when he asked God to take away the thorn of his suffering: *But he said to me, "My grace is enough for you: for power is at full stretch in weakness."* The Apostle explains, *It is, then, about my weaknesses that I am happiest of all to boast, so that the power of Christ may rest on me.* He concludes, *For it is when I am weak that I am strong.* (2 Corinthians 12:9)

Continue to trust God and practice love. As Saint Thérèse wrote, *Love is the vocation, which includes all others; it is a universe on its own, comprising all time and space—it is eternal.*[1]

---

[1]   Saint Thérèse of the Child Jesus, *The Story of a Soul.*

2 October—Memorial of Our Guardian Angels

 OPE FRANCIS DECLARED in accordance with Church tradition that we all have an angel who protects and watches over us, helping us to make the right decisions about our lives when we are perplexed or anxious about what action to take. He says this Guardian Angel is a reality for each of us, the voice of our guarding companion. *Do you listen to your Guardian Angel? Pope Francis asks. Do you ask him to watch over you as you sleep? Are you maintaining your friendship with this heaven-sent helper?*[2] We should be thankful for this presence, since *God has commanded his angels to keep you in all your ways.* (Psalm 90:11, Luke 4:10)

Saint Bernard of Clairvaux called this wonderful gift of a guardian angel a true charity. He urged us to study closely who gives us this gift and to remember to whom these angels belong and whose will they obey. *Think of it*, he writes, *those sublime beings, who cling to Him so joyfully and intimately, He has given charge over you! Walk carefully, in all your ways, as one with whom the angels are present.*[3]

---

[2]   Pope Francis, *Homily at Mass* 2015.
[3]   Saint Bernard of Clairvaux, *Sermon 12, On the Holy Guardian Angels.*

3 October—On not bearing false witness against your neighbour

 Y THIS COMMANDMENT all false testimony against any one is forbidden whether in a court of law or otherwise, but all private slanders and lies and all other ways of injuring one's neighbour by words are also forbidden.

Whispering, tale-bearing, and promoting misunderstanding and quarrels between neighbours are an evil so odious to God that he detests it. (Proverbs 6:16–19) But we often gossip and in doing so often slander people and forget God's commandment. Next time listen to the chatter in church as people gather for the service and discover that many Christians are guilty of this sin, some even *after* partaking in the Eucharist. How we love to gossip about other people!

All these unloving words we may utter are not innocent. They are to be condemned as crimes against the commandment not to bear false witness against our neighbour. Every one of such words are directly opposed to both charity and justice They oppose that rule of life that must govern all we do in this world: *Always treat others as you would like them to treat you; that is the Law and the Prophets.* (Matthew 7:12)

Therefore, remember that the person who wants to love life and see good days must keep his or her tongue from evil and his or her lips from speaking deceit. (I Peter 3:10) Do not be tempted to gossip.

4 October—Saint Francis of Assisi—Memorial

 OW WELL KNOWN are these words of Saint Francis in his often quoted prayer and yet so infrequently put into practice: *Lord, grant me the strength to accept the things I cannot change, the courage to change the things I can, and the wisdom to know the difference.*

Acceptance of the things you cannot change is neither to resist nor to surrender to grievous events that happen in your life or in the world. Such acceptance is to know when situations are beyond our ability to change them. This kind of acceptance should be an act of faith in God's grace and mercy. We turn over to God all the worries, anxieties and fears that prompted us to want to change or control a situation. We seek strength from him to leave the problem in his hands. The situation may not have changed, but by this kind of acceptance, we rest in God's peace and not in the frustration of trying to change what we cannot. Here is wisdom. Here is what Saint Francis was talking about in his prayer.

The actions of an individual, however, can change a situation and, indeed, have changed a whole world. Just think of that carpenter's son, Jesus, and how he showed by his life that every person matters to God.

All the lessons we need in believing we can change something are set before us by this example and teaching of Jesus. Holy Scripture is full of men and women, who had courage to change things for the better. They may have been called by God to do what they did, but we too are called by God to do good in this world and change for the better what, when, and where we can. This is the practice of charity. Here is what Saint Francis was talking about.

Finally, we come to that wisdom we all seek, which is to know the difference between what we can change and what we cannot. Such discernment is often very difficult. It is a spiritual probing of the reality of a situation and when we call upon the Holy Spirit to lead us to a decision about what we should do, we are calling for God's help. By calling on God, discernment will naturally arise in our hearts. Here is the holy key that opens the gates of wisdom for us. We will know, then, the difference between what we can change and what we cannot change, but we must follow the will of God in every choice to the best of our ability and good intentions.

Thus, we have trusted in God and in this way he will give us the discernment we need. So with Saint Francis we pray: *Lord, grant me the strength to accept the things I cannot change, the courage to change the things I can, and the wisdom to know the difference.*

5 October—On the prayer of Saint Francis of Assisi

ERHAPS THE MOST famous prayer of Saint Francis is this one:

> O Divine Master, grant that
> I may not seek to be consoled, as to console.
> To be understood, as to understand.
> To be loved, as to love.
> For it is in giving that we receive.
> It is in pardoning that we are pardoned.
> It is in dying that we are born to eternal life.

Let us reflect carefully on this prayer, which in both its parts and as a whole contains the essence of Christ's teachings and the holy law of God. It affirms what the Apostles, holy prophets, the messengers of God, and the holy saints have told us.

6 October—Optional Memorial of Saint Bruno of Cologne

AINT BRUNO FOUNDED the hermit Carthusian Order in 1084 of which the most widely known of the order's communities is the *Grande Chartreuse*. Carthusian monks and nuns live in silence and contemplation—a life given to God alone. Religious communities like this one, even though they do not participate in the world nor undertake monastic activities such as receiving guests, giving retreats or pastoral duties, have an important role to play in the mystical body of Jesus Christ, because such lives are devoted to contemplation, the fruits of which are liberty, peace and joy.[4] Such purity of self reflects Christ's *Sermon on the Mount* when he told the people: *Blessed are the pure in heart: they shall see God.* (Matthew 5:8)

Now such a life of contemplation, which depends on continuous prayer, is a full-time matter. It is only possible with a maximum of solitude, which means separation from the world, staying alone, not going out among others, and maintaining *a solitude of the heart*. The first two aspects, solitude and staying alone, are external ones. The last aspect of the Carthusian life, *solitude of heart*, is an interior one.

Most of us cannot live like a Carthusian totally separated from the world nor stay alone in our home or room and never have contact with the outside world. The realities of living make these things, even for a hermit, impossible to achieve fully outside of the monastic cloister of an enclosed religious community. In any case, God intended that we should live a life of joy and for most men and women that joy is to live in the world.

However, we can all attain, like the Carthusians, an interior solitude or *solitude of the heart* through our contem-

---

4   Vatican II, *Decree on the Renewal of Religious Life*, 7.

plation. This is to enter into that interior space of self through prayer, praise and our devotions. Here is where we can find that palace of God about which Saint Teresa of Avila speaks. Here is where we can find that lonely desert where Christ prayed. Here is where we find God waiting for us.

For this all to happen, we must have a purity of heart, that is we must keep our souls away from all things not of God or which do not lead to God. We can never find such interior solitude unless we make a conscious effort to separate ourselves from the desires and attachments of a life in this world.[5] If wisdom is found in silence, we must take the time to enter this precious space away from noise and distractions and away from the busy life of other people. (Job 13:5)

The degree to which each of us needs solitude to be with God differs from person to person. For some, like the Carthusian monk and nun, it is all the time. Such men and women become hermits in a community of like-minded hermits. Some men and women are called to life alone, seeking God and existing, preferable under their bishop, as hermits outside of a religious community.[6] They answer God's call to seek God in solitude.

For most Christians, much less solitude will do and, indeed, it should be so for we are meant to practice love toward others, which is impossible without other people. Resolve, then, to make time every day to have some degree of solitude and silence in a peaceful space in order to seek the presence of God. If you cannot find such a space in your home or other surroundings, then go to a church between its services when all is usually quiet. God is always with you and there is always somewhere you can be with him in the silence of self and *solitude of heart*.

---

[5] See Thomas Merton, *Letter to Dorothy Day*, 1965.

[6] See *CIC 603*; *Rule of St. Benedict*, Chapter 1.

7 October—On continuing to pray with Saint Francis

GAIN WE JOIN Saint Francis in prayer, O Divine Master, grant that I may not seek to be consoled, as to console. To be understood, as to understand. To be loved, as to love. For it is in giving that we receive. It is in pardoning that we are pardoned. It is in dying that we are born to eternal life.

To complete our plea to be instruments of love, as Christ himself was the greatest example, we ask to understand more than be understood and to love more than be loved.

To love others is to accept them and by seeing the Christ in them we overcome all obstacles to loving them. To love in this way, all that is dark and in shadow in others is pushed aside by the light of Christ so that what we love is the holy in them, that which makes them a child of God and, therefore, part of the divine itself. This is the triumph of love. This is the *understanding* we all need as Christians: To see the Christ living in each man and woman we see, met or know.

It is not an understanding that comes from the intellect but through our faith and in imitation of Jesus. We pray to be given the ability to love others for exactly what and how they are *in reality*. It does not matter who they appear to be in this world—rich, poor, prostitute, celebrity, infamous, prisoner of justice or of conscience, inadequate or powerful, king or beggar or thief, man or woman of greed or a person generous to a fault or the forgotten, lost and mad among us. We must *not* judge, because God forbids it. We must love them each and every one, no matter who they are, just as Christ loved each of us. (1 John 3:17; Proverbs 14:31; Psalm 83:12)

Therefore, our love must be boundless and without expectations, because as we pray with Saint Francis: *it is in giving that we receive.* The knowledge that we have done good is reward enough, since we have honoured God by such charity. To expect nothing in return and to have no expectations at all is to love. This is the kind of love we must profess and demonstrate throughout our lives as Christians, because we are disciples of Jesus and this is the kind of love he showed all of us.

Charity is always clothed with the robe of forgiveness, because when we pardon the offenses of others, God pardons us. (Matthew 6:14; Psalm 85:15) Yet, how often we take offense. With each passing year we seem to grow more sensitive to the slightest hint of criticism, even the mere use of the wrong word in a conversation may offend us. How can we be that sensitive about ourselves and yet so often insensitive to the feelings of others?

Indeed, such hardness of heart has perhaps always been so among those who enjoy a privileged life, because they are rarely criticized or rejected in anyway. If rich enough, they are surrounded by people, even friends and family, who tell them what they want to hear. Such privilege and such flattering words close the ears of the rich and the famous. They get confused about reality and vanity triumphs. They enter a prison of conceit. Worse still, they often forget God.

Among the poor, homeless, and destitute, however, it is a very different story. Rejection is so commonly encountered by such people that offensive remarks by others about them is accepted as the natural result of their low situation in life. This is why the rejected by society, like the tax collector and the prostitute, were surprised when Jesus looked upon them with kindness and compassion.

So the next time you feel offended by some rude or insensitive remark or other offense directed at you, are you humble enough to remain at peace and to turn the other cheek? (Matthew 5:39; Luke 6:29)

8 October—On avoiding lies

 OD CONDEMNS LYING. Jesus told us that all liars would burn with fire and brimstone. (John 8:44; Revelation 21:8; Proverbs 6:16–19) Since God detests lying, such use of the mouth eventually kills the soul. (Proverbs 10:18–21)

The reason why lies are so hateful to God is because God is essentially truth.[7] Our Lord confirmed this when he told us, *I am the Way, the Truth, and the Life.* (John 14:6) Hence, as all lies are opposite to truth, they are all opposite to God. So, when we lie we oppose God. There is no such thing as an *alternative truth.*

Consider for a moment how often we may have told little lies, the ones people call *little white lies.* These may be told with the best of intentions, but there are no lies whatsoever that please God, not even lies that may save the whole world. This is because good may not come from evil. So no matter how good our intentions we cannot make our lies into something good, even little white lies. We must not condemn our selves with our mouth.

---

[7]   St. Thomas Aquinas, *Summa Theologiae*, Article 5.

9 October—On honouring your father and mother

 ONOURING OUR FATHER and mother should be agreeable to our nature, reason, and religion, because in such honouring all will go well for us. (Ephesians 6:2–3) This commandment is the first that has a promise attached to it, that is if we give such honour then everything will be all right for us. In this way, it holds instruction for the present but also tells us about the future results of our action or inaction regarding the way we treat our parents.

It is natural to love those who have cared and protected us during the years of our childhood and vulnerability. In the best circumstances, a bond of love is established that lasts a lifetime. This natural instinct is not one of ceremony or bowing to authority out of fear, but one based on respect and reverence.

Yet, how often children grow distant from their parents, living a separate life and not sharing it with their father and mother. They set aside this natural instinct of relationship out of selfishness and forgetfulness. Such selfishness happens because they have ceased to realize how important they remain to their parents. Forgetfulness exists because their father and mother have taken such a low rank in their children's lives. The children now think their parents only marginally important. From time to time a sense of duty, usually felt out of social imperatives and pressures, obliges them to contact their parents, but it is short-lived, impatient, and without much fondness. Such contact is often polite but without real kindness or concern. The heart of the mother or father hears this insincerity with an inner ear of the heart and is wounded, yet says nothing for fear the child will be offended and not contact them again. Such is the love a mother or a father may have for a child.

As adults, we often mistake events in our childhood or misinterpreted them or simply imagine what took place. These feelings, false or misplaced though they may be, can lead in adulthood to an emotional estrangement from a father or mother. The child, now adult, persists in believing this false reality, which hurts not just the parents but the grown child as well. Resentment or anger or condemnation replaces love as a result of our putting aside our natural tendency to love those who cared for us as children. God's law absolutely forbids us to judge others and that includes our parents. (Matthew 7:1)

Have you unsettling memories of your childhood that still plague your heart? If so, then you are commanded by God to show mercy and to forgive. After all, what you need to remember is that every parent did his or her best as a parent, no matter whether it was good, average, or inadequate. In the end we have but one mother and one father in this world. We must do what is right in honouring those who cared for us as a child, no matter how great or limited their sacrifice for us. (Galatians 5:25; Ephesians 6:1)

10 October—What honouring your father and mother requires

HIS LAW OF God as regards our parents does not consist in cringing obedience and a polite ceremony of good manners, but implies a sincere love joined with respect and reverence. It means a sensible but ready obedience to their wishes in a way that does not clash with the holy will and law of God and still allows them to be an adult. It implies that we give our parents proper assistance in their physical needs as well as in their spiritual needs. In this respect, charity does indeed start at home. Our Lord does not welcome our gifts of devotion to him and to the stranger in need, if you do not offer the same to your father and mother. (Matthew 15:4)

Listen most carefully to these words of wisdom, which the Holy Spirit has told us: *The Lord honours a father above his children and he upholds the rights of a mother over her sons. Whoever respects a father expiates sins, whoever honours a mother is like some amassing a fortune. Whoever respects a father will in turn be happy with children, the day he prays for help, he will be heard. Long life comes to anyone who honours a father, whoever obeys the Lord makes a mother happy. Such a one serves parents as well as the Lord. Respect your father in deed as well as word, so that blessing may come on you from him; since a father's blessing makes his children's house firm, while a mother's curse tears up its foundations. Do not make a boast of disgrace overtaking your father, your father's disgrace reflects no honour on you; for a person's own honour derives from the respect shown to his father, and a mother held in dishonour is a reproach to her children. My child, support your father in his old age, do not grieve him during life. Even if his mind should fail, show him sympathy, do not despise him in your health and strength; for kindness to a father will not be forgotten but will serve as a reparation for your sins.* (Ecclesiaticus 3)

You have been told what to do, so conclude to make certain to carry out your obligation of love to your father and mother. Do not pass over this matter lightly in the examination of your conscience as many do who flatter themselves with a false security while they live in neglect of this duty to their parents. We must never forget that we have but *one* father and *one* mother on this earth.

11 October—What God requires from parents as regards their children

HE OBLIGATION OF parents is great for it concerns not just their own eternal welfare but also that of children under their care. Most parents try not to neglect their children as to their physical, educational, and emotional well-being.

But what about the nourishment of their children's spiritual life? This is a serious question that every parent needs to ask themselves, because the duty owed to children encompasses spiritual needs as well as physical and emotional ones. We must never forget that Jesus gathers all the children of God to himself. (Isaiah 40:11; Micah 5:3)

Therefore, it is parents who must be the first to instil into their children's minds the love of God and other people and not leave it to religious teachers and priests. (Ephesians 6:4) In this way, parents procure for their children an attitude to life that, while sensible, is not too harsh and aspires to trust in the power of love. Unfortunately, many parents train up their children to the values of the world, putting everything before God. This sets the worse kind of example for children and does not honour our children or God.

All too often Christians take their children to church and to catechism lessons when they are young, but as soon as they become more independent in the early years of their adolescence, many parents do not insist on their children accompanying them to church. They often give the excuse that their children are old enough now to make up their own minds about God and Church services or they simply give up the struggle and resign themselves to the situation. Such parents give up before their children have reached maturity. For example, isn't it bizarre that we consider a 13 year old child not adult enough to decide on their own whether or not to drink alcohol or when to go to bed, but we accord them a maturity of decision making about their spiritual life?

12 October—On the virtue of chastity

 HAT CHASTITY MEANS seems to change with the fashion of the times. However, chastity as defined by Holy Scripture does not. Chastity there is a *purity of self*. It means obeying God's law and the teachings of Jesus. Such purity excludes expressions or satisfactions of the flesh outside of marriage. This is extremely difficult for men and women for reasons of human nature and in the face of considerable pressure from most of the world that sexual satisfaction is permissible outside of marriage.

If you wish to follow Christ, chastity is what you are to practice as a Christian. Sadly many Christians do not. In the current cult of individuality, we believe that we have a *right* to express ourselves in anyway that we may feel as long as the law of the land does not object. One of those *rights* is increasingly to express our sexuality. Hence, chastity is not a popular option.

Yet, the chastity of unmarried men and women is demanded by God. It is hardly ever preached in churches anymore. If you do not believe this, then ask yourself when you last heard a priest, preacher, minister or pastor gave a sermon about fornication or adultery. It is our human nature to ignore what we do not like about virtue in order to indulge the satisfactions of the flesh. Indeed, nothing is new under the sun, including the problems about our sexuality. (Ecclesiastes 1:9; Ecclesiasticus 18:30)

Chastity is essential for the practicing Christian. According to Holy Scripture, it is not open to amendment or to a more contemporary tolerance or to the claims of psychology or to any new understandings of the nature of humanity, medical, scientific or otherwise

If we belong to the world, then we will surely fall into its ways and never be a man or woman of chastity and *purity of self*, because the ways of the world encourage the indulgence of our senses. Most of the world would have us believe that the physical expression of sexual desire is not only permissible, but a *right* without boundaries—anything and everything goes. While adultery, if married, is still frowned on by most people, all manner of excuses are made for fornication. How Christians wiggle and squirm in trying to turn divorce and second marriages into a secular issue and away from any spiritual concern. Since God's law has not changed, what the world is claiming in this matter is that God is wrong. Is this what we are saying by the life we lead?

Chastity, being purity of self, is, therefore, a virtue because it is obedient to God's wishes, which among others is to refrain from sexual intercourse outside marriage. Such chastity infers, of course, to the refraining from *any* sexual impurities as defined by Holy Scripture and it applies equally to men as well as to women. Being chaste may include virginity, abstinence, self-restrain, celibacy, and self-denials of our sexual expression.

Since God created sex, it must in itself be good, but only if such sexual expression is kept within an *appropriate place* by Christians. Holy Scripture tells us that the *appropriate place* is marriage. We may not like it. We may think it infringes our *rights* as individuals. We may find chastity unbearable and refuse it, succumbing to the temptations of our flesh. But being a Christian is not picking what we like in Holy Scripture, choosing what God says that pleases us and ignoring the rest. *Purity of self* is not a secular or cultural matter but one of the spiritual and inner life.

Many think chastity is simply about not having sexual activity- that is the abstinence from actual intercourse—but that all the other expressions of sexuality are permissible. This not true for the Christian, since there is no such thing as being partially in a state of purity or partially in a state of grace or pleasing God just a little bit while at the same time displeasing him a lot by what we are doing. Jesus reminds us of this when he tells us that true chastity involves the mind and the spirit as well as the body: *You have heard how it was said, "You shall not commit adultery." But I say this to you, if a man looks at a woman lustfully, he has already committed adultery with her in his heart.* (Matthew 5:27–28; Proverbs 5:18–21 & 6:20–35, Jeremiah 13:27) Since God does not accept half-measures, we are either chaste or we are not.

13 October—On chastity being more than abstinence

E ALL STRUGGLE with our sexual needs and desires. We are fragile humans in need of a more or less constant flow of forgiveness from God, but we need to accept that God create us as beings who are sexual. Everything in the world contrives to make any attempt at self-control in sexual matters a heavy burden for men and women. Our surrounding life is filled with temptations of every kind to give in to the desires of our flesh. Jesus said, *The spirit is willing enough, but human nature is weak.* (Matthew 26:41)

Inducements to sexual liberty are displayed daily to us. Moreover, the world would have us believe that sexual liberty, freed from religious constrains is good for us even if it means breaking God's commandments. The false promise the world makes is that we will be happier and healthier by succumbing to our sexuality.

To give up the overt expression of our sexuality and to stop our thoughts when they turn from admiration to lust is no little sacrifice. Yet, what a feeble sacrifice when compared to the Cross of Jesus Christ. This lack of physical expression of our sexuality is still only abstinence and, thus, only a part of the virtue of chastity. We still may lust with our thoughts. For example, as we know anyone who stares at a woman with lust has already committed adultery with her in his heart. (Matthew 5:28) Surely, this teaching equally applies to women looking with lust on a man, men looking at other men with desire, and to women lusting after another woman. Lust is lust and it does not matter who is the object of such desire.

14 October—On the temple of the Holy Spirit

 HERE IS AN even deeper significance to the virtue of chastity than just the self-denial of the physical and mental expression of our sexual desires. The purity that is the goal of chastity is that purity which arises because our body, mind and spirit, indeed our whole person, is the temple of the Holy Spirit. (1 Corinthians 3:16–17, & 6:19–20; 1 Timothy 4:7–9)

Now consider, if our body is this holy temple created by God, then we are not our own property. Therefore, we may not do as we see fit with ourselves, because we are God's property and his divine purpose resides in us. The Cross of Jesus stands before us in all things and each of us is the temple in which the resurrected Christ finds life. Therefore, we must willingly honour God with our body because it is holy. (1 Corinthians 6:19–20)

Now, the world will tell us, in one way or another from advertising to books, that we are allowed to do anything as long as we do not hurt anyone. But not everything does good. (1 Corinthians 6:12) Indeed, we will be reassured that our self-expression without restrain but within the secular law is a freedom that brings happiness and fulfilment. We will welcome this because we do not want to let anything or anyone make us a slave. We adore being comfortable.

Yet, our mind, body and spirit, belongs to God. We are *the many* for whom he gave his life. (Mark 10:45) Why then should we think ourselves different from Blessed Mary when it comes to a willing submission to the plan of God over our lives? As a temple of the Holy Spirit, we are participating in the life of God. Remember what we have been told: *Be holy, for I am holy.* (1 Peter 1:16)

15 October—Memorial of Saint Teresa of Avila

E ARE FILLED with devotion at the solemn rites of the Eucharist meal when we celebrate the life and death of Christ. (Psalm 46:6–7)[8] In this thanksgiving, we are nourished by the body and blood of our beloved Lord and strengthened in all we do in the service of God, whether we are having bad or blessed times. (John 6:32–58; Matthew 26:26-28; Luke 22:17–20; 1 Corinthians 11:24–25)

Saint Teresa of Avila reminds us that with such holy strength we can bear all things provided we have Christ dwelling within us as our friend and loving guide. If God grants us the grace, then all the things we face, whether good, bad or indifferent, will be easy for us. It will enable us to put to one side our self-concerns and do great things for him. (Matthew 3:17; Mark 1:11)[9]

If you would be a witness in the Church and desire to walk in the way of perfection, then kindle in yourself a fire for God so that you are reminded that God is with you and Christ is at your side. Then you may be given the grace to take those steps that Saint Teresa spoke of which lead to union with God. (Psalm 70:14–15; 1 Corinthians 6:17)[10]

---

8   Grimlaicus, *Rule for Solitaries*, Chapter 34.
9   St. Teresa of Avila, *The Life*, Chapter 22.
10   St. Teresa of Avila, *The Interior Castle*.

16 October—On the Sacrament of Reconciliation

 OMMONLY REFERRED TO as *Confession*, this Sacrament is an instrument of spiritual growth. It is a powerful and positive force to improve the quality of your life as a Christian in all ways and to bring you back to the fullest communion with God and your neighbour. Confession is not a negative process but a very positive one. It should not make us afraid, nervous or anxious, and never reluctant, but rather glad to ask God's forgiveness for our disobedience, no matter how slight or how grave that may have been. Whatever is troubling our conscience needs the healing that confessing brings to it, because such repentance brings forgiveness and this brings us reunion with God. We are reconciled once again.

17 October—On the importance of silence and contemplation.

 ODAY, WE CELEBRATE the life of Saint Ignatius of Antioch (c.50- 117?), who was one of the five Apostolic Church Fathers. He believed that the Christian lives in truth by allowing God's reality to speak and act in his or her life. To this end, he commended silence to the believer, saying: *It is better to keep silence and to be than it is to speak and not to be.*[11]

If we are not silent, how can we listen with the ear of our heart to what God has to tell us. (Prov. 4:20)[12] If we do not step outside the busy life of the world to be silent, how can we examine the most hidden aspects of ourselves? When we are distracted by the world, how can we enter that place where the Holy Spirit waits?

It is in this enfolding silence of self that we find ourselves in prayer. From prayer, we may enter contemplation, another inner gateway to God. This inner gateway is contemplation, a state of yourself where the true self awakes and the illusionary ego of self is no more.[13] In this way, we imitate Jesus when he sought the silence of the desert to pray. In contemplation the soul is flooded with the Holy Spirit.

Let us, then, follow the advice of Saint Ignatius, Saint Benedict and so many other holy men and women, finding the voice of God in the silence of contemplation and arising from that sleep that forgets God. Let us awake to our call to be holy. (1 Peter 1:15–16) Let us return to Holy Scripture and, hearing his voice, harden not our hearts. (Romans 13:11–12; Psalm 94:8)

---

[11] St. Ignatius of Antioch, *Epistle to the Ephesians*.

[12] *Rule of Saint Benedict*, Prologue.

[13] Thomas Merton, *The Inner Experience*, para 9.

18 October—Feast of Saint Luke, Evangelist

AINT LUKE WAS a Greek and a physician, who became a close companion of the Apostle Paul and accompanied him on his missionary journeys. (Philemon 1:24; 2 Timothy 4:11) Probably a Gentile, Saint Luke is the author of the third Gospel and the *Acts of the Apostles.* He tells us of the deep compassion of Jesus for sinners and those who suffer. He also places a strong emphasis on the role women played in the life of Jesus.

Therefore, in honouring Saint Luke, let us sing with Mary, that most favoured of women, her song which Saint Luke recorded for us and which we call, *The Magnificat.* (Luke 1:46–55)

My soul proclaims the greatness of the Lord,
my spirit rejoices in God, my Saviour.
Because he has looked upon
The humiliation of his servant.
Yes, from now onwards
all generations will call me blessed.
For the Almighty
has done great things for me.
Holy is his name,
His faithful love extends age after age
to those who fear him.
He has used the ower of his arm,
He has routed the arrogant of heart
He has pulled down princes
From their thrones
and raised high the lowly.
He has filled the starving with good things,
sent the rich away empty.
He has come to help
of Israel his servant,
mindful of his faithful promise.

19 October—On the vice of pride

 RIDE IS AN inordinate love of self in one form or another. For example, we may be conceited about some aspect of our selves such as a talent for drawing or running a very profitable business. Pride can be a desire for personal excellence, a wanting to win, a wanting to get ahead of others, or an ambition to triumph in the goals the world or our work or what other people, especially parents, may set as goals for us. So often what the world sees as achievement is actually just the vice of pride at our work.

Vanity comes dressed up in many ways and takes many forms. For example, pride can be taking delight in ourselves, a smug complacency stemming from some real or imaginary excellency, which we think, have or pretend to have. This can be pride in our virtues or our knowledge or in our commercial success and resulting material possessions. This kind of pride need not be just external and obvious, but can be hidden in us. It is even more insidious for that reason, because we often are not aware that behind our actions there is the vanity of pride shadowing everything we do and say. Other people, not so blinded by ideas of success in this world, may notice it before we ourselves recognize that pride is ruling us.

The worst possible pride must surely be spiritual pride, which makes us feel puffed up with the belief that we are pleasing to God, subsequently forgetting that we are sinners.

This is why people who are too publicly overly pious, whether in church or not, are often treated with suspicion by others. It has long been said that the habit of a monk does not make the man, but the man makes the habit. Rosaries, necklaces showing the Cross, veils, priestly robes, monastic clothing, and other outward signs of religiosity can be the result of pride and not a heartfelt symbol of love for God. As we parade our devotions in public, let us remember the beggar at the church door or in the street, who holds out his hand for our alms. Here is Christ himself for Christ lives in this man, as he does in every man and woman, as surely as he lives in us. Since we all belong to God, the vanity of pride has no place in the Christian life.

How often has pride blocked us from that hospitality we are commanded by God to offer others? Have we refused an angel without knowing it? (Hebrews 13:2)

20 October—How pride denies love

 HEN WE ARE filled with pride, it means we prefer ourselves to others. We may even come to despise others and judge them following such feelings. This kind of pride is the mother of all vices, because it is an expression of not loving others. It encompasses many other vices such as ambition, presumption, excessive vanity, condescension, the way we look, and social standing, power or possessions. Let us recall how often Scripture and the psalms reminds us that we are but dust and came into this world with nothing and leave it with nothing. (1 Timothy 6:7; Ecclesiastes 5:14–15; Job 1:21)

21 October—On four kinds of pride

 ope Saint Gregory the Great distinguished four ways of being guilty of pride. First, by attributing to one's self the good things we have from God either by nature or by grace. Secondly, by crediting to one's own talents instead of giving God the whole credit and glory for such gifts. Thirdly, by believing ourselves to have graces, talents, or perfections, which we do not have and being puffed up with this imaginary excellence. Fourthly, by valuing ourselves for the good qualities or gifts we really do possess and acting in such a manner with them as if only we alone have them and to dislike others or envy them, who may have similar talents or accomplishments.[14]

All these kinds of pride are of the worst kind of sin, because they oppose God in pretending a personal excellence that belongs to God alone. We learn from the Saint Paul that the proud in worshiping themselves as the creature, instead of worshiping God the creator, have been often abandoned by God and left to suffer in punishment of their self-conceit and arrogance. (Romans 1:25–26)

There is another form that pride can take, but this one is hidden in the shadows of self-love. It is called *false pride* and often affects the religious and ordained and those who lead what the world would term *a good and holy life*. Many a regular church-going Christian has fallen beneath the crushing wheel of *false pride*. This *false pride* means we have a pride in our interior life with God and we secretly believe that this is due to our own efforts of humility, prayers and worship. In so believing, even if we are not aware of it, is not to give all credit to the will of God for our interior spiritual well-being. It is as if we had decided to wear a halo and were always polishing it.

---

14   Pope Gregory I , *Morals* 24:8.

So *false pride* does not credit its holy source. In giving ourselves all the credit for the state of our soul, even when not conscious of doing it, is to deny the grace of God in its welfare. It is as if you cleaned up the palace of God in your soul where he should sit enthroned, then locked the door as if you were the keeper of the key to heaven and not Saint Peter.

How often false pride is hidden in a person, only to be discovered very late in life after years of apparently being obedient to God. If we think the vice of pride, including false pride, is not true of ourselves, there is no better proof of it than to imagine ourselves to be free of it.

22 October—Remedies against pride

N ORDER TO overcome pride, we must first be aware of it, because it often blends in with our virtues or talents so that we are unaware we are filled to the brim with this vanity. (Ecclesiastes 12:8) Admitting that we are filled with pride is very difficult. None of us want to feel that we are guilty of this vice, since we know that others, like our family and friends, will neither admire nor like it. Indeed, such dislike of our pride by others is often considered an insult, because pride hates to be criticized or attacked in any way.

What pride in us means is that we are corrupted by it, not just by the way we act and speak but by what it does to our spiritual life. Pride tries to snatch the crown of glory from the Holy Spirit and to parade with it in our heart and making us very pleased with ourselves. It is, therefore, the enemy of all that is holy. It blocks our attempts to be pure for God and causes our good intentions to go astray. In all of this, pride remains in us like a lion waiting to leap out and devour us. (Psalms 7:2; 1 Peter 5:8)

Hence, constantly watching out for pride and praying to be saved from it, needs the remedy of humility. We do this by turning frequently and regularly to the example of Christ and by listening to his words. All human greatness, power, and fame dwindles away and vanishes when God appears even earth and sky vanish, leaving no trace. (Revelation 20:11) If we remember that the seeds of virtue exist in every man and woman, placed there by the kindness of God and growing to bloom by the nourishment of the living waters of Christ, then we will not fail to defeat pride. (1 Corinthians 3:7)[15]

---

[15] St. John Cassian, *Confessions*, 13.12.5–8, 13.1.

23 October—Other remedies against pride

N ORDER TO overcome our pride, it will help us to frequently reflect on how vain and perishable those things generally are about which people are usually so proud. Among those things that invite pride to take hold of our life are worldly honours, wealth and property ownership, beauty and admiration, fine clothes and jewels, titles of nobility or election, and of being listed among those who are powerful and rich. For example, consider how having the financial ability to buy whatever takes our fancy leads quickly to a kind of pride called *snobbery*. Another example is to imagine how bloated with pride we become when everyday, like most celebrities, we are told we are fabulous, beautiful, charming, and wonderful. How easily we are seduced by such flattery.

The list of things to be proud of in this world is long and all of it is a great waste of our time, because all of it vanishes either before we are dead or most certainly after we are gone. No one remembers us after a few years and those who knew us will also die and with them any memory of us. Even stone monuments to us will eventually crumble with age or be destroyed by war or envy or vandalism. The cemetery is full of people who thought the world could not do without them.

We may say to ourselves, *but I can enjoy many of these things of the world and still please God if I am kind, loving, and compassionate.* Do we believe that? Who do you know that has acquired worldly things through being kind and loving? Do you honestly believe that anyone becomes president or prime minister or a leader, because he or she is compassionate? These are questions every Christian should ask, because the way of Christ is narrow and difficult and full of temptations, like pride, that can lead us out of God's holy light.

Generally speaking, those people who are proud are usually humbled eventually by God and other people. The powerful fall. The rich become poor. Nations, presidents, prime ministers, kings and queens, and dictators come and go. Nothing is settled and all is changing, because that is the nature of the universe and the *being* of God. His creating never ceases, but as far as this world is concerned every one ends in obscurity. Naked we were born and naked we return. Made from dust we become dust once again, save for our soul which rests in waiting for God's final judgment. (Ecclesiastes 5:14; Job 1:21; 1 Timothy 6:7)

24 October—On excessive vanity

XCESSIVE VANITY IS a vice into which many of us easily succumb, because our thoughts, words and actions are greatly influenced by our love of praise, honour and being held in esteem by other people.

We learn in the gospel that excessive vanity or vainglory was the vice of the Scribes and Pharisees, who did all their works that they might be honoured and esteemed by people. Therefore, their alms, fasting, prayers, and other good works were nothing in the sight of God. At the same time that they were esteemed as saints by the world, they were shameful in the eyes of God.

Now there is nothing wrong with other people recognizing our good qualities and acts, if they reflect the way we live as Christians, especially if they inspire others to live for the glory of God. Indeed, Jesus told us that *your light must shine in people's sight, so that, seeing your good works, they may give praise to your Father in heaven.* (Matthew 5:16) The desire for glory does not, in itself, make a sin, because that true glory we receive from God is the glory promised to us for our good works (2 Corinthians 10:17)

However, seeking human praise for its own sake is sinful. Saint Thomas Aquinas includes in his examples of vanity those people who expose themselves to needless danger just to show off.[16] So the real reason we have for climbing mountains may be very important in climbing the spiritual ladder to God. The world is full of temptations and traps just waiting to devour us like lions ready for the kill. (Psalm 21:14)

---

[16] St. Thomas Aquinas, *Summa Theologiæ.*

25 October—On remedies against excessive vanity

HEN WE CONSIDER how short-lived any human glory is and adds nothing to us in the sight of God, we see vanity or *vainglory* for it is—a puff of wind of no importance at all. Like morning mist, it soon disappears. When we realize that glory given by humans is merely passing vanity, it is not difficult to dismiss the causes of vanity in ourselves and take up again the truths of our faith.[17]

Those who do this, fearing the Lord, are not puffed up on account of their good works, says Saint Benedict, *but judging that they can do no good of themselves and that all comes from God, they magnify the Lord's work in themselves, using the word of the prophet: Not unto us, O Lord, not unto us, but unto your name give the glory.* (Psalm. 113:9)[18] The Apostle Paul gave himself no credit for his preaching, but claimed whatever he did was solely by the grace of God. (1 Corinthians 15:10) And again Paul tells us: *He that glories, let him glory in the Lord.* (2 Corinthians 10:17) So let us remember that he may condemn those who want praise by others and do not give credit to God for their achievements.[19]

---

[17] Thomas à Kempis, Book 1, c. 3).
[18] Introduction, *Rule of Saint Benedict*.
[19] St. Augustine, *Confessions* 1:10, Chapter 36.

26 October—On the vice of covetousness

 OVETOUSNESS FOR A Christian means a person is worshiping what he or she wants instead of giving that worship to God. Such envy is to set up your own desires as idols. Hence, such a greedy person is an idolater, worshiping the things of this world. Thus, covetousness is idolatry. We are, in effect, bowing down before the golden calf of false gods. (Ephesians 5:5; Colossians 3:5; Romans 1:25)

To be *covetous* and *covetousness* are not words much used these days. Nevertheless, covetousness as a form of envy is rampant in the world, because to be this way makes us greedy, grasping, mean, miserly, and we envy what others possess. But how the world admires those who have riches, power, and social status!

No one can escape being aware that the world is full of the many aspects of this vice. Its many manifestations are so common in the world that the only way to save yourself from them is to take refuge in God. (Psalm 45:2 & 90:1–2)

The covetous man or woman serves Mammon, the false god that makes them turn their backs against God and neglect his love and service. They are always ready to break his commandments for love of more money and, indeed, the *more* of everything. Such men and women harden their hearts against the necessities of their neighbours. The cries of the poor mean little or nothing to them, even when they may use their money to glorify themselves by creating charities and endowing public museums and libraries, usually named after themselves or their family. Such people often dislike contributing to the welfare of society through taxation as if they never used walkways, roads and other public spaces.

Covetousness is an envy so terrible that it can lead even to killing someone for what you want. (James 4:2) Our human history of full of such events—just consider the wars, kings and dictators, the rich and powerful, those who think of profits before the welfare of people or society or the environment, and those who have no regard for others as long as they achieve their goal of making more money. It really doesn't matter if the money is directly for themselves or indirectly through enhancing the values and profits made as shareholders or from a investors' fund, because we are responsible individually to God for what we do and envy in any form is contrary to God's commandments. We either live a life of the values set before us by God and Christ or we do not. (Matthew 6:24; Luke 16:13)

27 October—What Holy Scripture tells us about covetousness

E ARE TOLD that the ways of every covetous man destroy the soul of the possessor and that nothing is more wicked than a covetous man. (Proverbs 1:31; Ecclesiasticus 9:11; Isaiah 5:8) Jeremiah threatens the Jews with the worst of evils, because from the least to the greatest they all were given to covetousness. (Jeremiah 6 & 8) We find the other prophets tell of similar judgments and disasters that come from God against the covetous. (Amos 9:1–4; Habakkuk 2:5–12, especially 9–10) Christ himself reckons covetousness among the crimes of the heart that defile a man. Saint Paul puts the self-indulgent among others on the black list of such sin, telling us that these people are worthy of death and will never share in the heavenly inheritance of Christ or possess the kingdom of God. (Romans 1:28–32; 1 Corinthians 6:9–10; Ephesians 5:5–7) You would think that these terrible consequences against covetousness, which stems from the vice of envy, would deter Christians from this unhappy love of money, power, and social position but it mostly does not.

Consider further how the word of God tells us that wealth, which men and women so earnestly seek and want to possess, is not capable of making them happy or giving any lasting meaning to their lives. King Solomon declared that a covetous person will not be satisfied with money and those who love riches shall reap no fruit from them. (Ecclesiastes 5:9) The wealth of this world, instead of bringing content and peace to the soul, is generally accompanied with nothing but snobbery and vexation of the mind. (Ecclesiastes 2:11 & 5:10–11) More is never enough for those who suffer from such envy or covetousness and a sense of injustice about others escapes them.

With great wealth just as with any political or social power, not trusting in other people grows, the need for loyalty increases, truth becomes confused and lies abound. In the end, riches leave a person dissatisfied with his or her life and excluded from eternal life by a lack of repentance, all the consolation they ever have is in their short earthly life. (Matthew 19:24; Luke 6:24; 1 Timothy 6:9–10)

Let us pray, then, that we will listen to Holy Scripture truths and find our treasure instead in the truths of God. Let us do good works of love so that the gates of heaven will open for us. Let us trust in God. (Matthew 6:20; Luke 7:19–21; Psalm 76:14–15; 1 Timothy 6:7; Hebrews 8:5) We have no other security, because no other treasure will endure for us.

28 October—Feast of Saints Simon & Jude, Apostles

 ONSIDER THE WISDOM of God in rising up these apostles and the others from those without power or high social position and making them princes of his people. Saint Paul confirms that *God chose those who by human standards are fools to shame the wise; he chose those who by human standards are weak to shame the strong, those who by human standards are common and contemptible—indeed those who count for nothing—to reduce to nothing all those that do count for something so that no human being might feel boastful before God.* (1 Corinthians 1:27–31)

The Apostles, then, were not chosen by God because they were wise, rich, eloquent, learned, noble, considered important people by the world or even best qualified by their simplicity and humility and certainly not because they were especially pious. By the men Jesus chose to be his apostles, we learn that we cannot see, as Jesus could, into the hearts of men and women and by such vision understand their deepest good. This tells us that God honours what this world may despise and consider unimportant and treat with carelessness or contempt. Further, it shows us that our assumed grandeur, deceitful appearances, and ostentation of wisdom or piety are false. Since we cannot read what is in other peoples' hearts, it explains why we are unable to judge them, even if God had not forbidden us to do such a thing. (Matthew 7:1–2)

29 October—On the Christian's warfare

 HE LIFE OF a Christian is a perpetual state of war. (Job 7:1) A Christian's time of true and solid peace does not come until after many a conflict and many a victory. A Christian must fight his way to heaven against a set of cruel, deceitful, and obstinate enemies.

These enemies are the ones Saint Paul warns us about, telling us to put on the armour of God, so that we may be able to stand against the deceits of the devil. For it not against human enemies that we have to struggle, but against the principalities and the ruling forces who are masters of the darkness in this world, the spirits of evil in the heavens. (Ephesians 6:11–12) All these legions of demons dwell invisibly around us. These wicked spirits never cease to employ millions of tricks, artifices, traps, and allurements, all designed to draw us away from God. But they cannot hurt us unless we freely consent to them—that is by yielding ourselves to them.

On the other hand, we have on our side, not only all the host of heaven ready to guard and defend us, but even God himself. If God is for us, what does it matter who is against us?

Hence, Jesus requires that we should renounce all other things in the world to follow him, no matter how near or how dear to us. He has told us: *Anyone who comes to me without hating father and mother, wife, children, brothers and sisters, yes, and his own life too, cannot be my disciple.* (Luke 14:26–27; Matthew 10:37–38) This renouncing of self, even those one loves, is at the core of a Christian's fight to resist all and any temptations to be disobedient to the commandments of God. Winning this battle gives us the privilege to follow Jesus.

30 October—On the Christian's conflict

 E ARE MEANT to enjoy our life on earth, to be at peace with our self and with others, and to look forward to eternal life. (John 10:10) Such joy in living brings the contentment that is the lasting gladness of our mind, body and spirit, because we are living in the presence of God. (Psalm 17:11; 2 Timothy 1:11–13) By frequent prayer, participation in worship, and keeping Jesus as our closest companion, we are able to remain in the loving state of virtue that pleases God. (Psalm 36:4) Jesus gathers to himself those men and women who have been prepared by the Holy Spirit with a heart ready for God.[20] So if we make God's commands our song, we will have no conflict in living and surely be blessed. (Psalm 118:*Zayin* 49–56)

---

[20] Didache, Chapter 4.

31 October—On the Christian's armour

 F WE ARE to realize victory in our struggle with temptations, then we must provide ourselves with the proper armour like a true soldier going into battle. We learn from Saint Paul what this armour is: *You must take up all God's amour or you will not be able to put up any resistance on the evil day or stand your ground even though you exert yourselves to the full. So stand your ground with truth a belt around your waist and uprightness a breastplate, wearing for shoes on your feet the eagerness to spread the gospel of peace and always carry the shield of faith so that you can use it to quench the burning arrows of the Evil One. And then you must take salvation as your helmet and the sword of the Spirit that is the word of God. In all your prayer and entreaty keep praying in the Spirit on every possible occasion. Never get tired of staying awake to pray for all God's holy people.* (Ephesians 6:13–19)

We must not forget to provide ourselves with the helmet of *hope* by placing complete confidence in God and none in ourselves. Here is the ultimate protection against the evil of vice, because such hope is the source of our courage and the metal from which all holy armour is made.

NOVEMBER

Theme: Renewing faith

Your deeds, O Lord, have made me glad;
For the work of your hands I shout for joy.
O Lord, how great are your works!
How deep are your designs!
The foolish man cannot know this
And the fool cannot understand.

Psalm 91: 5–7

1 November — Solemnity of All Saints

N THIS DAY we honour the saints and all those in heaven, a vast assembly from all nations that no person could possibly count. (Revelation 7:9) *All Saints Day* and *The Commemoration of All the Faithful Departed* are times to give special thanksgiving. By this celebration, we are encouraged to follow the examples of those God has chosen to be with him. This gives us the hope of joining them in heaven.

Speaking to the church, the Saint Paul tells the people that we have come to God, to the spirits of righteous men and women made perfect, to Jesus the Mediator of the new covenant, and to the blood that speaks a better word than the blood of Abel. He says, *Do not lose your fearlessness now, then, since the reward is so great.* (Hebrew 8 & 10:35) Here is the church triumphant in praise and love of Christ, the mediator for everyone in the world through the sacrifice of his blood on the *Cross of Love*.

On this day, we reflect on this glory in heaven with which God rewards his servants here on earth, remembering there is but one God in this and all universes. So the God you serve is the *same* God who is served by all those now rewarded by being with him in heaven. We have the *same* Saviour in Jesus the Christ as they had, the same beloved who sits at the right-hand of God. We have the *same* sacraments and the *same* help and means of grace as they had. All those now in heaven suffered the *same* weaknesses, desires, and passions as tempt us. If the one God is the *same* as always, then we should aspire to the *same* glory and happiness as the saints and all those who are in heaven.

2 November — Commemoration of All Souls

 HIS IS A celebration full of charity, because we remember all those who have died and we pray for God to welcome them in heaven. (2 Maccabees 12:41–46) Such praying for the souls of the departed is one of the spiritual works of mercy and, as such, is one of the most acceptable to God for he is the lover of souls.

When we pray for the departed, we obtain mercy ourselves as well. We are clearly told this in the Beatitudes: *the merciful shall obtain mercy.* If we forgive others their trespasses, then God will forgive our own trespasses. Isn't this what we are doing when we pray the *Lord's Prayer*? (Matthew 5:7 & 6–9) To be merciful, then, is to love and to love is to please God. When you show mercy you give God ample reason to give you mercy in return. (2 Samuel 22:26, Psalm 112:4–9; Proverbs 11:17; Proverbs 14:21; Psalm 17:25; Psalm 37:25)

When we pray for those who have died, we cannot help but think about our own death, but we need to remember that God takes no pleasure in destroying the living. For us to exist and to live in joy is his intention and to this end he created all things and us. (Wisdom 1: 12–15)

However, the godless among us argue that life is short and wearisome and death, like birth, is mere chance, the luck of the draw. *In any case,* they often claim, *no one will remember you after you are gone.* So they point out that we should enjoy the good things of this world like them while we can and never mind the poor, the helpless, those in need, the orphan or the old. Forget charity and mercy for others, since the most important rule for them is to always make self-love come first regardless of the consequences for others. They exalt such self-love as the greatest asset and most important aspect of living.

All of us know such godless people. Indeed, they abound everywhere. (Wisdom 2: 1–9) They believe themselves more important than even God. They do not realize that their local cemetery is full of people who thought the world could not do without them. They forget God or reject him, but God showed us through the resurrection of Jesus that he has power over death. (Isaiah 25:8) We know now that the triumph of eternal life can be our destiny. This is the *Good News* that God sent to us.

On this special day of *All Souls*, we need to remember what Saint Paul told us about death that to live is Christ and to die is gain. (Philippians 1:21)

3 November—On the duty of Christians to be saints

 EFORE THE WORLD was made, God chose each of us in Jesus Christ to be holy and faultless before him in love. (Ephesians 1:4) Again and again Christians are called to be saints, because all people who love God are called to be holy. (Romans 1:7) *You are a chosen race,* Saint Peter declares, *a kingdom of priests, a holy nation, and people to be a personal possession.* (1 Peter 2: 9) How often God has declared that all his people ought to be saints. *Set no bounds to your love, just as your heavenly Father sets none to his,* he instructs us. *Be perfect, just as your heavenly Father is perfect.* (Matthew 5:48)

Our being saints is not merely a matter of us attaining greater perfection. It is a divine command in every sense. Not all of us are chosen by God to work miracles or to exercise extraordinary austerities of self-denial for the sake of our spiritual life or to retreat into deserts to pray continually or to retire from the world to a consecrated life as a nun, monk or hermit or to sell all we have and give it to the poor, or to imitate the actions of many saints in making themselves more virtuous by self-deprivations and the denial of the virtuous pleasures of this life. God calls people individually and each is chosen for whatever the plan of God may be for them.

Yet, we are all commanded to love God with our whole heart, our whole soul, our whole mind, and with all of our strength. This is the shortest and surest way to all sanctity and perfection. It is this love of God that makes saints and it is a strict obligation for us all to try to be one of those saints. (Matthew 22:37; Mark 12:29–31; Luke 10:27) God calls each of us to do nothing less. Therefore, let us never forget how we have to try to be saints, because that is the goal of our life, the fulfilment of virtue, and our true destiny by the desire of God himself.

4 November—On the means we all have to become saints

F OUR LORD calls upon us to be saints, he is not demanding the impossible. He always gives us the means to achieve such a goal, if we make good use of his help. He increases our strength through our desire to be earnest in prayer and other spiritual exercises. He supports our acquisition of virtue if our perseverance to obtain it and our faithfulness to his command to love are constant and abiding. God leads us to hunger and thirst after justice but to leave the judgment of such justice to him. (Matthew 5:6)

Consider further the many helps to sanctity which we have waiting for us in the church of the people of God: the holy sacrament of the body and blood of Jesus Christ which nourishes and sustains us; the Word of God which is preached to us or studied by us and reflected upon; the lives of the saints, those great examples of living as servants of God; the mysteries relating to our redemption that we so often celebrate in public worship; and the praise and praying together with others. All these are there to help you become the saint that God wants you to be. Indeed, becoming a saint is not beyond our reach. (Deuteronomy 30:11–14)

5 November—On the perfection of our ordinary actions

GREAT MANY CHRISTIANS make the error of putting sanctity in an action, event or thing that is not really part of it. For example, many suppose that in order to be a saint one must work miracles. This is not true. Just recall that John the Baptist, one of the greatest of saints, did no miracles. (John 10:41) Others imagine that sanctity consists in having visions, revelations and ecstasies or in the gifts of prophecy, the speaking in tongues, and knowledge of the most sublime and divine truths. Not necessarily. Many people believe all these are signs and symbols of God and, therefore, must be full of sanctity, especially when they often find such things as these in the lives of saints.

But none of these things made the saints. Many saints have had none of them. Moreover, sanctity does not consist in much fasting or in self-denial or in the giving of large alms nor in reciting long prayers nor in any other extraordinary practices or observances. All these, however good in themselves they might be, can be found as well in men and women who are slaves to pride, self-love, hypocrisy and passion.

Consider then that if sanctity does not depend upon us doing extraordinary actions, it must depend upon our *ordinary* actions. Our life passes away in these daily ordinary actions, which take up our time from morning till night. We rise from sleep to carry out the day's work and responsibilities. We eat and drink. We make love. We raise our children. We complain. We are glad. We are sad. In other words, we go about life in a repeated pattern and habit. Many days are good. Some are not so great. We get by.

But God wants us to be happy and content, full of joy in living. This is what we hope for in our ordinary lives, because joy is the gift of God. (Psalm 36:4; Psalm 15:11; Proverbs 10:28)

Now, if everything in ordinary life is done extraordinary well with observance and remembrance of God in every task we undertake, then all of our time will be well spent. Nothing more than to live in a state of love will be required to make us saints, because the perfection of our ordinary actions depends upon the purity of intention with which we perform them and our attention to God in all that we do. We learn to look at the world as God does. (Psalm 91)

6 November—The sanctification of ordinary actions in our life

 ANY CHRISTIANS OFTEN wonder just how they can make the acts of ordinary living a continuous presence of God. That is, how are we to keep an awareness of God consciously present in our lives while doing house cleaning or cooking a meal or any of the other many mundane acts of daily living?

Many Christians find it helpful to make a little rule of life as they go about the ordinary business of living that brings a consciousness of God's presence. As we are in a real world and sometimes do not have much support from others about what we are doing, we need to keep it very simple. Here is a routine you can follow at home and work, giving offense to no one, but underpinning your faith and an awareness of God.

Prayer: Begin and end each day with as short prayer, offering God the work, success, failures and sufferings of your day.

Blessings: Begin each meal by thanking God for your food. You can do this silently if you wish. God always hears you whether it is your lips speaking or the voice of your heart.

Recollection: Take time at least once a day, even 15 minutes will do, to sit and be still. Put aside all preoccupations and anxieties of every kind. Invite Jesus to sit beside you.

Patience: Be patient with yourself in all you do, remembering that when you draw near to God, he draws near to you. (James 4:8)

7 November — On following the light of Christ

ONSIDER THESE WORDS of Jesus Christ, *I am the light of the world: anyone who follows me, will not be walking in the dark, but will have the light of life.* (John 8:12) These are beautiful words, because they inspire and bring hope. Jesus said them not just to the chosen few. Not just to the poor or needy, not just to the rich and powerful, not just for the master or the slave. He said these words to every man and woman in the entire world. These words have the same meaning today and tomorrow as they did at the moment Jesus said them.

This true light, which is Jesus the Christ, brings all men and women out of the darkness of ignorance and into the gladness of truth and wisdom. This light directs our feet in the way of peace. (Luke 1:78–79) We know at last the light of his divine grace and the purpose and aim of our earthly lives. (2 Peter 1:19)

We are born with this light in our hearts, because each of us is a beloved creature, created by God. This light, which is the presence of God in our lives, waits to be recognized and once awakened shows us the path of life, the path that leads to heaven, the path that pleases God and brings peace and contentment to us while we are here on earth. The teachings of Jesus, once we know them, are the guides and consolations that are with us every step of the way on this divine path. (Psalms 119, 104:1–2; Proverbs 3:6, 15:24; Matthew 7:13–14)

The holy light of God waits to lead each of us to heaven. It gives meaning to why we exist. So we need to follow it and be God's true subjects. If we come close to God, he will come close to us. (James 4:8) When we humble ourselves before the Lord, he will exalt us. (James 4:10) Never forget, then, when you stumble or fall or find life hard that Jesus Christ is there for you as the way, the truth, and the life. (John 14:6) The light of his life is shining on us to show us the way forward and his consolations are there to help us on our way to eternal life.

Pray for God to send always forth his light of truth and wisdom, letting these be our guide to bring us to God's holy mountain, to the place where he dwells. (John 3:19; Psalm 41:9–12)

8 November—Only one thing is necessary

HEN JESUS CAME to a village where a woman named Martha lived, she opened her home to him. She had a sister called Mary, who sat at the Lord's feet listening to what he said, while Martha was busy with all the preparations of hospitality for him. Eventually, Martha came to Jesus and asked him: *Lord, do you not care that my sister is leaving me to do the serving all by myself? Please tell her to help me!"* But the Lord replied, *Martha, Martha, you are worried and fret about so many things, and yet few are needed, indeed only one. It is Mary who has chosen what is better, and it is not to be taken from her.* (Luke 10:38–42)

Open your eyes to the great wisdom of Jesus when he tells Mary, and thus all of us, that *only one thing is necessary* and that *one necessary thing* is God. We are to listen to God. We must pay attention to what he says and teaches through Jesus the Christ and his prophets and messengers. We are not to work for food that perishes, but for food that endures in eternal life, which Jesus the Christ will give us for God has placed his seal of approval on him. (John 6:27)

But like Martha we are very often too concerned with our multitude of cares and concerns about worldly matters. A variety of amusements and work distract our thoughts. We generally live by a lot of dissipations and distractions. We frequently give a higher priority to responsibilities and duties of this world than to what is spiritual and holy. How little there is about God in our daily conversation. How few of our words or actions refer to him. How often, like Martha, we are so busy with worldly affairs that we forget to listen to God. How often we forget *only one thing is necessary.* We need to remember that even if we gain the whole world, it does not profit us if we lose our soul. (Matthew 16:26)

Take care then to make your first priority this *one thing necessary*, because our Saviour told us to seek first the

Kingdom of God and his justice, and all those things of goodness, peace, mercy and contentment would be given to you. (Matthew 6:33)

9 November—Strive to enter by the narrow gate

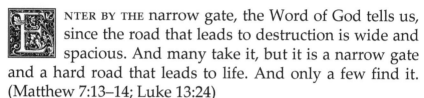 NTER BY THE narrow gate, the Word of God tells us, since the road that leads to destruction is wide and spacious. And many take it, but it is a narrow gate and a hard road that leads to life. And only a few find it. (Matthew 7:13–14; Luke 13:24)

Here we see there are two ways in which men and women walk in this life and there are two gates out of this life into eternity. One of these ways is broad and spacious, agreeable to the world and to the flesh and crowded with great multitudes of people, who are slaves to the world and to passions. No sooner do they enter this gate than they slip down into the bottomless pit of a miserable eternity.

The other way is narrow and difficult, because it restraints the liberties and passions of those who travel it. It is disagreeable to the desires and passions from which all men and women suffer. It demands virtues and the fulfilment of God's laws to the best of your ability. The few who succeed in staying on this narrow path are walking toward the gate of eternal life, comforted and accompanied by Christ. This is the way that leads to God.

Conclude to walk in the narrow way as a child of holy light. Do this by living always in the fear of God and by keeping his commandments.

10 November—No one can serve two masters

 O ONE CAN serve two masters and this is clearly explained to us in Holy Scripture: A person who tries to serve two masters will hate the one and love the other, or he will be devoted to the one and despise the other. So that we are left in no doubt about what this means we are then told, *You cannot be the slave both of God and of money.* (Matthew 6:24)

Now money is the measure of success by the standards of this world. It defines power and position. It separates the rich from the poor. Those with great wealth most often presume to have the authority to judge and rule over others. The desire for money creates greed, jealous, envy, distrust of others, and much devious behaviour. Eventually, a person is ruled by the desire for *more*. They never have enough money. No matter how much privilege and material possessions they have, they still want *more*. This wanting of *more* is the nature of greed. No one can escape once this curse takes possession of him or her. Money is the fuel of greed and the vice of greed is like a great fire, demanding more of that fuel until it consumes everything in its path. It is the enemy of God.

We have no obligations to greed and money and all the many temptations of the flesh. They are all enemies of our true welfare and the salvation of our souls. If we serve them, they will make us miserable forever. Jesus confirmed all this when he told his disciples: *How hard it is for those who have wealth to enter the kingdom of God. It is easier,* he added, *for a camel to go through the eye of a needle than for a rich person to enter the kingdom of God.* (Mark 10:17–30)

God is our only true master. He is our first beginning and our last end. He is our creator and our redeemer. He is infinitely good in himself and infinitely good to us. He is the source of our life. He is the will to live in everything on this earth. He is being itself.[1]

---

[1]   Albert Schweitzer, *Reverence for Life*; St. Thomas Aquinas, *Summa Theologiae.*

11 November—On accepting the will of God in all our sufferings

 HEN EVENTS IN our life turn out well, we are pleased with the will of God, but when we suffer, then it can be very hard to accept that God ordains everything that happens to us, except for sin. After all God is suppose to love. So we ask why we suffer.

First, it is true that God ordains all our sufferings of whatever kind, even those sufferings inflicted on us by the wickedness of other men or women. It may shock us that these are allowed by God. To realize that God wills or should allow the afflictions, trials, or injustices that we suffer is deeply difficult to accept. It is especially hard to understand when at the same time we know that he is a God of mercy and forgiveness, the God of love. We have tried our best and yet we suffer. It seems so unjust and not at all in keeping with the loving God we have learned about. Many Christians turn away from their faith, because they do not accept a God, who permits suffering, cruelty, wars, famine, injustice and, especially, the deaths of those we have loved.

Think how many formerly devote Christians get so angry at God when someone they love dies that they turn away from anything to do with him, the church, or any acknowledgment of eternal life. It is quite common for this to happen to people and we probably know someone who feels this way.

When times turn bad, we often blame God and make him the scapegoat for our situation. We refuse to continue to believe in his love and to accept his gift of hope. Instead of going to his embrace in thanksgiving for what is good in our lives, we dismiss him for what we do not like or refuse to accept. We show no trust in God. Our faith wavers and, finally, may fall from our heart. We make ourselves sad and unhappy. Such people refuse God, because they believe a loving God would not let them suffer. They do not want to talk about religion or faith or church services. Indeed, they are very angry with God.

Yet, if we are to continue to run the good race, to seek the laurel of winning heaven, and if we are to remain disciples of Christ, we must look through the visible hand of those people or situations which strike us with seemingly unjust suffering. We must see the invisible hand of the just God that allows us to be so afflicted. (Genesis 50:15–21) Then, we must embrace such suffer as God's will for us, because true faith is being certain of what we do not see and may not understand. (Hebrews 11:1–2)

Hard as it may be, we need to accept that we know all things work for the good of those who love God and are called according to his purposes. (Romans 8:28)

12 November—Finding resignation to the will of God

N ILL-HEALTH AND in all those things we don't want or expect that happen to us, we need to turn to Christ. Here is our hope for better times and the comfort we need to get us through difficult times. By imitating him in bearing up with our suffering and continuing to trust in God, our resignation to the will of God will sustain us through sad or desperate times. On all such occasions we should consider Christ as offering us a bitter cup of remembrance of his own suffering. To accept it is to desire to receive it for his sake and not our own. Let our wounding then, no matter what it is, become holy in this way. In this smaller enactment of his greater sacrifice, we move closer to Christ, making our acceptance of God's will an act of love, just as he did on the Cross.

The first way to do this is to support our self with a patient mind. To strength our patience we can say with the prophet: *I will bear the wrath of the Lord, because I have sinned against him.* (Micah 7:9) and with the psalmist when under such afflictions, *I was silent, not opening my lips, because this was all your doing.* (Psalm 38:10)

The second way is a willing obedience to the plan of God, following the examples of Mary and Jesus. They showed us by their willing obedience to the will of God the invisible hand of God which brought forth the man Jesus who taught us how to live, and the risen Christ who brought us salvation. (Genesis 50:21)

The third and most perfect way of resignation is when we willingly accept suffering from the hand of God and rejoice in such suffering for the love of him. How hard this is for us but it surely tests our faith. In this gladness at God's plan for us, we finally leave behind the emotions and thoughts that go with resignation, because the accomplishment of God's will has finally become the whole object of our desire.

Remember, God will never test you beyond your strength. (1 Corinthians 10:13)

13 November—The way to happiness

 APPINESS IS IN the observance of the commandments of God. Nothing else can ever make us content. Listen to the apostle when he tells us that there will be trouble and distress for every human being who does evil, but glory, honour, and peace for everyone who does good. (Romans 2:9–11) Awake then, singing out in prayer to the Lord, rejoicing in your gift of life:

> Sing a new song to the Lord for he has worked wonders.
> His right hand and his holy arm have brought salvation.
> The Lord has made known his salvation; has shown his justice
> to the nations.
> He has remembered his truth and love for the house of Israel.
> All the ends of the earth have seen the salvation of our God.
> Shout to the Lord all the earth, ring out your joy. (Psalm 97)

14 November—The kingdom of heaven is like a treasure

E NEED TO understand the heavenly kingdom of God that is in us. A heavenly kingdom, which we are commanded to seek and for which we pray for in the *Lord's Prayer* when we ask, *Your kingdom come.* (Matthew 6:10) Now this kingdom of grace in us is like a great treasure, because its value is without price. (Matthew 13:44) It is worth more than all the kingdoms of the earth, because it brings God to reign in us. But it is often a hidden treasure, because the people of this world are strangers to the true value of it. While they may have heard of the field made of virtue and devotion where such a treasure is to be found, they are far fonder of the amusements and distractions offered by the world than of this unseen treasure buried within them.

Therefore, most men and women are unwilling to incur the personal cost of digging for this treasure. A cost measured not in money but in personal virtue and devotion to God. A cost that involves seeing deeply into the inner self, discovering all the darkness there, feeling repentance, and praying for forgiveness. Our giving up self-love and aspirations for worldly status and possessions make this a very high price to pay. The coinage of this price is humility.

Now, this was not true for the man in the gospel story, who discovering the existence of this treasure, sets his whole heart on it and sells all he has to buy the field in which it is hidden. (*Ibid*) Do you consider, like this man, that your heart is set upon the treasure? For we have been told that where our treasure is, there also will be our heart. (Matthew 6:21) Are we as willing as the man was in the gospel story to purchase at any price that blessed field where this treasure lies? The blessed field and the great treasure buried there is the kingdom of God within us. The priceless treasure awaits us there. (Luke 17:20–21) There is no time for distractions in the search for this great treasure, because the lion of the night, which would devour your soul, is constantly on the prowl. (Peter 1:3–8; Psalm 123)

15 November—On the parable of the marriage feast

TRUTH OR MORAL hidden inside a story is waiting to be discovered and making this discovery is always more interesting to the listener or reader than just telling them directly the meaning or message of the story. In Jesus's day telling a story through a parable was a way to teach an idea or moral concept. This is what the story of the marriage feast is all about. In many cultures today, especially in those where many people may not know how to read or write, this oral tradition remains the way teaching is done. This is particularly true in spiritual and religious matters where there is a moral principle or lesson to be given.

In short, the teachings and miracles of Jesus contain a hard core of important spiritual truths for the way in which we should live our lives in order to please God. Once we understand not just the superficialities of the parable—for example, what, where, and who was involved—but what Jesus is trying to teach us by this story, then the hidden meaning becomes comprehensible to us as a spiritual truth and a moral guide. So it is with the parable of the marriage feast. (Matthew 22)

Now read this story again in the bible. Do you get the message?

16 November –Lessons from the parable of the marriage feast

N THIS PARABLE Jesus compares the kingdom of heaven to a marriage feast that a king makes for the wedding of his son. To this feast, he tells us, many are invited who refused to come for one reason or another. Many take no notice of the invitation, but go their own way. For example, one went to his farm and another to his business. Many of the messengers the king sends to invite people are abused, some even put to death. Naturally, the king is furious as well as sad. He declares those he invited do not deserve now to come to the banquet. He rejects the whole guest list. In its place, he orders his servants to find strangers on the streets and invite them to the banquet. But when the king joins his guests, he notices one man not wearing wedding clothes. The man cannot explain how he was able to get into the banquet improperly dressed. So the king has him thrown out into the darkness and declares: *For many are invited, but few are chosen.* (Matthew 22:14)

The marriage in the story is symbolic for the one that the king of heaven, God, makes for his beloved Jesus. That is, the anointed Jesus the Christ came down from heaven to marry himself to our human nature by the mystery of his incarnation. The divine became human flesh, but this human flesh remained divine. The two are one. In this way, Christ is married to each man and woman as individuals by the union of holy grace and divine love.

The feast with which this marriage is celebrated is begun here on earth in the souls of those who come to Christ with faith and love. To this marriage feast, the prophets and messengers of God long ago invited Jews. Now all nations and all people are invited to the same banquet, because there is but one God and the invitation to this great feast of salvation is intended for all men and women everywhere in the world. (Isaiah 53; Revelation 19)

Every person, who answers this heavenly invitation, should come readily to this great feast, but those who do come must arrive with the proper qualifications, which are signified by the wedding garment they wear. They must be dressed in love and bejewelled by obedience to the commandments of God. They must no longer have a heart divided between the world's values and those of God. They must carry the mark of Jonas upon their hearts. (Matthew 12:38–41; Jonah 3:4–10)

Yet, just as in the parable, there is still the foolishness of many men and women who neglect this divine invitation. People who cast aside such a call and hurry away to carry on with their life like they always have. Here, we must exclude those who have not yet heard of Jesus the Christ and, therefore, have not yet received this divine invitation. However, we must include those who have heard the Word and, thus, have been invited to this great feast, but have refused this holy call. How often we hear the plea, *I am too busy*. Such people prefer to be busy with worldly affairs rather than feast with the bread of life and the living waters at this divine wedding banquet.

Then there is the guest, who arriving unsuitably dressed in neither love nor faith and whose real hope is still in the things and values of this world. Such a guest with his or her divided heart is thrown out into the darkness. Therefore, Jesus concludes this parable with that frightening announcement that strikes the hearts of all who want to go to heaven: *Many are called, but few are chosen.* (Matthew 22:14) Jesus says this in order to inspire us to endure in our faith and to convince us that if we are not of the number of the elect the fault is entirely ours in not answering the invitation of heaven to this divine marriage feast.

We must ask ourselves if we are one of those invited, but who refused on the excuse that we were too busy with matters of the world. Perhaps we are someone who has arrived for this feast unsuitable dressed, that is have we arrived with a heart divided partially with this world's values and partially with a lukewarm commitment to God. Are you ever this lukewarm in your faith?

What and who are we if we are not among the chosen? Jesus warns us, *Not everyone will enter the kingdom of heaven, but only those who do the will of my Father who is in heaven.* (Matthew 7:21–23)

17 November — On the barren fig tree

LL CHRISTIANS ARE like fig trees planted in the vineyard of Christ and he expects that each should bear fruit. Jesus is never content with a show of just beautiful leaves or with a poor harvest. He requires that everyone so planted, just like a fig tree, should bring forth good fruit and he declares that every tree that does not bear such a harvest will be cut down and burned. (Matthew 7:19) Indeed, the axe of heaven is already laid against the roots of the barren trees, but not yet used. (Matthew 3:10)

As we see in the story of the fig tree, God in his mercy lets barren trees live for a few more seasons in the hope of their coming in time to bear good fruit. This shows how patient God is with us. But such patience is not without limits. After repeated disappointments in poor harvests, God may suddenly cut down the barren trees to be the fuel of a fire, the fire of eternal damnation. (Luke 13:6–9) This cutting down is our dying and then our holy judgment.

Consider how God planted you in his vineyard and how he has taken care of you over so many years. His guiding hand has been gentle with mercy as you struggled to grow in faith and to follow holy values and not the constantly changing ideals of the world. His love has been living waters that showered you with hope when you have needed it. His forgiveness has been the healing medicine you have needed from time to time, especially when you have stumbled on the path of life shown to you by Jesus.

All these gifts of care were given to us so that we might bear wonderful fruit when the time of our harvest arrives. Jesus is the very best of gardeners. He gives us ample time to bear our fruits. God meant us to bloom in joy, scented with love for each other. There is no other way that leads to our being a good harvest. We need to go back to God now while time and opportunity is on our side so we can bloom where the great gardener planted us.

18 November—The harvest God wants from you

HAT FRUITS HAS all this holy care produced in us? How have we responded to all these favours of heaven? Have we merely contented ourselves with the unproductive leaves of outward performances like those of the Scribes and Pharisees, a beautiful display that might please the eyes of the world without bearing any real fruits of solid virtue? If so, remember the axe still stands near us with its fateful sentence.

But where these fruits are wanting, because pride, passion, or self-love still prevails, neither alms nor frequent fasting nor long prayers nor regular frequenting of the sacraments nor speaking in tongues nor prophesying nor working of miracles nor even raising the dead to life will secure any tree from the dreadful judgment of being cut down and cast into the fire. Jesus makes it clear that even if we prophesy in his name or drive out demons or even perform many miracles in his name, he will tell us on judgment day *I never knew you. Away from me, evildoers!* (Matthew 7:21–23)

Nothing can save us from such a fate if we do not change the way in which we live to the way Jesus taught us is the path to eternal life. The fruit we will bear is our being a witness by our complete obedience to the two commandments for our life: *Love your God with all your heart and with all your soul and with all your mind and love your neighbour as yourself.* (Matthew 22:37–40; Mark 12:29–31)

19 November — On the parable of the prodigal son

N THE FIRST part of story of the prodigal son, we find echoes of what happens frequently between many parents and children. (Luke 25) Many children, like the prodigal son, separate from their mothers and fathers for various relationship reasons. These reasons for a child leaving are often minor in the beginning, but often grow from innocent disagreements into unloving differences of opinion. The parents and their child finally cannot get on together. They are alienated. Most of us know of such cases among our friends and neighbours, perhaps such problems exist in our own family.

In this parable, Jesus is telling us about how we should act toward children who find us, as a father or mother, too difficult or as parents who find their children not living up to their parents' expectations. This story Jesus tells is about love and the forgiveness that must go with it.

Jesus tries repeatedly to teach us that love should not have expectations of any kind. Love must be free of self-interested goals and aims. We must love one another, whether we are a child, a parent, or a neighbour. We must love even our enemy. (Matthew 5:43–45)

To love without expectations and to continue to love no matter what happens is the meaning of the second commandment of God *to love your neighbour as yourself.* In order to give such love to others we must have a forgiving heart, a heart empty of all grievances, a love created in us by our forgiveness, no matter what offense has been visited on us.

This story of the prodigal son is about such forgiveness and the resulting expression of love. It is told through the image of the son who chooses to go to a far land where he lives a wild life, squanders all he possesses, and abuses all the gifts that God, his father, his family, and friends have bestowed on him. Such a son represents the misery of every poor sinner, who by wilful sin goes away from his father's house, which is God's house, into a far country of godless values. The son in this parable wastes everything by making everything he possesses subservient to his passions and desires. But one day a great famine strikes the country where the son is living. Eventually destitute, he binds himself to a farmer who gives him the work of feeding pigs. Even then the son does not have enough to eat. Everything he does is in vain, because he still serves the values and expectations of this world and not those of God.

The famine in this story is more than just a want of food and shelter. It is an emptiness of the soul for want of love. It is a famine of hunger and thirst, not just of the body but of the spirit as well. It is so deep that it can only be satisfied by repentance and going back to God, that is by going back to virtue and love. Repentance with reconciliation with family, neighbours and God is the nourishment that is needed. It is all about love.

When the son finally reaches the place where his hope is do dimmed that he sees no future for himself, his heart is suddenly opened to the light of God and the promises that God gives to him and to everyone. He is stricken by an overwhelming desire to return to his father. With a heart filled with humility, he returns to his earthly father and, in doing so, he returns to God, his heavenly father.

He carries a deep sorrow for his sins as he makes his way home. As he goes he cries out, like King David, that he has sinned. (Psalms 32 and 51; 2 Samuel 12: 13) When he meets his father, he declares that he is not worthy to be called his son and asks to be simply one of his father's hired servants. Instead, his father embraces him, welcoming him home with forgiveness and love, just as his father in heaven forgave him and welcomed him back as his beloved child.

We must pray that all those now living a life of self-love will turn away from their vices and imitate the prodigal son in his repentance and that they will seek their true father in heaven as well as be united with their parents and children through love. We must make love triumphant, because love is the only ointment that heals all wounds.

20 November—On the parable of the shrewd manager

 N LUKE 16, we learn about a manager, who accused of wasting his master's possessions, thought to be shrewd by discounting a considerable part of what the master's debtors owed. By acting in this way, he thought the excused debtors might be willing to receive him into their houses and to entertain him. By doing this, the manager acted wickedly with regard to his master and showed no respect or love for him, but the manager acted wisely by what the world calls wisdom. The lesson we learn here is that, if you have not been trustworthy in handling worldly wealth, who is going to trust you with the true treasure that is the holy wealth of eternal life? (Luke 16:11)

21 November—Memorial of the Presentation of the Virgin Mary

HEN SHE WAS about three years old, Mary's parents, Joachim and Anna, dedicated her in gratitude to the service of God at the Temple. In honour of this dedication, the *Presentation of the Virgin Mary* has been remembered on this day for many centuries.[2] We are reminded by this story of the many great advantages to be found in piety early in life as well as the duty of all parents to present their children to God in thanksgiving and to train them up in the love and fear of God. Are the parents in our church doing this? Next Sunday look around at church and see how many children are there. The more the better for the children set us the example of natural virtue by their sheer joy in being alive. So do not frown or complain or worry if the children make noise or run around, but remember how much they are pleasing to God. We too must become like children in our innocence and virtue, because Jesus told us that unless we change and become like little children, we never will enter the kingdom of heaven. (Matthew 18:3)

---

2   *Protoevangelium* of James and other apocryphal works.

22 November—The parable of the rich man and Lazarus, the poor beggar

 CRIPTURE TELLS US there was a certain rich man, who dressed in expensive clothes and feast magnificently every day. At the gate of his house, there was a poor man called Lazarus, covered with sores. Lazarus longed to fill himself with what fell from the rich man's table of food—but he was never offered a thing. One day Lazarus died and was carried away to heaven. The rich man also died, but he ended up in Hell. The rich man, looking toward heaven, saw Abraham comforting the poor beggar Lazarus. Burning with eternal fire, the rich man cried out to Abraham to take pity on him and send Lazarus to dip his finger in water and cool the rich man's burning tongue with it. But Abraham said to him, *My Son, remember that during your life you had your fill of good things, just as Lazarus had his fill of bad things. Now he is being comforted while you are in agony. Between us is a great gulf, a space that has been fixed so that no one is able to cross from your our side to yours or your side to us.* (Luke 16: 19–26)

The rich man was being punished for ignoring God's commandment to love your neighbour as yourself. He had known this commandment and the plight of the poor man Lazarus, but he had ignored both and done nothing.

Here, we learn the first lesson of this parable: Do to others as you would do to yourself.

Stricken by what had happened to him, the rich man begged Abraham to send Lazarus to his five brothers, whom he loved dearly, and to warn them so that they would not wind up in Hell as he had. Abraham replied that his brothers had Moses and the prophets and they should listen to them. But the rich man declared they would not repent unless someone came to them from the dead. Then Abraham told him, *If they will not listen to either Moses or to the prophets, they will not be convinced even if someone should rise from the dead.* (Luke 16: 27–31)

Here, we learn the second lesson in this parable: Listen to the Word of God and live a life pleasing to God and in accord with his commandments if you wish to have eternal life.

Finally, there is a third lesson: self-declared and persistent atheists, who have not been convinced of God through Scripture and the prophets and the history of Christianity, will not be convinced even by the resurrection of Jesus Christ from the dead.

While there is hope of holy mercy and salvation for every sinner, those who persist in denying God, insists on belonging to the values and morality of this world, and have refused the Word of God, may remain in sin *even if someone should rise from the dead.*

This is why we do not argue with such people about the merits of our faith, but instead we pray for them.

23 November—Another lesson from the parable of rich man and the poor beggar

 BRAHAM'S FINAL WORDS to the rich man should make us pay attention and repent, because many among us have continued to be disobedient to God in spite of knowing about Christ. All is foretold about him in Moses and the prophets and, if we do not listen and act on what they tell us, then we are like the rich man's brothers. *Keep watch on yourselves*! Abraham warns us. (Genesis 22; Luke 21:36)

Ask then if we are keeping watch on our life so that we, like the rich man, are not sent to the punishment of Hell. Ask if we too pass by the poor man, the homeless, and the weak and fragile without giving them what they might need. Do we go to church regularly and enjoy the good things of life, but suffer from a miserly or even a closed hand when it comes to the needy? Are we all lip service and no action? Consider most carefully how you think about refuges, people of another religion, and the strangers in the street who do not speak your native language. Ask yourself how Jesus would have behaved toward them, recalling the story of him and the Samaritan woman at the well. How much of what we enjoy do we actually share with those less fortunate? These are all questions that a Christian must answer, because Saint Paul tells us *to be kind and compassionate to one another, forgiving each other, just as in Christ, God forgave you.* (Ephesians 4:32)

While having all these blessings of this life we work and pray for heavenly wisdom so as to conduct our life in such a manner that all is in the service of God. Do not forget charity for it pleases God.

24 November—On the parable of the persistent widow

ESUS SHOWS IN this parable that we should never give up. It is about having an enduring faith in God. Jesus told about a certain judge who neither feared nor cared about people or God. This judge repeatedly refused a widow who came to him regularly to plea for justice. Finally, one day he was so tired of the continual trouble she was causing him, he decided to give her justice. He thought this would stop her bothering him. The judge did not do this because he cared about the woman or about justice. He cared only about not being bothered any more by her pleading. Just think, asks Jesus, if an unjust judge can finally give in to pleading, will not God bring about justice for his chosen ones who cry out to him day and night? (Luke 18:1–8)

25 November—Why we should pray for the rich

 OW FREQUENTLY THE prayers we hear in church are for the poor. How often men and women privately plead to God for those in need. For example, those in poverty or refugees from war. How often our thoughts turn to those in need, because of their poverty or their situation that seems hopeless. Now, all this is much to the good and pleases heaven, since you ask out of love for the poor that God should answer their needs. We know that if God does send them blessings that this will include not just worldly benefits but hope as well. And it is hope, above all, that those in poverty need. All this is pleasing to God and responds to the love that Jesus taught us to have. (Mark 2:17; Luke 19:10)

However, do we ever pray for the rich? Why you may ask should we pray for such people as these, who seem to have all the best of worldly possessions and who appear to have lives filled with comfort and never seem to want for anything that money, power, and social position can easily obtain. They appear to everyone as needing nothing. Many are most charitable with what they possess and many are devoted churchgoers. Most of them seem to have no needs and so we do not pray for them.

Yet, Jesus told the man of wealth: *How hard it is for the rich to enter the kingdom of God. Indeed, it is easier for a camel to go through the eye of a needle than for a rich man to enter the kingdom of God.* (Luke 18:24–25)

Since this is the true situation of the rich, whether rich through their own efforts or by inheritance, they must surely be in great need of our prayers, because most remain reluctant, like in the story of the rich young man, to follow Jesus when he asks them to give up worldly wealth for treasure in heaven. (Luke 18:22–23) But Jesus reassures them that nothing is impossible for God. (Luke 18:27) This means that God may have mercy even on the rich, who do not appear to qualify for heaven because of their wealth and their present refusal to give it up.

As if these words of Jesus were not enough to bring us to pray for the rich, let us consider the rich as men and women like ourselves—fragile, often stressed or in poor health or in a relationship that is not working. In spite of appearances which may disguise their interior life or the realty of their private life, wealthy people still feel depressed or in need of comfort. We forget that the rich are no different from us as humans and they need to be understood and loved as much as anyone else.

So not only do we pray for God to show mercy to the wealthy, we also pray for blessings in their lives, knowing that material possessions do not in themselves bring happiness. In praying for them, we are acknowledging that they are our brothers and sisters. After all, the souls of the rich are no different than the souls of the poor. Both are in need of our prayers.

26 November — The gift of contemplation

 OD GIVES THE gift of contemplation to many and not just to the vowed religious nor to people who go to church. Even the saints have no exclusive privilege to this grace. But to receive this gift we cannot earn it just by refusing to be involved in the values and things of this world. It takes a bit more than that to rid us of our entrenched desires and inappropriate passions. We may hide these temptations and wrongful acts deeply in ourselves by forgetting about them, like things left in a closed cupboard. Nevertheless, they remain with us and God does know about them.

Our life must be turned toward heaven in every way. There must be no hidden vices, no closed cupboards of secrets within us. As a disciple of Jesus, we must be *in* the world but not *of* it. (1 Peter; Romans 12:22; Galatians 1:4; James 4:4; John 17:14–16 & 15:18) We must be filled with the joy of life and deeply thankful for life and for all people and the natural world around us. Our concern is to run the good race and win the laurel of eternal life and to always be in thanksgiving for the salvation given to us by the sacrifice of Jesus. We need to shed the old self and become the *new man* and the *new woman*.

This then is the way to open ourselves in contemplation of God, which is awareness of his holy presence, a time of listening with our heart, a conversation with heaven if we are lucky. This is the nature of the grace of contemplation for a Christian.

27 November—The three vices that prevent contemplation

HILE INTENDED FOR vowed religious men, the writings of the Carthusian monk Guigo de Ponte many centuries ago remain good advice for all Christians aspiring to progress in their spiritual life.[3] He suggests that we should examine three vices in particular that can stand in the way of contemplation. These are *Pride of Self*, *Vanity of Intentions*, and *Vice of Gluttony*. Should we find ourselves guilty of any of these vices, we must stop them if we are to advance spiritually and be able to enter into contemplation with God.

Pride of self is when we believe heaven favours us over others because we are so good, so holy, and so prayerful. Indeed, so pious. Christians often forget that Jesus told us: *No one is good but God.* (Mark 10:17–18; Luke 18:18–19) It is true that many regular churchgoers are proud of their religious practices, but being proud of our devotion can be the outward sign of *pride of self*—a disastrous form of self-love. Such pride is sometimes called *false pride*. Let us remember not to forget the Word of God tells us, *When you are invited to a wedding feast, sit down in the lowest place.* (Hebrews 1:3–9; Luke 14:10) The best way to avoid pride of self, then, is to esteem others better than yourself. (Philippians 2:3)

As to the *Vanity of Intentions*, Holy Scripture says everything we need to know about this vice: *Vanity, all is vanity!* (Ecclesiastes 1–12)

The word *gluttony* is hardly used anymore. It may have fallen of out fashion as a word, but unfortunately not as a vice. We do not like to this word, because it stands for *greed, greediness, overeating, over-consumption, binge eating, being a gourmand, gluttonousness, voracity, wolfishness, insatiability, and piggishness.* The problem is that some of these words in our

---

3   Guigo de Ponte, *De vita contemplativa*, Book 3: 240–244.

time have turned from being negative to being positive. For many people *more is better*, that is to be never be satisfied with what you have and always want more, more, and even more. Another example is the flattery of being called *a lover of good food*. Is this an accusation of greed or a compliment? It works both ways today. Now fashion may change the meaning of words, but if the effect is still negative and against God's commandments, then it remains a vice. So *gluttony* in any form is still a vice.

These demons of vice hide under many disguises and seduce even kings. (Revelation 16:14) Whatever we call them makes little difference. They still make slaves of many Christians. (1 Timothy 4:1)

28 November—*The vice of a vanity of intentions*

 ET US EXAMINE further this *vice of vanity of intentions.* It is concerned with those people who are eager to make a show of their virtue, often doing in public what they do not do in private. In other words, a person seems devout and virtuous when in reality they are actually doing all this religious devotion simply to seek praise from people around them. They want to please people not God. They need to be the centre of attention. When given the chance they often are given to very long prayers aloud in the assembly of the faithful. When we discover how they actually are, we often refer to them as *hypocrites.*

When we try to be holy with the best of intentions and truly mean what we are doing, we can still fall prey to this vanity. For example, when a person believes others disdain them, they often feel sorry for themselves and fall into self-pity. Such self-pity is a form of self-love. It means we have not accepted the will of God in our life. Thus, such a man or woman succumbs to the vice of the *vanity of intentions.*[4]

The remedy for this vice and a return to virtue both rest in the practice of humility and in boasting only in the Lord. (1 Corinthians 1:31) In that way, *a vanity of intentions* will no longer blocked the way to contemplation.

---

4   Guigo de Ponte, *De vita contemplativa*, Book 3: 242.

29 November—The vice of gluttony

ET US EXAMINE even further this third vice of *gluttony*, which most of us generally regard as eating and drinking too much. This does not mean we do not appreciate food and drink, both of which are blessings from God. After all, Jesus enjoyed going to feasts and the taking of a meal together unifies people. But *gluttony* means consuming more than you could possible need and making a pig of yourself. The French sometimes call someone a *gourmand* who eats a lot just because they like food and not because they need it. In America and Britain such a person might be called a *foodie*. To prevent gluttony and make food a virtue, we need to strike a balance between our need for nourishment and our enjoyment of it. It is this balance that turns a potential vice into a virtue.

While many people are fastidious and fussy over what they eat out of a desire for a certain type of body image or a concern for health or environmental reasons, many just seem to live to eat. The more money they have to spend on food, the more luxurious and fancy the food and the more rare and costly the drink or they may over-indulge in fast food or food to take-away. Eating becomes an idol, a little god to worship. Cooking food can also become an idol of worshipping over-concern with food, another form of *gluttony* but one that parades in disguise.

Saint Benedict in his rule admits that the amount of food and drink needed differs greatly between individuals, but that whatever is taken should be moderate and according to health and age. In other words, we should strike that golden balance between need and enjoyment. This advice serves all Christians well and not just those in religious orders. A sensible moderation about food and drink keeps us healthy as well as spiritually aware. This pleases God.[5] In this moderation or balance with eating, *the vice of gluttony* should no longer block our way to contemplation.

---

[5]   *Rule of Saint Benedict*, Chapters 39 & 40.

30 November — Feast of Saint Andrew, Apostle

VEN BEFORE HE followed Jesus, the Apostle Andrew had been a disciple of John the Baptist and had heard him say of Jesus, *Look, the Lamb of God!* So when Andrew had spent time with Jesus and knew this was the person rightfully claiming his loyalty and service, he told his brother Simon, who is known today as Peter. When Jesus left the place where they met him, Andrew and Simon Peter gladly followed him. In this way Andrew and Simon Peter became the first disciples.

Saint Andrew was spiritually ready before he met Jesus through his association with John the Baptist. (John 1: 35–40) His heart was ready for Our Lord. (Psalm 57:7) It was this that helped him recognize and follow Jesus in his earthly mission. By his actions, the Apostle Andrew echoed the prophets and King Solomon in having been trained in devotion and spiritual matters from an early age. (Lamentations 3:27; Proverbs 21:6)

What this tells us is that we need to pay close attention to the spiritual life of children and young people and not let them wander in a daze of ignorance about God. If they remain ignorant of God, they are bound to become self-centred victims to worldly values and to pay no attention to their spiritual life. They need a stable spiritual foundation, like Saint Andrew, on which to chose what they value and what serves to give them a life that is whole, joyous, and healthy in body, mind and spirit.

Without a spiritual awareness, we are leaving the young to fate. Some eventually will discover God if he calls them. Others will remain slaves to this world, never finding peace, contentment or satisfaction. We must strengthen our children by making certain that they have a solid spiritual foundation as they grow into adulthood.

Consider how St. Andrew had no sooner found Christ himself than he immediately sought to share this happiness with his brother and brought him to meet Jesus. (John I: 41–42) This sharing and witnessing to Jesus Christ pleases heaven, because the saving of a sinner is the greatest of goals. (Luke 6:28, 19:10; Galatians 6:1)

THE SEASON OF CHRISTMAS

Themes: Rebirth & Joy — the fulfilment of prophesy

Cry out with joy to the Lord, all the earth.
Serve the Lord with gladness.
Come before him, singing for joy.

Psalm 99 (100)

1 December—On the time of Advent

 DVENT IS A time set aside by the church for celebrating the glorious arrival of Jesus the Christ. The start of the liturgical year in the church, it is a time of devotion in which we look forward to celebrating the birth of the Saviour. It is a season of our greatest joy.

We prepare for this celebration through repentance and reconciliation with God. It is our annual pilgrimage toward the greatest event in the history of the world. It is a renewal of our faith in God and his promises.

Heed the words of Saint Paul as you begin Advent: *The hour has already come for you to wake up from your slumber, because our salvation is nearer now than when we first believed. The night is nearly over; the day is almost here. So let us put aside the deeds of darkness and put on the armour of light. Let us behave decently, as in the daytime, not in carousing and drunkenness, not in sexual immorality and debauchery, not in dissension and jealousy. Rather, clothe yourselves with the Lord Jesus Christ, and do not think about how to gratify the desires of the flesh.* (Romans 13:11)

2 December—On what we must do to prepare the way of the Lord

HE BEST DEVOTION for the time of Christmas is that which brings Jesus Christ into our souls by his spiritual birth. We can begin this birth by cleaning up our lives and discarding excessive self-love and all the desires, passions and vices that belong to it. In this way, Jesus Christ may find nothing that may hinder him from being spiritually born in us.

Conclude to put in practice at this holy time all those lessons of love, worship, and faith that you have learned and know in your heart to be pleasing to God. An Advent spent in this manner cannot fail to bring you a happy and joyous Christmas.

3 December—On the problem of spiritual dryness

 PIRITUAL DRYNESS IS a well-recognized experience of many devout people. This includes the saints. St. Thérèse of Lisieux is just one example of such suffering. What it means is that a faithful person for no apparent reason suddenly finds that somehow their conversation with God has dried up, especially in prayer. They seem to have nothing else to say to God and God appears to have nothing to say to them. This state of the soul is called *spiritual dryness*.

If this experience happens to us, we should not despair, because this time of spiritual dryness is an opportunity to persevere in devotion. It is a testing time, a time of trial such as Moses had at Meribah. (Numbers 20:2–13) It is valuable time and worthy of all who do not give up when it happens, but who persist in their prayers and devotions. They endure because they have put all their trust in God and persist in their faithfulness. Let us plead with the psalmist then, *O that today you would listen to his voice! Harden not your hearts as at Meribah* (Psalm 94[95])

The Roman Catholic Church in confirming the existence of spiritual dryness explains it this way:

> Another difficulty, especially for those who sincerely want to pray, is dryness. Dryness belongs to contemplative prayer when the heart is separated from God, with no taste for thoughts, memories, and feelings, even spiritual ones. This is the moment of sheer faith clinging faithfully to Jesus in his agony and in his tomb. "Unless a grain of wheat falls into the earth and dies, it remains alone; but if dies, it bears much fruit."[1]

As Christians, we know that this dying is the death of the self for a new life in Christ. It is the letting go of all self-concern

---

[1]   CCC 2731.

and the acceptance of God's will. Our dying in this way is like a seed falling on the fertile earth of our faith, where it flourishes, grows strong, bears the flower of love, and finally produces the fruit that pleases God. (Matthew 13:1–23, Mark 4:1–20, Luke 8:1–15) It is our submission to the will of God that brings this about. This acceptance eventual changes spiritual dryness back into fruitful prayer and contemplation in God, because God never really leaves us.

However, the Church goes on to warn us that *if dryness is due to the lack of roots, because the word has fallen on rocky soil, the battle requires conversion.* So spiritual dryness provides us with an opportunity to cling ever closer to God, who has assured us many times that we are not deserted and that by such whole-hearted seeking we will return to his embrace. (Jeremiah 1, 24:7, 29:13; Zechariah 1:3; James 4:8; Matthew 5:6) So our repentance by turning to a more fervent way of life and by our endurance and forbearance in prayer and devotions will eventually bring back our feeling of the presence of God in our life.

If you should experience spiritual dryness, then keep on praying and being devoted. Never give up for God never gives up on you. Jesus Christ confirms this when he says, *Seek and you will find. Knock and the door will be opened.* (Matthew 7:7; Luke 11:9)

4 December—On helpful practices for endurance in prayer

T IS ALWAYS possible to find benefits in monastic practices for increasing the presence of God. Such practices have proven beneficial over many centuries. Many have been adapted for ordinary life outside a religious life. For example, there are now books about how we might benefit in daily living by utilising the *Rule of Saint Benedict*, still the most widely used monastic rule. For example, below is the ancient brief *Rule of Saint Romuald* written about 1006, which can be especially helpful.[2]

1. Sit in your cell as in paradise. Put the whole world behind you and forget it

2. Like a skilled angler on the lookout for a catch keep a careful eye on your thoughts.

3. The path you follow is given in the psalms—don't leave them.

4. If you've come with a beginners enthusiasm and can't accomplish what you want, take every chance you can find to sing the psalms in your heart and to understand them with your head.

5. If your mind wanders as you read (Holy Scripture) don't give up but hurry back and try again.

6. Above all realize that you are in God's presence. Hold your heart there in wonder as if before your sovereign.

7. Empty yourself completely.

8. Sit waiting, content with God's gift, like a little chick tasting and eating nothing but what its mother brings.

Your *cell* is wherever you can be alone, silent and solitary, and have space in which to pray and wait upon the Lord. No

---

[2] See Bruno of Qerfurt, *Lives of the Five Brothers*, Chapter 9.

mobile phones ring. No television is heard. There are no distractions. If a bird chirps you will be able to hear it, because all around you is quiet. If you cannot find such a place at home, then go to a church when there are no services. Sitting and waiting on God, you will be in dressed in the habit of silence, content to be alive in this moment of time. Full of joy, because you know you are in the presence of God. Your heart will fill with wonder so stay still in this little cell of your inner self and all that God has planned for you will come true. Indeed in this time of peace with God you are having a little taste of paradise.

5 December—On the state of your heart

HE HEALING OF the man with leprosy by Jesus is a particularly instructive miracle, because leprosy in those days was considered more than just a dangerous contagious disease. (Luke 5:12; Matthew 10:8) It was seen as a symbol of sin as well and there were many Levitical laws about it. (Leviticus 13:44–46; and 14) So the diseased person was considered impure, not just in body but in spirit as well. A leper was isolated from the community. (Numbers 5:2,3) He or she had to avoid touching others and must cry out to anyone who approached them: *Unclean! Unclean!* Such uncleanliness was not just about the disease of the body, because people thought then that it was also a disease of the soul and marked by God on the person's flesh to show that he or she was a sinner. (Deuteronomy 24:8,9)

Unlike today, there were no medicines then that helped in this dreaded affliction. Anyone thought to have contracted leprosy in those days had to go to the priest for a diagnosis, because it was a spiritual matter, not just a health issue. Subsequently, if anyone thought they were cured, they too had to appear before the priest for a judgment and, even if declared cured of the disease, they still had to submit to ritual cleansing of what was considered their spiritual leprosy of sin.

If you consider that we have progressed to no longer thinking a disease of the flesh is an outward sign of inner sin and that today we treat ill people differently, just remember what happened when gay men were first discovered to have Aids. They were shunned and for many years many left untreated to die. They were excluded from community life. Many Christians still make a forbidden judgment, thinking that such men were being punished by God for being homosexual. Those who suffered from Aids were the lepers of our modern day. Our hearts can still be hard as at Meribah in the desert. (Numbers 20:13; Psalm 94:8; Psalm 105:32;

Deuteronomy 32:15) So we must ask ourselves these questions: What state is your heart in right now? Do you judge others when God has forbidden it?

6 December — On being blessed by God

 N ANOTHER MIRACLE when Jesus heard the pleas of ten lepers for healing, he told them to go show themselves to the priest. They did as he bid and on their way, they were suddenly cured. When he realized what had happened to him, one of the men returned at once to Jesus. This cured leper, a Samaritan, fell down before Jesus in worship and thanksgiving and glorified God in a loud voice.

Jesus asked him: *Were not all ten made clean? The other nine, where are they? It seems no one has come back to give praise to God, except this foreigner. And he said to the man, "Stand up and go on your way." Then he said to the cured leper, Your faith has saved you.* (Luke 17:11–19)

Let us learn by this example the love and gratitude with which we ought to praise and glorify God after being cleansed by his mercy from the unhappy disease of our sin and reconciled to him. Are you the leper who returned in thanksgiving for God's mercy or are you one of the others who was blessed with mercy, but went on their merry way?

7 December—On preparing ourselves for receiving Jesus Christ

OD PREPARED THE Blessed Mary to be the mother of Jesus by keeping her pure from the moment of her conception. We too must be pure in order to qualify for the spiritual conception and birth of the same Lord in our souls. Just as we could never have been happy if Jesus had not been born into this world, so we never can be happy if he is not also spiritually born in us.

Therefore, we must put off the old Adam, the disobedient one, and put on the new Adam that is Jesus Christ, the obedient one. This cannot happen to us until we are at peace with God and remain pure of heart like Mary. We, ourselves, must be the proper place for the spiritual birth of Jesus. It is by a repentant conscience and a whole-hearted purity that we prepare the way of the Lord.

So the first and most essential branch of Christian purity without which God has no part in us, is a purity of conscience at least from mortal sin joined with a determination to remain pure. (Job 31:2) This means that no honour, no pleasure whether of flesh or mind, no fear, no promises of gain, no power, and no terrors and threats from anything or anyone can make us consent to sin and let it take purity from us. To maintain such purity takes great faith and an absolute trust in God. Blessed Mary had these virtues and there is no reason on earth or in heaven why we too should not possess them. Let us return then to the road of Christ, which although a demanding and narrow way, is hedged by mercy and surrounded by a landscape of love.

8 December—Solemnity of the Immaculate Conception of the Blessed Virgin Mary

HRISTIANS OFTEN CONFUSE the *Immaculate Conception of Mary* with the virgin birth of Jesus, but the celebration today is about the conception of Mary, his mother, and not that of her son. So let us begin by understanding what this term, *The Immaculate Conception*, means because without such knowledge we may not grasp the importance of today's celebration.

The Catechism of the Catholic Church explains the Immaculate Conception in this way:

> To become the mother of the Saviour, God enriched Mary with gifts appropriate to such a role. The angel Gabriel at the moment of the annunciation salutes her as full of grace. In fact, in order for Mary to be able to give the free assent of her faith to the announcement of her vocation, it was necessary that she be wholly borne by God's grace. Through the centuries the Church has become ever more aware that Mary, full of grace through God, was redeemed from the moment of her conception.[3]

Pope Pius IX proclaimed in 1854 that the most Blessed Virgin Mary was, from the first moment of her conception, by a singular grace and privilege of almighty God and by virtue of the merits of Jesus Christ, Saviour of the human race, preserved immune from all stain of original sin.[4]

The unique holiness by which Mary is enriched from the first moment of her own conception comes wholly from God, because she is redeemed in this exalted fashion by reason of the coming merits of her son, Jesus. God blessed Mary more than any other person *with every spiritual blessing in the*

---

[3] *CCC* 490.
[4] *CCC* 491.

heavenly places and chose her in Christ before the foundation of the world to be holy and blameless before him in love. By the grace of God Mary remained free of every personal sin during her whole life.[5]

In spite of the scandal her pregnancy and the birth of a child might create, Mary set aside all those worldly and social standards about how she should behave, especially the opinions and gossip of other people. Even in the face of becoming a social outcast, Mary dared to be obedient to the will of God. By such obedience, she became the new Eve and was to give birth to the new Adam.

Mary shows us the perfect example of obedience and trust in God that we should imitate. Just as she gave birth to Jesus, we should give birth to a new life as a new man and a new woman through our obedience to God and his beloved Messiah.

To honour Mary on this day, wonderfully filled with praise as it may be, is not sufficient celebration unless we become as faithful as she was in her life. This is the honour and real celebration Mary wants us to give her, because it pleases God as she did.

---

[5]   CCC 492, 493.

9 December—On the miracles of Jesus Christ

ROM THE VERY beginning of his mission to preach the good news Jesus did miracles through the grace of God. He healed those possessed by devils, the mentally ill and those who were paralyzed, blind, and wounded and raised the dead to life. (Matthew 4:23)

His fame grew so great that vast multitudes of people brought their sick to lay them down at his feet, begging Jesus to heal them. (Matthew 15:30) Those who touched him were healed as well for his holy power went out to them. (Luke 6:19; Mark 6:56) This was a profound lesson in the complete and instant power of God. It shows that what may be impossible for men and women is possible for God. (Luke 18:27 & 1:37; Job 9:9 & 40; Psalm 7:8; 2 Corinthians 9:8–9) Such examples of God's power in the miracles done by Jesus encourages us, strengthens our faith, and helps us to be his willing servants.

His miracles in particular were done to confirm our hope in God and, if we look carefully into them, we find Jesus' miraculous cures were not just about the problems of the flesh but for those of the soul as well. Jesus clearly shows us that there is no division between the body, the mind and the spirit.

Yet, we are usually concerned with physical health and rarely examine the state of our spiritual health as well or seek healing remedies for what is needed by the body, mind and spirit as a connected, integrated and inseparable whole. We forget the lessons of the miracles that there is no separation between these aspects of ourselves.

Since Jesus Christ is just as ready to heal us now as he was during his mission on earth, why not go to him at once? You know the way and where you may stumble into darkness, God will pick you up and light your way to the healing you need. *Ask and it will be given to you, search, and you will find; knock, and the door will be opened to you.* (Matthew 7:7–8; Luke 11:9–10)

10 December—On Jesus cleansing the lepers

 MAN WITH LEPROSY came to see Jesus and kneeling before him pleaded: *Lord, if you are willing, you can make me clean.* Jesus put forth his hand and touched the man. In that instant, the leper was cured.

By this miracle, Jesus uses leprosy, the most dreaded disease of his day and one thought to have resulted from spiritual sin, to show us how we are to appeal to God if we wish to be healed of our physical or spiritual diseases. We see with what a strong faith and honest humility this leper presented himself to Jesus. His few words were more than just a plea for a cure. He was speaking from a belief in Jesus as the sacred vessel of God's power. He appealed to him for a cure of all his disease, whether of body, mind or spirit. If we wish God to act on our behalf, we too must have faith and absolute trust in God's power like the man with leprosy.

The lessons of this miracle of the first leper does not end with his cure, because Jesus told the leper after the healing to tell no one about what happened, but to show himself to the priest and render thanksgiving to God. This conformed to the prescription of the Law of Moses and other parts of Scripture that even when we are cured of a physical disease, we must still show thanksgiving to God for his healing. (Numbers 6:24–26; Exodus 23:25; Deuteronomy 7:15) In this way, our whole self in body, mind and spirit are healed.

11 December—On Jesus stilling the storm at sea

HE APOSTLE MATTHEW tells us about Jesus stilling the storm at sea just by speaking to it. *Jesus said to the disciples in the boat: ' Why are you so frightened, you who have so little faith?' And then he stood up and rebuked the wind and the sea; and there was a great calm.* (Matthew 8:23–27)

As Christians, we are all embarked as it were on a ship during our mortal life on a sea that is sometimes calm, but often stormy and frightening. This ship, called *earthly life*, is sailing towards the haven of a blessed eternity, a port of peace, a paradise promised to us by God. During this great voyage, we have Jesus on board with us for companionship and consolation. Our Lord assured us that no matter where we were or what was happening to us, he was with us even to the end of the world. (Matthew 28:20)

On this voyage of life, we are often exposed to storms. These storms threaten us sometimes not just us as individuals, but even collectively as the people of God. For example, in cases of persecutions, heresies, terrorism, or other evils where everyone who is a Christian is under attack. At other times we are in danger from our own temptations and tribulations, which are like the winds and waves of a storm at sea coming suddenly without warning and from which threat no one is exempted in this earthly life.

But we need not worry nor be afraid, because we have Jesus the Christ on board with us and we have nothing to fear if we keep company with him in a lively faith and with confidence in his unqualified love for us.

Although Jesus may often seem to defer his help, as if asleep, we must survive this trial of our faith by continuing to have confidence in him. We must remain patient. This may be a testing time, a trial of faith like the one of our ancestors at Massah and Meribah. However, as a result of such a trial we are made more aware of our need for God in our lives.

(Exodus 17:7; Psalm 94:8) Be patient then, because Christ never fails us. In his own good time he will rise up to command those winds and seas raging in our lives to be calm. Remember when Saint Peter tried to walk on the water and fell in and Jesus told him: *You have so little faith,* he said, *why did you doubt?* (Matthew 14:31)

12 December—On Jesus feeding the multitude

 HEN WE HEAR the story of how Jesus fed five thousand people with five loaves of bread, we must not have any lingering doubts about the power of God to do such a thing. After all, Jesus did clearly tell us, *What is impossible for people is possible for God.* (Luke 18:27)

In this story Jesus uses the loaves of bread, the common basic food, as a symbol. He tells us we are not to seek or follow him for the sake of loaves—that is for the sake of earthly gains whether of food, power, prestige, wealth or other advantages. To do this would be catching the shadow of his teaching but losing the substance of it. (John 6:26- 27) Jesus reminds us that we are not to work for food that spoils, but for that spiritual food that endures to eternal life, which the Son of Man will give us. (Luke 6:1–5) *The Lord does not allow the righteous to hunger for what they need.* (Matthew 6:33–34: Luke 12:21; Proverbs 10:3)

13 December—On purifying the interior powers of the soul

 E NEED TO be quite clear in our minds about what it means to always abide in Christ and to have Christ always to abide in us. This means we must become profound in our vision of the holy. It is a vision of the meaning of our life and the holy that is not cluttered by distractions, desires, and inconsequential and petty things. We can have this clarity of vision about life by getting rid of our false opinions and ignorance, because these fill us up and leave little room for the presence of God.

We must also purify our memory, erasing from it the too frequently remembered wounds by others whether of their real or imagined words or actions. Along with casting out these useless memories that belong forgotten in our past, we must also get rid of our dreams of self-concern, especially those that begin with *If only.* When we indulge ourselves in regret and think *if only I had acted differently* or *if only so-and-so had not done this or that,* we fall into ways that are bad for us and take us from peace and contentment into sorrow, regret, and depression. This kind of negativity and foolish wishful thinking is difficult to avoid, because we are modelled as humans by what has happened to us or what we imagine to be our experience of life, rather than through the truths that Jesus told us about. Our eyes have turned to worldly concerns and not toward heavenly values.

So we must recover from these past experiences if they lead us into spiritual confusion and crowd out God from our interior self. We need to forgive those who we feel have betrayed us. We must bless our enemy because this returns us to God through the charity of our mercy. This is to obey God. In such forgiveness the way is cleared for a greater remembrance of God. Such is the nature of repentance and reconciliation.

14 December—On the purity of the heart

HE CENTRE OF us is a spiritual place from which immortal life flows. When it is pure such a heart is filled with the presence of God, invisible to the eye but affecting who and what we are during our life on earth. This is the dynamic principle that drives us to seek understanding of ourselves.

Such understanding is never complete and remains unattainable except through faith, since such wisdom goes beyond any human knowing. Indeed, we continue to fail in understanding completely the nature of the life around us, let alone ourselves. For example, our full understanding of an ant remains a mystery. There is still so much we do not know. We have hardly begun to understand what an octopus feels or how a tree may speak to another of its kind. Our wisdom of this world remains incomplete, as does any full understanding of our self. We never can know what is in the heart of another person. Only God knows that.

Yet, we are called to love, most often that which we do not fully understand. This calls the pure heart to trust in the mystery of God.

To hold a pure heart out to God, even one that barely understands anything, is to be humble and to exercise that powerful wisdom which is humility. As is written in Scripture: *Since gold is tested in the fire, and the chosen in the furnace of humiliation. Trust in him and he will uphold you, follow the straight path and hope in him.* (Ecclesiasticus 2:4–5)

We should try, therefore, to unite a pure heart to a pure mind with a body free of unwarranted and unwanted desire. *I have fought the good fight to the end; I have run the race to the finish; I have kept the faith.* (2 Timothy 4:7) Surely, this is what all Christians aspire to when we speak of the purity of the heart?

15 December—On the purity of our actions

HE GREAT SABBATH foretold by Isaiah will only come when humanity leads a holy life on earth. (Isaiah 66) But this cannot happen until we end selfishness and this will not happen until we rid our nature of two concepts— *mine* and *yours*, those two little words that signify all that is self-love.

Consider how these two words are the cause of many wars, great agonies of body and spirit, constant quarrelling and fighting, envy and hatred, disunity and disruption. So whoever deals in *mine* and *yours* deals in avarice and is disobedient to God's commandment, because whoever loves God must also love his brother. (1 John 4:20–21) In the matter of love, there can be no *mine* and *yours.*

This is not possible when we are guilty of greed and, most certainly, those words, *mine* and *yours*, bring greed into relationships of every kind. When we are reluctant to share what we possess with others, we show the world that we esteem our worldly possessions more than we care about charity. Love always involves sharing, hospitality and equality. When we use those two little words, *mine* and *yours*, we fail to live up to the requirements of our Christian faith, which is founded on love.

For example, if we think that dropping a bit of money in the collection on Sundays at church or contributing to a charitable cause is enough or giving a bag of supermarket products to the annual Christmas charity collection is sufficient, we need to think again! John the Baptist told people that whoever had two coats should give one coat to another person who has none and whoever has food, should do the same. See how clear it is![6] (Luke 3)

---

[6] See Peter Walpot, *True Yielders and the Christian Community of Goods* (1577), 3; deals with Hutterian Anabaptism.

Let us consider how we actually live in terms of the goods we possess. Look in the wardrobe. Do you see how many dresses, shirts, coats and other clothes you possess? What about those socks, shirts, and underwear at the back of the drawer that you never wear? When did you last invite a stranger to share your lunch? Do we pass the man or woman who begs and think them unimportant and a nuisance—or even worse do we judge that if they drink or take drugs that they are unimportant and best ignored? Do we consider some people *undeserving* who claim to be in need?

Such questions are very important for a Christian, because we cannot claim not to know that we are to love our neighbour as ourselves. After all, there are some twenty-five verses in the bible about sharing what we possess and it is one of the commandments given by God himself. Remember what Jesus told us: *I was hungry and you gave me food, I was thirsty and you gave me drink, I was a stranger and you made me welcome, lacking clothes and you clothed me, sick and you visited me, in prison you came to see me.* (Matthew 25:35)

But the righteous, not understanding the real meaning of what Jesus said and believing they had served him faithfully, asked him: *When did we see you hungry and feed you, or thirsty and give you something to drink? When did we see you a stranger and invite you in, or needing clothes and clothe you? When did we see you sick or in prison and go to visit you?* (Ibid 37–39) Jesus replied: *In truth I tell you, in so far as you did this to one of the least of these brothers of mine, you did it to me.* (Ibid 40)

Such actions of hospitality about which Jesus speaks, make for mercy and love, because they are based on loving our neighbour as ourselves and seeing in others the living Christ. We may not want to believe it, but both science and our religion tell us the same thing—the man or woman sitting near you in church or on the bench at the Mall is in fact our *brother* or our *sister*. They may not be Christians and some may even claim they do not believe in God, but we have not yet begun to understand the message of Jesus unless we see in them the risen Christ, always present whether as yet spiritually awakened in that person or not. This is why we must treat every stranger as Christ himself. (*Rule of Saint Benedict*, Chapter 53:1; Matthew 25:35–40)

So this purity of our actions springs from a sincere love of others. It prepares the way for Christ to live fully in us and we to live fully in him. We have thrown out those divisive words, *mine* and *yours*, and along with them the kind of selfish thinking and actions that they create in us.

However, our love must not be confined to the interior powers of the soul and reside only in our intentions or only in our prayers for others. They must extend also to the whole body of our actions. As the tree ought to be pure, so ought the fruit also be full and perfect, because a tree is known by its fruits. (Luke 6:43–45; Matthew 7:16, 12:33) Now ask yourself how you are doing when it comes to loving others, bearing in mind the words of the Apostle James: *As a body without spirit is dead, so is faith without deeds.* (James 2:14–26)

16 December—On the purity of our intentions

CCORDING TO JESUS, the purity of our actions principally depends on the purity of our intention: The lamp of the body is the eye, he told us. It follows that if your eye is clear, your whole body will be filled with light. But if your eye is diseased, your whole body will be darkness. (Matthew 6:22; Luke 11:34) When that inner vision, which forms our intention, is turned away from God and looks elsewhere, a vision of goodness is lost and our actions fall into darkness. In this way our intentions lose all virtue. There is no holy light to guide us. The eye of our soul has been blinded.

The practice of a purity of intentions requires that we should begin each day by offering ourselves and everything we do to the service of God. Next, we should consult his will in all things before acting. Do this by means of prayer, contemplation, and reflection on Scripture, letting the Word of God guide you. Make love the balance scale on which you weigh all choices. When you do act, watch carefully over yourself as you progress and swiftly exclude all self-love if you find it arising in what you are doing.

Finally, you should often renew the directing of your attention to God by seasoning all your actions with his presence. As the monk, Brother Lawrence of the Resurrection, reminded us so many centuries ago: *There is not in the world a kind of life more sweet and delightful, than that of a continual conversation with God.*[7]

---

[7] See Br. Lawrence of the Resurrection, *The Practice of the Presence of God*.

17 December—On the wonders of God in the incarnation of Jesus the Messiah

 FTER Mary's consent to God with these words to the angel Gabriel, *You see before you the Lord's servant, let it happen to me as you have said.* Thus, the history of this world was changed forever. (Luke 1:38) It was the miracle of miracles, because the eternal Word was made man and man was made divine. (The Gospel of Matthew)

In this way God made us brothers and sisters through Jesus the Christ. By assuming our humanity, that is by the incarnation of Jesus as human flesh and blood, God has made us in some measure participators of his divinity. At the same time, Mary in her perfect obedient to the will of God became the second Eve, the new woman. This gift of the birth of the Messiah was our invitation to heaven.

18 December—Further wonders of God in the incarnation of his Messiah

 OD DID NOT imbue his Spirit to Jesus in any kind of limited way as he did with his prophets, messengers, and saints. He gave all things to Jesus in complete fullness of all grace and truth. (John 3:34 & 1:16–17; Ephesians. 4:7) The graces from God to his Messiah included the following:

1. Purity from all sin or imperfection whatsoever.

2. Sanctity, exceeding that of all the angels, saints and prophets put together. Hence, Christ may be called *the holy of holies*, because the Holy Spirit of God rested on him with every possible gift, grace and benefit. (Daniel 10; Isaiah 2:3)

3. A beatific vision of the divine essence of God.

4. Knowledge of the wisdom of God.

5. The power of working all kinds of miracles and of raising the dead to life along with a command over all nature and elements on water, land and in the sky.

6. The power to forgive sins, to convert sinners, and to change their hearts, to ordain sacraments and sacrifices, and to give many men and women special graces and super-natural gifts.

7. The honour of being the perpetual Head of all the church both in heaven and earth, that is Christ was made by God as eternal High Priest of all men and women.

8. The source of all blessings, gifts, and graces that have been given, are given at present, or shall at any time in the future be bestowed upon his mystical body or any of its members who form his church, which is the body of Christ.

We thank God, the eternal Father, with endless praise for all these wonders of holy grace which he gave to the man Jesus, who was made flesh like us so we might understand the meaning of our lives. He showed us the way to please God. He instructed us in God's commandments, so that we might live in union with God to bring that joy, peace, and harmony with all on earth that God intended for his Creation. Jesus, the perfect model of love, overcame death itself so our salvation was won. The Messiah, returned to Heaven, sent the Holy Spirit to watch over us. As if all this were not sufficient to show God's love, Christ, the Messiah promised by God, lives in us forever.

Let us rejoice in Jesus, that holy child given to us by God. His name shall be called Wonder-Counsellor, Mighty-God, eternal Father, Prince-of-Peace. (Isaiah 9:5–6)

19 December—*Our saviour as our king and priest*

 ONSIDER HOW JESUS Christ by his incarnation came to be our king, priest, teacher, and Master of Love. As such, he gave us a multitude of blessings, including making us kings and priests to God. (Revelation 1: 6) He is our true Melchisedech, sovereign king and high priest forever. Of this great king and his reign the royal prophet sings:

O God, give your judgment to the king
To a king's son your justice,
That he may judge your people in justice
And your poor in right judgment.
May the mountains bring forth peace for the people
And the hills, justice.
May be defend the poor of the people
And save the children of the needy
And crush the oppressor.
He shall endure like the sun and the moon
From age to age
He shall descend like rain on the meadow,
Like raindrops on the earth.
In his days justice shall flourish and peace till the moon fails.
He shall rule from sea to sea,
From the Great River to earth's bounds.
Before him his enemies shall fall,
His foes lick the dust.
The kings of Tarshish and the sea coasts shall pay him tribute.
The kings of Sheba and Seba
Shall bring him gifts.
Before him all kings shall fall prostrate,
All nation as shall serve him.
For he shall save the poor when they cry
and the needy who are helpless.
He will have pity on the weak
And save the lives of the poor.

From oppression he will rescue their lives,
To him their blood is dear.
Psalm 71:1–14

Here then is the Messiah promised to us and given by God to everyone on this earth. *Blessed be his holy name and may the whole earth be filled with his glory. So be it for us and all men and women.* (Psalm 71:19) Let us ask everyday for Jesus the Christ to continue his reign in us, to deliver us from our sins, and to bring us home to our Father in heaven.

20 December—On choosing the yoke of Christ

 UR LIFE ON earth has been called *A Vale of Tears*, because everyone suffers in this life. (Psalm 84:6) Thomas à Kempis put it well when he wrote:

> The days of this world are short and evil, full of sorrows and miseries, where man is defiled with many sins, ensnared with many passions, assaulted with many fears, disquieted with many cares, dissipated with many curiosities, entangled with many vanities, surrounded with many errors, broken with many hardships and fatigues, troubled with many temptations.

This heavy yoke of labour and sorrows has been our lot since the first Adam. (Ecclesiastes 1: 8–9).

There is only one remedy for all this sad inheritance and that is to run to Christ. With him we will find consolation and refreshment of mind, body and spirit. He will rescue us from slavery to the world's false ideas of what is meaningful in living. He shows us that, if we change the yoke of the First Adam that demeans us for the yoke of Jesus, the Second Adam, we will find a humility and goodness, which brings us rest for our spirit. In short, going to Jesus Christ brings us to God. So run to him as fast as you can. Then, we will find our yoke is sweet and our life bright with his light.

21 December—Feast of Saint Thomas, Apostle

 HEN THE OTHER disciples opposed our Saviour's going back to Jerusalem where the Jews had lately sought his death, St. Thomas said to the other disciples: *Let us also go to die with him.* (John 11:16) Such was his love for Jesus and was such his courage.

At this very moment somewhere in the world, a man or woman is witnessing their faith in the face of danger, even death. But we need to ask ourselves if our faith and courage are as strong as that of the Apostle Thomas or as strong as those fellow Christians who face martyrdom. How can we be certain of such courage when we are so often frightened by every little threat or difficulty in our life? Moreover, we often turn away from Jesus and deny him, just as Apostle Peter did. This shows our faith as weak or none existent in the face of danger. So, when we read about St. Thomas, the question remains: Are you among the blessed who have not seen and yet believe? (John 20:29)

22 December—On the cause of our great joy

 AINT PETER, THE first disciple of Jesus Christ, told us about our heavenly inheritance: *Blessed be God the father of Our Lord Jesus Christ, who in his great mercy has given us a new birth as his sons, by raising Jesus Christ from the dead, so that we have a sure hope and the promise of an inheritance that can never be spoilt or soiled and never fade away, because it is being kept for you in the heavens. Through your faith, God's power will guard you until the salvation, which has been prepared, is revealed at the end of time. This is a cause of great joy for you, even though you may for a short time have to bear being plagued by all sorts of trails; so that, when Jesus Christ is revealed, your faith will have been tested and proved like gold—only it is more precious that gold, which is corruptible even though it bears testing by fire—and then you will have praise and glory and honour. You did not see him, yet you love him; and still without seeing him, you are already filled with joy so glorious that it cannot be described because you believe; and you are sure of the end to which your faith looks forward, that is, the salvation of your souls. Free your mind, then, of encumbrances; control them, and put your trust in nothing but the grace that will be given you when Jesus Christ is revealed. Do not behave in the way that you liked before you learnt the truth; make a habit of obedience: be holy in all you do, since it is the Holy One who has called you and scripture says: Be holy, for I am holy.* (1 Peter 3–4)

As we near the celebration of the birth of Our Saviour, we should meditate on what Peter has told us. This helps us to prepare ourselves to witness again the grace given to us by God in the birth of Jesus. We are to be saved by this incarnation in order that we should live a new life in joy and contentment by following Jesus Christ in all we do and say.

Be holy for this is the practice of love.

23 December—On preparing for the birth of Jesus

OW CAN WE expect to have peace with another person if we are not at peace with our selves? Moreover, such a peace is most fully achieved by our awareness of the presence of Christ in our lives. We feel completely certain that he lives within us, just as we are alive in him.

This inner peace is to be at peace with yourself and God. The more you are at peace with yourself the more you will be at peace with others. As this peace grows so does our awareness that the source of such peacefulness is love. In this state of peace, which is a state of love, we please God and honour Jesus the Christ. The kingdom in you awaits its rightful king. You are ready in all ways to receive the presence of Christ.

This is how we are to be prepared for his birth, a birth that is historic, mysterious, miraculous, physical, and spiritual. A birth we celebrate each year to remind us that as Jesus, the New Adam, was born so we too can be reborn into a new life. In this new life in Christ, we have a great reconciliation with God, because we are celebrating and uniting with love itself.

But we cannot say we are peace until we have seen in our enemy the presence of Christ. We must turn the other cheek when confronted with injury of any kind from another person. (Matthew 5:39–42) If we cannot do this, then we have extended only *conditional* love, a love depending on how the other person acts and on how we feel about him or her. When Jesus died on the cross, he showed that true love is always *unconditional*, depending not on how the other person acts or how we may feel but on the commandment of God to love our neighbour as ourselves. Here is the oil of gladness poured on our life. (Psalm 45:8; Isaiah 61:1–3)

This triumphant virtue of love, the very crown of a life in Christ, requires us to change and the change we seek for ourselves is the result of our repentance. Although we often regret what we have done, said or perhaps left unspoken, repentance is quite out of fashion with many people today. Most men and women do not like to admit to anyone, especially to himself or herself that they have been wrong. Moreover, most people do not like to feel sad or bad about an action or choice they have made and repentance always involves regret.

The only way forward is to repent for the sake of reconciliation with God and with yourself, both the exterior and interior man or woman that you are in truth and honesty. Now, regret and apology are often considered a sign of personal weakness and a diminishment of individuality and independence. This is so today, because the world admires strength and power. This is why dictators succeed and kings remain on their thrones. The bully in a leader inspires fear and fear rules us, not because we are weak but because we do not trust in God.

However, we are never independent from God's will. As to individualism, it most often leads to self-devotion, which is to love yourself above all else in this world or the next. But it can only exist if such a person lives by worldly values, which means being ruled by pride, power, possessions, and acts of desire and passion without regard for others.

Repentance, which is our regret put into the first stage of action, infers a desire to change. The way forward in this change is to get back on the narrow road of Jesus where we find life and truth. (John 14:6) This we do by our repentance, asking God to forgive us. So when we repent, we are announcing that we are changing our lives, the way we think, and the choices we make. Our act of repentance means we have acted on our regret. We are looking for that change in ourselves which brings us reconciliation with God and changes our sorrow of regret into the joy of living for which we were created.

Such a change in life is very difficult for people, because by and large no one really much likes change in their lives, especially as they get older. But what we seek in such a change, a breaking away from old habits that do not please heaven, is a return to God and to his holy ways of living that his Word taught us, a way of living that the apostles, prophets, messengers and saints showed us. This change is what God wants for us, so he will help with our perseverance. When we fall, he will pick us up again and return us to the narrow road of Jesus Christ. We once again have the chance to be holy as he is holy.

Thus, when we are reconciled with God, we are embarking on a new life, a different way of thinking about our selves and others, and a way of showing our faith in the promises of God and the consolations of Christ. Only then, are we ready to celebrate the birth of Jesus with a whole heart.

24 December—On the birth of Jesus

 N THE SILENCE of the night, the eternal Word of God came to dwell among us. The brightest star in the heavens showed the way to his modest birthplace. Poor shepherds and wealthy men gave him honour. Even animals gather in peace before this child. The gifts placed before Jesus and his mother were *gold, frankincense,* and *myrrh*—symbols of the life, death and holiness of Jesus.

The gift of *gold,* which was used in adorn holy temples and which is incorruptible, told of the moral perfection of Jesus. (1 Kings 7:48–50)

The gift of *frankincense,* a resin gathered from trees, was burned in the temple to invoke the presence of God. Such incense was required at every sacrifice in the temple. The fragrant smoke of Frankincense was considered to carry prayers to heaven. (Isaiah 60–6; Leviticus 2:1) This gift told of the presence of God in the child, Jesus, and foretold of his eventual final sacrifice.

Myrrh, the third gift, is a sap drawn from another desert tree. It was a key ingredient in preparing the sacred oil that imparted holiness. This anointing oil was only used to sanctify the temple and its altars and never used outside the temple. Most importantly, myrrh was used to anoint and consecrate the high priest. (Exodus 30:26–33) Thus, Jesus from his birth was acknowledged and consecrated forever as God's high priest.

Consider what kind of a place God ordained for this wondrous birth. It was not the palace of a king, although Jesus was born the eternal king. It was the poorest of places, a place really only fit for animals. We learn from this that God gave us not only the humanity of Christ in his being made man, but he showed us by his place of birth that Jesus was one with the entire Creation whether it was other humans or creatures like sheep, cows and donkeys. By this God tells us that we too are one with everything in his Creation.

This birthplace of Christ showed us as well that the environment God wants for us is one of peace, humility, simplicity, and virtue. It is a place that does not reflect worldly values nor the power struggles and cruelty of men and women. We are shown by God that love conquers all and that the reason for love is love itself.

This birthplace of the promised Messiah became the holiest of places and was chosen by God with love. It is in love that Jesus was born. It by love he was raised by Mary and Joseph. It is through love that he died and saved us. It is with love that God ordained we should live. Such love is a gift beyond gold, frankincense, and myrrh for love is the gift of life itself, the being of God himself. In the incarnation of Jesus Christ, God showed us that we too are made of love, that we too may live by heavenly values, and that we too may be holy and pleasing to God. Love, then, is all.

Let us welcome Jesus at his holy birth with the great rejoicing of love.

25 December—Solemnity of Christmas Day

 ING OUT WITH joy and endless praise for our Saviour, Our Lord, Our King, has been born! Sent by God, Jesus the Messiah has come to be with us forever, the Word itself taking human form to teach us how we may live in virtue and love and in obedience to the commandments of God.

Let us place ourselves near the crèche of our Lord, kneeling before the infant with the Wise Men, honouring this holiest of gifts and paying our homage to Mary and to Joseph as well. Let our mind, body and spirit be filled with joy, since by this birth all men and woman were saved forever.

Joyfully embrace this gift of love that is Jesus the Christ. Share it with everyone you meet, because Christ lives in that relative, friend, or stranger just as Christ lives in you. (Matthew 25:35–40) Be merciful as God is merciful. (Luke 6:36) Be holy for that is why you were born and why Jesus Christ was sent to show us the way to God. (1 Peter 1:16)

26 December—Feast of Saint Stephen, the first martyr

 AINT STEPHEN WAS the first witness to the divinity of Jesus by laying down his life for him. Stephen *has been given the living fountains of eternal waters through his death for love of the Lamb of God.* (Revelations 7:14–17)

Saint Paul tells us that Stephen was a man full of faith and of the Holy Ghost. He was full of grace and fortitude, and did great wonders and miracles among the people. By his zeal the word of the Lord increased, and the number of the disciples was multiplied in Jerusalem exceedingly and though many adversaries rose up, who disputed against him, there are none of them able to resist the wisdom and spirit that spoke. (Acts 6 & 5:7–10)

St. Stephen's zeal in his faith in Jesus was rewarded with a heavenly vision. Filled with the Holy Spirit, he *saw the glory of God and Christ standing at his right hand.* (Acts 7:55–56) Even in his terrible death, St. Stephen bore witness to his faith, invoking the Lord as he was stoned and crying out, *Lord Jesus, receive my spirit. Then, he knelt down and said, Lord, do not hold this sin against them. With these words, he fell into sleep and died.* (Acts 7:55–60)

How distant are most Christians from this perfection of charity shown by Stephen. How few of us are willing to suffer even the least inconvenience for the sake of Christ, let alone to die for him. Even as we stumble and fall prey to temptations and need forgiveness for our sins, we still remain unwilling to sacrifice ourselves for Christ's sake. So let us at least love all those martyrs like Saint Stephen, who even today still die rather than deny Christ. We may never be martyrs or be declared saints, but we can remain faithful and make Jesus Christ our beloved.

27 December—Feast of Saint John, Apostle & Evangelist

HERE ARE MANY reasons to celebrate this wonderful apostle, Saint John. First, he was called to follow Jesus in his youth and he obeyed at once. His purity of body and spirit made him a special favourite of his Lord. Indeed, we think it was John who leaned in devotion against Jesus at the *Last Supper*. It was to the care of the Apostle John that Jesus entrusted his mother when he was dying on the cross. We should pray for God to give us such purity and holy love as Jesus found in his beloved Apostle John.

Consider next to what a height John was raised by divine grace. He was made an apostle, one of the three that were chosen by Jesus to witness both the glory of his transfiguration and his anguish on the Mount of Olives. (Matthew 17:1–13; Luke 22:39–44) He was also chosen by God to be one of the gospel writers, a prophet, and a martyr.

Saint John tells us that God first loved us and that what we owe him in return is to keep his commandment that we should love one another. (John 1:4–5) This spirit of love for one another runs through all his writing and, indeed, makes the Apostle John the *Disciple of Love*. Try to keep close to this truth of love so heralded by Saint John, because in such love, we will find the peace and contentment that comes from obedience to God.

28 December—Feast of the Holy Innocents, Martyrs

 esus the Christ, who came into this world to be the Saviour of the world, was no sooner born than he began to be persecuted by this world, starting with King Herod. The king, *perceiving that he was deluded by the wise men, who had found the new-born Jesus, was exceeding angry for he wanted to make certain he secured his kingdom for himself and his family. He ordered all the male children under two years old that were in Bethlehem to be killed.* (Matthew 2:16–18)

These murdered children are the Holy Innocents, whose feast we celebrate this day, bearing testimony to the birth of Jesus, not by their words but by their blood, These are the first victims to the coming of the Lamb of God. These Holy Innocents are the first flowering of martyrs to be followed afterwards around the world by countless other followers of Christ, who have maintained their faith by the testimony of their blood. (Revelations 14:4–5)

As Saint James tells us: *Count it all joy, when you meet trials of various kinds, for you know that the testing of your faith produces steadfastness. And let this unwavering endurance have its full effect, that you may be perfect and complete, lacking in nothing.* (James 1:2–4) So then assure yourself that God knows what is best for you. Endure in your faith. (Romans 5:3–5)

29 December—On preparing to change the way you live

ou are a New Man and a New Woman! Looking at the world around you with an open mind, a frank reflection, and a spirit reflecting the values and the promises of God, you prepare for a new life in Christ.

Here is what the Cistercian monk Brother Louis, the writer Thomas Merton, had to say of our world:

> We live in a time of no room, which is the time of the end. The time when everyone is obsessed with lack of time, lack of space, with saving time, conquering space, projecting into time and space the anguish produced within them by the technological furies of size, volume, quantity, speed, number, price, power and acceleration. The primordial blessing "increase and multiply" has suddenly become a haemorrhage of terror. We are numbered in billions, and massed together, marshalled, numbered, marched here and there, taxed, drilled armed, worked to the point of insensibility, dazed by information, drugged by entertainment, surfeited with everything. Nauseated with the human race and with ourselves, nauseated with life. As the end approaches, there is no room for nature. The cities crowd it off the face of the earth.[8]

You were created by God to be happy and at peace. Now is your chance!

---

[8] Thomas Merton, *Raids on the Unspeakable,* New Directions, USA, 1964, Burns & Oates, UK, 1977), p. 49.

30 December—The Holy Family—Feast

 ODAY WE HONOUR of the Holy Family of Jesus, Mary, and Joseph. The primary purpose of this celebration is to present the Holy Family as a model for Christian families.

Pope Benedict XVI explained it this way:

> We can still identify ourselves with the shepherds of Bethlehem who hastened to the grotto as soon as they had received the Angel's announcement and found Mary and Joseph, and the Babe lying in the manger. (Luke 2:16) Let us too pause to contemplate this scene and reflect on its meaning. The first witnesses of Christ's birth, the shepherds, found themselves not only before the Infant Jesus but also a small family: mother, father and new-born son. God had chosen to reveal himself by being born into a human family and the human family thus became an icon of God! God is the Trinity, he is a communion of love; so is the family despite all the differences that exist between the Mystery of God and his human creature, an expression that reflects the unfathomable Mystery of God as Love. In marriage the man and the woman, created in God's image, become "one flesh", that is a communion of love that generates new life. The human family, in a certain sense, is an icon of the Trinity because of its interpersonal love and the fruitfulness of this love. (Genesis 2:24) The Christian family is aware that children are a gift and a project of God. Therefore it cannot consider that it possesses them; rather, in serving God's plan through them, the family is called to educate them in the greatest freedom, which is precisely that of saying "yes" to God in order to do his will. The Virgin Mary is the perfect example of this "yes". Let us entrust all

families to her, praying in particular for their precious educational mission.[9]

If you have children is this how you raise them? If you have grandchildren is this how you educate them when they are with you? Is each and every child precious to you? Do you care and support family life no matter your own situation? Do you set an example of love? These are the questions that confirm or deny our obedience to God's Creation.

---

[9]   Pope Benedict XVI, Angelus Address, 27 December 2009.

31 December—On living your life in fullness and joy

 ESUS CAME INTO your life so that we might live in full measure to enjoy our life on earth. (John 10:10) This living fully brings the contentment that is the lasting gladness of our mind, body and spirit. It comes from the joy of living in the presence of God. (Psalm 15:11) By keeping Jesus Christ as our dearest companion and delighting in him as the one who brings all the desires of our heart, we will find the discipline to remain in the state of love that most pleases God. (Psalm 36:4)

When we have been reconciled with God, surely we may count on being saved by the life of his Messiah. Now that we have been justified by his death, we shall be saved through him from the retribution of God. What is more, we are filled with exultant trust in God, through our Lord Jesus Christ, through whom we have already gained our reconciliation. (Romans 5:9 &11)

A new life in Jesus Christ is before you. This is a life of joy. Do not refuse what God has given you, because all your hope and salvation are in him.

BIBLIOGRAPHY

Unless otherwise noted the biblical references and brief quotations in this book are acknowledged as mainly from *The New Jerusalem Bible: Reader's Edition*, Darton, Longman & Todd Ltd, London 1990 and the psalms from *The Psalms*, Collins, Fount Paperbacks, London, 1963. However with biblical references, any authorized bible translation will serve. All references are acknowledged as given below with the other sources used in writing this book. All these form a selected biography.

Athanasius: *Vita s. Antoni, Saint Athanasius, Nicene and post-Nicene fathers of the Christian Church*, Vol IV, *Select works and letters*, P. Schaff and H. Wace.

Augustine, *Confessions* of St. Augustine, Trans. F. J. Sheed, Sheed & Ward, London & NY, 1944; *Confessions*, St. Augustine, 10:27; *Divine Office*, Readings for Wednesday, Week 8; *Sermon 304*; *Sermon 169*.

A Carthusian , *They Speak by Silences: Live 'In Conspectu Domini'*, Longmans, Green & Co, London, 1955.

—*From Advent to Pentecost:Carthusian Novice Conferences*, Trans. Carmel Brett, Cistercian Publications, Kalamazoo, Michigan, 1999.

—*Interior Prayer: Carthusian Novice Conferences*, Trans. Sr. Maureen Scrine, Darton, Longman & Todd, London 1996.

Benedict: The Rule of Saint Benedict: *Households of God*, David Parry OSB, Darton, Longman & Todd, London,1980.

—*The Rule of St. Benedict*, Trans. Justin McCann, Sheed & Ward, London,1970, 1976.

—*The Rule of Saint Benedict*, Trans. Abbot Parry, OSB, Gracewing, Leominister, 1990.

—*La Règle de saint Benoit, VII, Commentaire doctrinal et spiritual*, Adalbert de Vogue; Les Editions du Cerf, Paris 1977.

Bernard of Clairvaux, *Sermon 12, On the Holy Guardian Angels, The Twelve Degrees of Humility & Pride*, and *On the Love of God: De diligendo Deo*, Trans. A Religious of CSMV, Mowbrays, London & Oxford, date of translation unknown.

—Bernard of Clairvaux, *Bernard of Clairvaux: Essential Writing*, Dennis Tamburello OFM, Crossroad Publishing, NY, 2000.

Code of Canon Law 603.

Cassian, John, *Confessions: The Wisdom of the Desert*, Xlibriscom, USA, 2000.

—*John Cassian: The Conferences*, Trans. Boniface Ramsey OP, NewMan Press NeY, 1997.

—*John Cassian: The Intitutes*, Ancient Christian Writers Series, The Newman Press, NY, 2000

Catechism of the Catholic Church, Articles 490, 491, 492, 493, 322, 329, 330, 326, 327, 328, 2176, 2177

Chrysostom, John, *De incomprehensibili in l'incompréhensibilité de Dieu. Homélies I-5*, A.-M. Malingrey, J. Daniélou and R. Flacelière, SC, Paris, 1970. Available in Bodleian Library, Oxford.

Desert Fathers, *The Sayings of the Desert Fathers*, Trans. Bendicta Ward, SLG,Cistercian Publications, Inc., Kalamzoon, Michigan USA, Revised Edition, 1984

Didache, *The Didache: Teaching of the Twelve Apostles*, Chpt. 4, Trans. Maxwell Stamford in *Early Christian Writings*, Penguin Classics, London, NYC, 1987)

Divine Office (Liturgy of the Hours), Vols 1,2 & 3: International Committee on English in the Liturgy, The Vatican, Rome. For Thursday, Week 17 *Memorial of St. Alphonsus Liguori; Midday Prayer, The Divine Office III*, p.127.

De Foucauld, Charles, *Charles de Foucauld: Exploreur du Maroc, Ermite au Sahara*, René Bazin, Plon-Nourret et Cie, Paris 1921.

Charles de Foucauld: le Prèdestiné, René Pottier, Fernand Sorot, Paris 1944.

De Foucauld, Charles, *Meditations of a Hermit*. Trans. Charlotte Balfour, Burns & Oates, London & New York, 1930 & 1981.

Bibliography

Fourth Lateran Council 1215, *Decrees.*

Francis de Sales, *The Mariology of St. Francis de Sales,* Edward J. Carney OSFS.

—*Sermons for Lent 1622.*

—*An Introduction to the Devout Life,* Tan Classics, USA, 1994.

Grimlaicus, *Rule for Solitaries,* Trans. Andrew Thornton OSB, Liturgical Press, Collegeville, Minnesota, USA, 2011.

Ignatius of Antioch, *Epistle to the Ephesians; Spiritual Exercises, No. 234; Sermo de Ascensione Domini,* Vatican Archives, Rome.

John of the Cross, *The Collected Works of St. John of the Cross,* Trans. Kieran Kavanaugh OCD, & Otilio Rodriguez, OCD, ICS Publications, Institute of Carmelite Studies, Washington DC, 1991.

The Koran, Trans. J. M. Rodwell, J. M. Dent & Co., *Everyman's Library,* London & NY, 1909 & 1963.

Lawrence of the Resurrection, *The Practice of the Presence of God, Letters of Br. Lawrence of the Resurrection,* compiled in French by Fr. Joseph de Beaufort with numerous translations in English.

Maximus of Turin, *Sermons of St. Maximus of Turin,* annotated by Saint Boniface in *Christian Writers: The Work of the Fathers,* Trans. Walter Bughardt & Thomas Comerford Lawler, Newman Press, NY, 1989

Merton, Thomas: *Raids on the Unspeakable,* 1964, New Directions, USA, 1964, Burns & Oates, UK, 1977.

—*The Inner Experience: Notes on Contemplation,* William H. Shannon (Editor), Harper San Francisco. Reprint edition, 2004.

—Thomas Merton in letter to Dorothy Day, 1965.

—*The Wisdom of the Desert: Sayings from the Desert Fathers,* Trans. Thomas Merton, New Directions NY, 1960, reprinted from *Harper's Bazaar.*

Newman, John Henry, *On the pleasant Care of Boys* in *Sayings of Cardinal Newman,* given in an address at Oratory School Society 1879, The National Institute for Newman Studies, Original Manuscript on Digital Collections, 2020.

Pope Benedict XVI: *Angelus* speech, 2005; General Audience, 2006; *Angelus,* 27 December 2009; General Audience 13 August 2008.

Pope Francis: *Mass Homily 2015; Gaudete et Exsultate, Apostolic Exhortation on the call to today's world, 19 March 2018,* The Vatican, Rome.

Pope Gregory I: *Morals,* The Vatican, Rome.

Pope Saint Gregory the Great, *Homilies on the Gospel, The Divine Office, Vol III,* The Vatican, Rome.

Pope Leo 1: *Sermon 1, Nativitate Domini,* The Vatican, Rome.

Pope Saint Leo the Great: *Sermon 10 on Lent, The Church Fathers,* Trans. Charles Lett Feltoe, Trans. Charles Lett Feltoe, Edited by Philip Schaff and Henry Wace, Christian Literature Publishing Co., Buffalo, NY, 1895.

Psalms: *The Psalms, A New Translation,* Gelineau *et al,* The Grail, Collins Fount Paperbacks, London 1963.

The Psalms: A Commentary for Prayer & Reflection, Henry Wansbrough, The Bible Reading Fellowship, Abingdon UK, 2014:

Schweitzer, Albert, Dr. Albert Schweitzer, *The Ethics of Reverence for Life (The Philosophy of Civilization and Ethics),* Macmillan New York, 1929.

—*Out of My Life and Thought: An Autobiography,* JHUP, 2009.

—*The Quest of the Historical Jesus: A Critical Study of Its Progress from Reimarus to Wrede,* The John Hopkins University Press, Baltimore & London, 1998.

Qutb, Sayyid, *In the shade of The Qur'an,* Vols 1, 5 & 11, Trans. Adil Salahi & Ashur Shamis, The Islamic Foundation, Leicester, UK, 2000. (*Note:* Sayyid Qutb is one of the greatest scholars of *The Qur'an* in the 20th century.)

Teresa of Avila, St. Teresa of Avila, *Interior Castle,* Trans. E. Alison Peers, Image Books, Doubleday, NY, London, 1961, 1989.

Bibliography

—*The Life of Saint Teresa of Avila by Herself,* Trans. J.M. Cohen, Penguin Books, London 1957.

—*Selected Writings of Teresa of Avila,* W. J. Dohenny, Bruce Publishing, Milwaukee, USA, 1950.

Thérèse of the Child Jesus, *The Story of a Soul,* The Autobiography of St. Thérèse of Lisieux, Trans. Michael Day, Cong Orat. Tan Classics, NY 2010.

Thomas Aquinas, *Star of the Sea: Ave Maris Stella,* the words of this hymn used as a prayer.

—*Summa Theologiae,* 4 vols.

—*Summa contra Gentiles,* Commentary on Romans in New Testament.

Thomas of Villanova, Attributed saying, *Divine Office, Feasts of the Year.*

Vatican II, *Decree on the Renewal of Religious Life.*

Walpot Peter, *True Yielders and the Christian Community of Goods, Early Antibaptist Spirituality: Selected Writings,* Trans. Daniel Liechty. Paulist Press, New York & Mahwah, New Jersery USA, 1994.

Wencel, Cornelius, *The Eremitic Life: Encountering God in Silence and Solitude,* Fr. Cornelius Wencel, Ercam Editions, Bloomingdale, Ohio, USA, 2007

Lightning Source UK Ltd.
Milton Keynes UK
UKHW011043300322
400832UK00002B/3